REBUILDING THE LOCAL LANDSCAPE

To my wife, Joanne

ETC UK

This book is an ETC UK project. ETC UK is a not for profit company established in North Shields, England. It is part of the ETC International Foundation Group, with headquarters in Leusden, The Netherlands. There are sister offices in other countries throughout the world. ETC UK has been in operation for 10 years and has handled 200 projects. ETC Foundation and its sister companies specialise in sustainable development with a strong emphasis on participation by local people in project design and development. This emphasis on participation leads to an end use, bottom up approach to development. Sectoral expertise in low external input agriculture, environment and conservation, land use planning, social forestry, energy and evaluation of humanitarian assistance. ETC UK is particularly involved in environmental management and impact assessment. Its services are usually requested for innovative policy making and project design, particularly in circumstances of significant social change. ETC UK's main objective is to encourage and support local initiatives which aim to build sustainable development.

Chris Howorth works as a consultant for ETC UK, specialising in natural resource management and sustainable development. He has worked on projects in many countries in east, west and southern Africa. He has also lectured on environment and development in Newcastle University and the University of Northumbria.

Rebuilding the Local Landscape
Environmental management in Burkina Faso

CHRIS HOWORTH

LONDON AND NEW YORK

First published 1999 by Ashgate Publishing

Reissued 2018 by Routledge
2 Park Square, Milton Park, Abingdon, Oxon, OX14 4RN
711 Third Avenue, New York, NY 10017, USA

Routledge is an imprint of the Taylor & Francis Group, an informa business

Copyright © Chris Howorth 1999

All rights reserved. No part of this book may be reprinted or reproduced or utilised in any form or by any electronic, mechanical, or other means, now known or hereafter invented, including photocopying and recording, or in any information storage or retrieval system, without permission in writing from the publishers.

Notice:
Product or corporate names may be trademarks or registered trademarks, and are used only for identification and explanation without intent to infringe.

Publisher's Note
The publisher has gone to great lengths to ensure the quality of this reprint but points out that some imperfections in the original copies may be apparent.

Disclaimer
The publisher has made every effort to trace copyright holders and welcomes correspondence from those they have been unable to contact.

A Library of Congress record exists under LC control number: 98074636

ISBN 13: 978-0-367-00005-9 (hbk)
ISBN 13: 978-0-367-00007-3 (pbk)
ISBN 13: 978-0-429-44504-0 (ebk)

Contents

List of Boxes Figures, and Tables   *vii*
Preface   *x*

1 The Resilience of the Peasantry in Burkina Faso (or les paysannes sont fortes)   **1**
    Introduction   1
    Burkina Faso   2
    History, Environment and Movement in West Africa   6
    The Peasant Mode of Production   8

2 The Province of Sissili   **19**
    Introduction   19
    Physical Environment   19
    Human Resources and Human Systems   29
    Issues of Resource Use in Sissili   38
    An Introduction to the Three Case Study Villages   56
    Islam in Sissili   58
    Summary   64

3 Culturally Locating Production Patterns   **66**
    The Nuni   66
    The Mossi   76
    The Fulani   85
    Summary   95

4 Lon   **97**
    Introduction   97
    Legal Arrangements and Administrative Decision Making   110
    Ethnic Interrelationships in Lon   113

5 Boutiourou 116
Introduction 116
Legal Arrangements and Administrative Decision Making 128
Ethnic Interrelationships in Boutiourou 132

6 Saboué 133
Introduction 133
Legal Arrangements and Administrative Decision Making 144
Ethnic Interrelationships in Saboué 146

7 Conclusion: African Realities and Western Dreams 149
Introduction 149
Local Environmental Management and the Emerging
   Development Paradigm 154

Appendix: Land Classification Units According to de Boer, 1992 157

References *162*

List of Boxes, Figures and Tables

Boxes

2.1	*Gestion de Terroirs*	39
3.1	Néré or African locust bean – *Parkia biglobosa (jacq.) Benth*, Mimosaceae family	75
3.2	Karité or Shea nut – *Butyrospernum parkii (G.Don) Kotschy*, Sapotaceae family	77
3.3	Roles and responsibilities of Fulani herders	90
4.1	The oral history of Lon	98
5.1	The oral history of Boutiourou	117
6.1	The oral history of Saboué	134

Figures

1.1	Burkina Faso	3
2.1	The province of Sissili	20
2.2	Total annual rainfall in the province of Sissili, 1960 to 1993	21
2.3	Population growth in Sissili, 1975 to 1990	30
2.4	Population growth in the department of Cassou, 1985 to 1991	32
2.5	Agricultural tools	41
2.6	The soil catenary sequence and soil profile, land use and vegetation in Sissili	46
2.7	Indigenous and scientific soil classification in Sissili	51
2.8	The province of Sissili showing Lon, Boutiourou and Saboué	57
2.9	The range of religious mixes: Animist, Muslim and Western	63
3.1	The Nuni agricultural calendar	72
3.2	The forest food gathering calendar	74
3.3	The evolution of the occupation of space after the reception of Mossi immigrants	79
3.4	The evolution of the agricultural organisation of the Mossi immigrants	80

3.5 Relative labour allocation for livestock and agriculture amongst the Fulani 89
3.6 A comparison between farmers' and Fulani labour allocation for agricultural activities 93
3.7 The Fulani seasonal labour calendar in Sissili 94
4.1 Village transect of Lon, 1993 to 1995 100
4.2a The evolution of the landscape in Lon, 1955 to 1993: 1955 102
4.2b The evolution of the landscape in Lon, 1955 to 1993: 1985 103
4.2c The evolution of the landscape in Lon, 1955 to 1993: 1993 104
4.3 Networks and linkages of the Nuni in Lon, 1995 107
4.4 The origins and linkages of the immigrants in Lon 109
4.5 A diagrammatic representation of the power structures in Lon 111
5.1 Village transect of Boutiourou, 1993 to 1995 118
5.2a The evolution of the landscape in Boutiourou, 1955 to 1993: 1955 120
5.2b The evolution of the landscape in Boutiourou, 1955 to 1993: 1985 121
5.2c The evolution of the landscape in Boutiourou, 1955 to 1993: 1993 122
5.3 Networks and linkages of the Nuni in Boutiourou, 1995 126
5.4 The origins and linkages of the immigrants in Boutiourou 127
5.5 A diagrammatic representation of the power structures in Boutiourou 129
6.1 Village transect of Saboué, 1993 to 1995 135
6.2a The evolution of the landscape in Saboué, 1955 to 1993: 1955 138
6.2b The evolution of the landscape in Saboué, 1955 to 1993: 1985 139
6.2c The evolution of the landscape in Saboué, 1955 to 1993: 1993 140
6.3 Networks and linkages of the Nuni in Saboué, 1995 142
6.4 The origins and linkages of the immigrants in Saboué 143
6.5 A diagrammatic representation of the relative integration of the three ethnic groups in Lon, Boutiourou and Saboué 145
6.6 A spatial representation of the relative interaction of the three ethnic groups in Lon, Boutiourou and Saboué 146

Tables

1.1 Base data for Burkina Faso 5
2.1 The departments of Sissili and their land surface 20
2.2 A classification of land cover: Burkina Faso and Sissili 24
2.3 General overview of the environmental and human situation in Sissili 25

List of Boxes, Figures and Tables   ix

2.4 The detailed occupation of space (in per cent) for the departments
of Cassou, Léo and Biéha and for the province of Sissili 26
2.5 Vegetative production of the herbaceous layer in kilograms of
dry matter per hectare per year in Sissili (kg dm/ha/yr) 28
2.6 Vegetative production of the woody layer in kilograms of
dry matter per hectare per year in Sissili (kg dm/ha/yr) 29
2.7 Areas of employment in the resident, active population of
Sissili (of 10 years old or older) by sex, 1985 30
2.8 Village size and frequency in Sissili, 1985 31
2.9 Population growth by ethnic group in the department of Tô,
1985 to 1991 32
2.10 Population growth by department, 1975 to 1985 33
2.11 Climatological data from the province of Yatenga, 1979 to 1988 34
2.12 The positive and negative effects of immigration 35
2.13 Intended destination of people with the intention to migrate in
four provinces: Sissili, Namantenga, Yatenga and Soum 36
2.14 A summary of some agricultural characteristics of the three
main ethnic groups in Sissili 43
2.15 Nuni soil nomenclature in Lon, Boutiourou and Saboué 49
2.16 Prices of animals on the market in Léo, 1992 52
2.17 Vegetative production for different pasture zones in million
kilograms of dry matter in Sissili 54
2.18 Recovery of perennial grasses and the percentage of burnt
land in Sissili 55
2.19 Fodder calendar for Sissili 56
3.1 Crops and their roles in the first ring/household field 82
3.2 Crops and their roles in the second ring/village field 83
3.3 Crops and their roles in the third ring/bush field 84
3.4 The Fulani yearly activities 87
3.5 The Fulani seasonal calendar 88
3.6 The agricultural division of labour in Fulani communities by sex 92
4.1 The growth in the different categories of land cover in Lon,
1955 to 1993 105
4.2 Ethnic interrelationships in Lon 114
5.1 The growth in the different categories of land cover in
Boutiourou, 1955 to 1993 125
5.2 Ethnic interrelationships in Boutiourou 131
6.1 Trees and their uses in Saboué 136
6.2 The growth in the different categories of land cover in Saboué,
1955 to 1993 141
6.3 Ethnic interrelationships in Saboué 147
A.1 Characteristics of land classification units as described by
de Boer (1992) 160

Preface

Africa's environmental challenge too often produced meta-narratives that have little to do with the lives and livelihoods of Africans. Frequently viewed as large scale rural factories initially by colonisers then transnational corporations and now by an African elite of large scale landowners, the environment offered a productive utopia for modern production – exports and individual wealth beckoned. The contrasting meta-narrative was that of doom and gloom – a Malthusian nightmare resplendent with overcrowded slums, polluted rivers, collapsing subsistence production and soil erosion. Neither, of course is correct but both meta-narratives still have their promoters.

Of late there has been a willingness to try and understand what peasant farmers are designing and building in their local landscapes. Extreme physical events, such as the 1980s Sahelian drought, allow insight into environmental management strategies in subsistence production systems. Response to drought and recovery towards a development agenda show a mosaic of environmental management strategies that build on past cultural norms but acknowledge opportunities and constraints in a new environment.

Chris Howorth's work details such an experience in Burkina Faso. Building on ecological and farming systems research in three villages he examines changing environmental management strategies including changing frameworks of customary land law as the land resource becomes scarce. The emerging mosaics described defy the uniformity of a modernisation process without denying the benefits of modernity. Potential ethnic conflict is muted by building inter and intra village practices that are broadly commensual.

This work, originally produced as his doctoral dissertation, was based on Chris Howorth's fieldwork as a UNAIS technical assistant. It combines academic rigour with a commitment to participatory development action; abstraction with action. There is much to recommend in such an approach, not least as the chances for detailed African fieldwork decline. More interaction between universities and field agencies is necessary if the richness of produced landscapes is to be understood. On a more local note I am pleased that Chris Howorth chose to complete his work at the University of Northumbria building capacity with others – notably Sam Moyo – for work on the political economy of African environmental management. Where he has led, others are certain to follow.

Phil O'Keefe
Newcastle upon Tyne
September 1998

1 The Resilience of the Peasantry in Burkina Faso
(or les paysannes sont fortes)

Introduction

The first part of this book explores the idea that the peasant mode of production[1] has shown itself to be efficient in providing subsistence to the household and ensuring family survival. It is also argued here that development can occur within the peasant mode of production, as it has always done. Historically, the peasantry of Africa have been highly mobile and highly adaptive in creating lifescapes which are mobile in both time and place and it is these which make the peasant mode of production so effective. The resilience of the peasantry is due to its proven ability to survive and prosper over millennia. Far from being an outdated mode of production, it is constantly modernising itself, assimilating what global developments offer, to make it a more effective system.

As African landscapes continue to be studied in detail, new findings emphasise the creative and productive human influence, rather than the negative impacts of humans. As Tiffen *et al* (1994) showed in part of Kenya, more people meant less erosion: Fairhead and Leach (1996) showed that local people were the reason behind the increasing presence of forests in parts of Guinea. This study attempts to show that the presence of three times as many people in one area, compared to 15 years ago, contributes to a vibrant economy and a productively managed environment.

To understand how people manage their local landscapes, it is important to understand the rationale and driving forces behind the peasant mode of production in an historical context.

---

1 A mode of production is an abstraction identifying the basic logic and structures of given social formations (Hyden, 1980:12).

2   Rebuilding the Local Landscape

Burkina Faso

Physical Geography

Burkina Faso is a land locked country in the West African Sahel region, north of Ghana, between the Sahara desert and the Gulf of Guinea, south of the loop of the Niger River. It is located on a plateau that rises gently from an elevation of 800 feet in the southwest to 1150 feet in the northeast (Atampugré, 1994:4). It covers 274,200 square kilometres and shares borders with Mali, Côte D'Ivoire, Niger, Ghana, Benin and Togo (Figure 1.1). The country has generally poor soil with many areas being infertile semi-desert. The climate is hot and dry, with average annual rainfall 650–1150 mm but less than 250 mm in the north. Water is therefore scarce in many parts of the country and, where it is available (for example, in the Black Volta River valley), infestations of river blindness or sleeping sickness prevent its use for agriculture. There are three distinct seasons: warm and dry from November to March; hot and dry, from March to May; and hot and wet, from June to October.

Population

Burkina Faso is also one of the more densely populated countries in the Sahel with an estimated population of just over 10 million, three quarters of whom live in the rural areas. The Mossi plateau, in the centre of the country, has the highest population density of 32.5 people per square kilometre and accounts for almost half the country's population (Atampugré, 1994:4). Burkina Faso has a very young population with some 47 per cent being under five years old. There are three major urban areas: Ouagadougou, the capital (population 500,000), Bobo-Dioulasso (population 250,000) and Koudougou (population 75,000). The urban population has been estimated to be growing at 5.4 per cent per annum since 1980 (EIU, 1991–92). Burkina Faso's population is not well provided for in basic services like education or health. The adult literacy rate is very low at only 16 per cent, with only 7 per cent of women being literate. There is only one doctor for every 54,000 people and one nurse for every 3,000.

Burkina Faso is home to 60 different ethnic groups which belong to two major West African cultural groups – the Voltaic and the Mand. Burkina Faso is dominated by the Voltaic group which include the Mossi who make up 52 per cent of the population. The Mossi were originally a warrior tribe that migrated from Ghana to present day Burkina Faso and established an empire that lasted more than 500 years, from 1400 AD to 1900 AD. They still retain allegiance to their king, the Moro Naba, who holds court in Ouagadougou. The other major ethnic groups include the Fulani, Bobo,

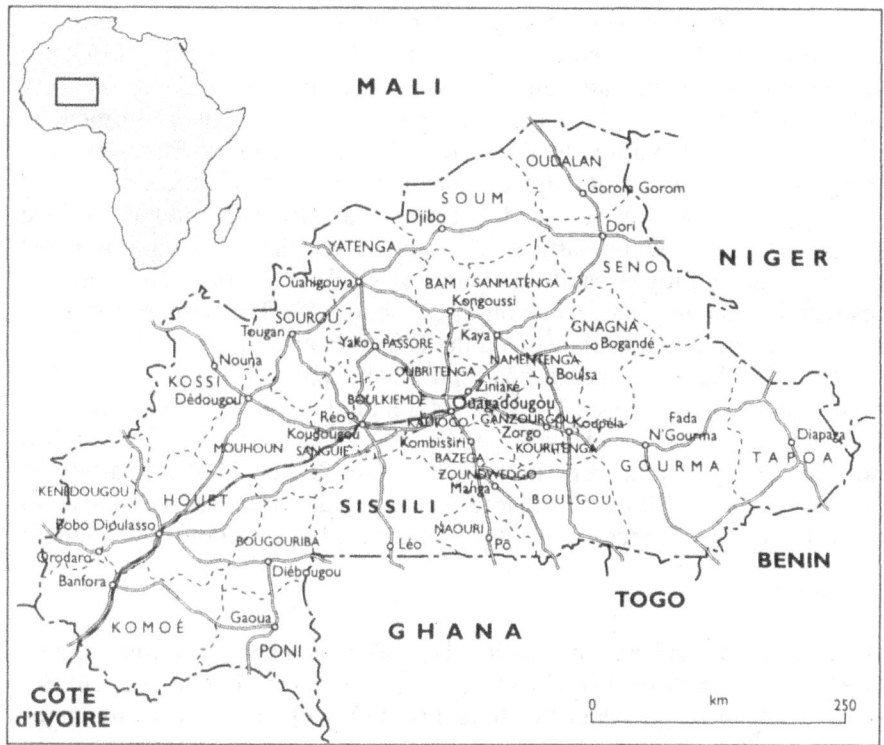

Figure 1.1 Burkina Faso

Gourounsi, Bisa-Samo, Gourmantché and Senefou. Ethnic groups that were previously Animist have mostly been converted to Islam although many of these still retain many of their old animist traditions. About ten per cent of the population follows Christian religions. French is the official language and most of the plethora of tribal languages belong to the Sudanic family, which is spoken by 90 per cent of the population.

History and Politics

The area now occupied by Burkina Faso was one of the oldest kingdoms in West Africa, dating back to the eleventh century. In 1400, the Mossi ethnic group came from what is now Ghana to settle in the area. They created 19 separate kingdoms each depending on the most powerful central kingdom of Wogodogo, today's Ouagadougou. By 1600, the Mossi created what was effectively a centralised state with a strong administrative system that resisted conquest by neighbouring African empires. It was colonised by

France in 1896 and was used as a labour pool by the French to service the coastal colonies. It gained independence in 1960 as Upper Volta. After a succession of corrupt and unsuccessful governments, a group of army officers led by Thomas Sankara seized power in 1983. Sankara formed the socialist Conseil Nationale de la Révolution (National Revolutionary Council – CNR) which attempted to develop a self-sufficient economy.

In 1987, tensions surfaced between Sankara and Captain Blaise Campaoré, his erstwhile partner, who represented the relatively privileged government employees and trade unions (UNAIS, 1996). The tensions resulted in Sankara's assassination in October 1987. The basic needs strategy of Sankara was abandoned and the IMF was invited in.

In 1991, there was a significant political change which saw a referendum on a new constitution. The June referendum in the same year gave a 93 per cent vote in favour of multi-party democracy. A new constitution has now been adopted and there are now well over 20 new political parties. In November 1991, Blaise Campaoré was elected unopposed for a second term. Table 1.1 provides the most recent detailed base data for the country.

Economy

Burkina Faso has a very weak national economy and has an external debt of US $116,173 million (World Development Report, 1992). Agriculture provides about 40 per cent of GDP and is mainly of a subsistence nature or is traded in the informal local economy. Cash crops include cotton, ground nuts, sesame and shea (or karité) nuts. The main food crops are cereals such as sorghum and millet but livestock raising is also important, especially for the nomadic ethnic groups. Formal industry, dominated by unprofitable government controlled corporations, accounts for about 15 per cent of the GDP and employs four per cent of the population. However, this 4 per cent of the population consume almost 50 per cent of the budget through their salaries. It was projected by the political West African journal, *Jeune Afrique*, that 1993 salaries would reach 64 per cent of current expenditure and 70 per cent of national income (*Jeune Afrique*, 1993).

Burkina Faso's industries include mining, agricultural processing plants, brewing and bottling, light industry and trade. The informal sector has become an increasingly important source of income for many Burkinabé people, particularly with the growth of the urban areas (UNAIS, 1996). The country holds limited natural resources which have been underexploited due to poor infrastructure. These resources include manganese, gold, limestone, marble, phosphate and zinc. Economic development is hindered by a poor communications network within a landlocked country.

Table 1.1   Base data for Burkina Faso

	Unit	Period	Figures
AREA/POPULATION			
Area	Thousand km²	1985	274
Total population	Thousands	1985	7936
Population density	Persons/km²	1985	29
Life expectancy	Years	1985	48
Infant mortality	–/1000	1985	152/1000
AGRICULTURAL PRODUCTION			
Groundnuts	Tonne	1987–88	379
Cotton seed	Tonne	1987–88	148,015
Cotton fibre	Tonne	1987–88	58,464
Shea nut	Tonne	1987–88	1,825
Sesame	Tonne	1987–88	625
Maize	Tonne	1987–88	176
Millet and sorghum	Tonne	1987–88	2,239
ENERGY			
Electricity production	Million kWh	1989	148.1
Consumed petroleum products: petrol, kerosene, diesel;	Thousand m³	1989	146.4
fuel oil, diesel oil	Thousand tonnes	1989	56.3
TRANSPORT AND COMMUNICATIONS.			
Rail transport:			
Total merchandise	Thousand tonnes	1987	428
Aeroplane passengers:			
leaving;	Number	1989	63,951
arriving	Number	1989	63,625
Aeroplane freight:			
leaving;	Tonne	1989	4,556
arriving	Tonne	1989	3,912
COMMERCE			
Value of imports	Billion FCFA	1989	175.3
Value of exports	Billion FCFA	1989	30.2
Value of principal imports:			
food products;	Billion FCFA	1989	29.3
energy products;	Billion FCFA	1989	10.8
raw materials;	Billion FCFA	1989	2.7

Table 1.1   Base data for Burkina Faso (continued)

machines/transport vehicles;	Billion FCFA	1989	82.8
other industrial products;	Billion FCFA	1989	–
Value of principal exports:			
food products;	Billion FCFA	1989	3
raw materials	Billion FCFA	1989	17
WAGES AND PRICES			
Variation in price indices	per cent	1990	–0.83
Minimum wage	FCFA/hour	1988	130.69
FINANCE			
National budget	Billion FCFA	1990	159.5
Budget previsions:			
Total resources	Billion FCFA	1990	98.5
Total spending	Billion FCFA	1990	111.1
Foreign debt	Billion FCFA	1988	241.7
Balance of payments	Billion FCFA	1987	16.6
NATIONAL ACCOUNTS			
Gross Domestic Product at market prices	Billion FCFA	1985	455.9
General Purchasing Power at factor cost	FCFA	1985	57,447

Source: INSD, 1993.

History, Environment and Movement in West Africa

Current land-use practices and environmental arrangements in West Africa reflect a long and complex history and it is therefore necessary to examine historical perceptions about how African communities used and adapted themselves to the prevailing environmental conditions. Western experts and colonial administrators before them, have considered the African farmer as a despoiler of environment; far from being a custodian, the farmer is a destroyer of the very resources that sustain him. Collingwood (1940 – quoted in Fairhead and Leach, 1996:13) says, this is a root assumption in western thought. It follows that the more people there are, the more damage they will do: hence, fears of population growth. Fears are intensified when these large populations start to move and migrate and images spring to mind of a swathe of forest ants clearing away all vegetation that lies in their path. It is necessary to examine our own perceptions of Africans and environmental degradation (discussed further in chapter seven) because it is these, more than anything else, that have led to 'Africa in crisis' conclusions.

According to Giblin *et al* (1996:2), there have been two great debates by historians over environment and demographic growth: firstly has been the 'Merrie Africa' approach, which sees stable pre-colonial communities as having lived in harmony with nature before suffering depopulation, ecological disaster and economic exploitation under colonial rule; and there is the 'Primitive Africa' approach which depicts precolonial Africans as having inhabited a hostile environment in perilous proximity to famine, epidemic and demographic reversals before achieving greater security in the colonial period. The 'Merrie Africa' led to the assumption of a stable social system and economic organisation as well as permanent ecological equilibrium and the 'Primitive Africa' illustrated the perpetual darkness and hopelessness of Africa unless it be saved through conversion, conquest and foreign rule (Sutton, 1990:2). Apart from these perceptions being vast distortions of reality,[2] both negate the capacity and capability of Africans to transform prevailing external (and internal) conditions to suit their own purposes. In this sense, western perceptions of the African situation imply stasis, i.e. there was a before and after, a then and now, and 'dynamism' was replaced in the vocabulary by 'development'.

Environments, economic and political situations, cultures (through invasion and religious contact) and climate have constantly changed throughout African history and what is seen today is the result of thousands of years of complex history. Communities have continually used their economic, political, cultural and moral resources to prosper in ever-changing ecological circumstances (Giblin *et al*, 1996:3). Unfortunately, the historical dynamism that should be used to locate African development is ignored. Instead, present socio-economic and ecological conditions are assumed to be relics of a by-gone era which may have been slightly changed by colonial intervention. It is upon these assumptions that development projections are based. Sutton (1990) says that there persists the notion of an essentially unchanging, a supposedly 'traditional' African past, the details of which need little researching since they can readily be assumed. Once we begin to think about farming and pastoral societies inhabiting ever-changing environments, we are led to consider how economic institutions, political and gender relations, intellectual leadership and moral imperatives may have been involved in the process of environmental adaptation (Giblin *et al*, 1996). It is for precisely this reason that the recent process of north to south migration in the province of Sissili in Burkina Faso, which is the focus of this study, needs to be contextualised.

---

2 Sutton (1990) calls this antiquarianism, a sentimental quest for the past which denies history and with it an understanding of change and development and the pressures stimulating them.

West Africa is one of the most sparsely populated regions in the world and historians of all persuasions are united in attributing its underdevelopment in part to a low density of population, which has inhibited growth of the economy, state formation and intensification of agriculture (Hart, 1982). The aspects of historical blindness, the assumption of stasis and the myth of over-population cloud modern interpretations of a very dynamic region. In such a clouded interpretation, there is a limited view of Africa and, it is categorised, sadly and unfairly, as an irrelevant corner of the globe (Sutton, 1990).

In the following section we examine the internal dynamics of Burkinabé communities in an attempt to describe and explain their modes of production in a wider context.

The Peasant Mode of Production

The Peasantry

The 'peasantry' have been studied intensely in academic and political history since the 1850s, most notably by Karl Marx in 'Peasantry as a class' in 1850 and Chayanov in the early 1900s with the 'Theory of peasant economy'. More recently the study of the peasantry has been popularised by Scott (1976), Hyden (1983), Richards (1985) and most recently Chambers (1983, 1989, 1994, 1997). It is necessary in this study, not to provide a commentary of the past and present debate on theories of peasantries, but to illustrate what is meant by peasantry in this particular context. Shanin (1975:240) provides a useful introduction:

> The peasantry consist of small agricultural producers who, with the help of simple equipment and the labour of their families, produce mainly for their own consumption and for the fulfilment of obligations to the holders of political and economic power.

For the peasantry, for want of a better word, the family farm is the basic unit of ownership, production, consumption and social life and the individual, the family and the farm appear as an indivisible whole (Shanin, 1975). The family's objective is survival through subsistence and consequently their economies have been little understood through neo-classical economic study which is focused on markets. What is unique about the peasantry is that the unit of consumption is also the unit of production. The family begins with a more or less irreducible subsistence consumer demand, based on its size, which it must meet in order to continue as a unit (Scott, 1976:13). The subsistence ethic, coupled with the family as the producing and consuming unit, makes the peasant's motivations both unique and universal at the same time. This universality of family solidarity coupled with an existence in a natural economy, or biomass economy (O'Keefe *et al*, 1982), makes for the segmentation of peasant society into small units with a remarkable degree of self-sufficiency and ability to withstand crises (Shanin, 1975). Vierich (1986) agrees saying that the organisation of peasant societies into smaller units (or compounds) also provided more vulnerable units with a form of buffer against misfortune.

The studies of the Russian peasantry of the late 1800s have been found to share similarities with contemporary African peasantries, with southern Burkina Faso being no exception. For example, Shanin (1975:244) notes that the family of the Russian peasant at the beginning of the twentieth century was generally 'the people who eat from the same pot'. This is common throughout Africa and the Third World, with the Mandikas in the Gambia using the name **sinkiro** (Howorth, 1992) to mean the same thing. Similarly a Malayo-Polynesian ethnic group use the term **mweenga** (Goodenough, 1955). Likewise, Fei (1953:32) in his study of Chinese peasantry, says that 'the peasantry ... is a way of living'. It is clear that there are universals in peasant modes of production.

One of these fundamental universals in peasant economies is their relationship to land. Moyo (1995) stresses that land fulfils different roles in peasant economies which apply to the spectrum of peasantries throughout the world. Moyo notes:

- land as a store house of nature for reproduction of future generations;
- land as an agricultural production tool for subsistence food and exchange incomes to meet broader subsistence needs and for re-investment;
- land as a receptacle of direct household utility needs; water, woodfuel, organic fertiliser, medicine, shade, fruit, housing and home and meat; and
- land as social and political territory of governance and community reproduction.

Land is central to the peasant economy and attempts at severing the indivisible links that attach human to land has come up against fierce resistance, as noted by Scott (1976) in Southeast Asia.

To return to the household economy of the peasant, the family unit is crucial to understanding the processes and dynamics of the family's production system.[3] As Galeski (1963:140) notes, 'the family is the

---

[3] In several African languages, the common word for 'poor' implies a lack of kin or friends (Von Braun, 1991:409).

production-team of the farm and position in the family determines duties on the farm, functions and rights attached. The rhythm of the farm defines the rhythm of family life'. Shanin (1975:246) increases the depth of analysis to say that the individual in his own right 'doesn't count' because the key to peasant economies is the family and the survival of the family. The individual becomes almost unimportant but at the same time he/she is vital. Like Hyden's (1986) analysis where he says that although villagers normally have an astonishing ability to ensure everyone's livelihoods, the absence of a key household member can have adverse effects on other family members.

> Not every member of the household does everything. Husbands and wives combine to carry out most tasks falling within the sphere of the household economy; children are drawn in to care for crops, animals and smaller children, and combinations of relatives or neighbours help each other with farming, construction or other heavy jobs. (Hyden, 1986:18)

The impact of male seasonal migration on households, for example, can be severe. This integration of the individual and the family unit being 'more than the sum of its parts' is in contrast to capitalist economies where the individual becomes the basic nuclear unit of society, free to interact with any others in the huge new complex of social hierarchies and structures (Shanin, 1975). From this premise alone, it is difficult to understand peasant economies from a capitalist vista.

The peasant economy operates a risk minimisation approach to subsistence. In this approach the peasant (farmer) prefers to minimise the probability of having a disaster rather than maximising his average return (Scott, 1976). Thus, the profit and accumulation motives rarely appear in their pure form, which makes the neat conceptual models of maximisation of income, normal in a market economy, of doubtful applicability to a peasant economy (Shanin, 1975). Another reason why capitalist modes of thought do not 'connect' with peasant economies is raised by Clifton and Wharton (1971:570) who note that the peasant's consumption is fairly constant; in good years the farmer may have some surplus to sell, and in bad years little or none, but at least his family is fed. They also calculated that the peasant family consumes 80 per cent of its produce and say that such a consumption level can be regarded as his minimum subsistence level, i.e. a level he will strive not to fall below. Scott (1976) calls this the 'safety-first' maxim and says it is a logical consequence of the ecological dependence of peasant livelihoods and it embodies a relative preference for subsistence security over high average income. This characteristic of peasant communities finds expression in a wide array of actual choices, institutions and values.

Clifton and Wharton (1971:566) identified three characteristics of peasant communities:

- they are historically proven to be successful, i.e. the members have survived;
- they are relatively static (but the general pace of development is below that which is considered desirable by modern economies); and
- attempts at change are frequently resisted, both because the known institutions and processes have proven dependable and because the known elements constitute something akin to an ecological unity in the human realm.

This resistance to change was seen by Scott (1976), who identified the similarities between the peasantry of eighteenth and nineteenth century Europe with that of contemporary Asia. He comments that the Southeast Asian protest movements were less about equality of wealth and landholding but more about the 'right to subsistence'. This is the same 'right to subsistence' that the peasantry hold as the fundamental element of peasant society and can be seen with the settlement of Mossi and Fulani immigrants in Sissili (see later). Scott (1976) goes on to say that all village families will be guaranteed a minimal subsistence niche insofar as the resources controlled by villagers make this possible. 'Village egalitarianism ... is conservative not radical, it claims that all should have a place, a living, not that all should be equal' (Scott, 1976:5). This is clear when looking at Nuni society (see chapter three) where there is a strong belief in hierarchies; subsistence, however, is at the root of peasant society. The historical patterns of resistance by the peasantry are also coupled with peasant producers enjoying an unusual degree of autonomy from other groups, such as the state, in society. Hyden (1986) says that this is partly due to the rudimentary technology that characterises most of peasant production. To illustrate this, and the subsistence level, Hart (1982:78) tells us:

> They build and repair their houses; they prepare food and fetch water, fuel and other domestic supplies; they spin, weave and sew clothing; they keep animals, slaughter them and tan their hides; they make tools, pots, baskets, furniture and ornaments; they generate remedies for their ills; they run their own systems of conflict resolution and work hard to keep a variety of spiritual agents appeased.

Scott's 'moral economy' (1976) was one where subsistence was guaranteed as far as possible within village communities. 'They [the informal social guarantees] represent the peasant view of decent social relations embodying the right of all to a subsistence niche and the pooling of risks ... they are standards of moral judgements' (Scott, 1976:41). However, this morality is not always apparent, 'they aid [each other] because there is a tacit agreement about reciprocity and their assistance is as good as money in the bank when the situation is reversed'[4] (Scott, 1976:28). Amartya Sen (1982, 1983, and Dreze and Sen, 1989) called this arrangement (and similar arrangements) *entitlements* and looked at the loss of such arrangements as the root cause of poverty and famine. Following Sen, the entitlement to exchange, reciprocity and aid is central to peasant economies.

Scott's interpretation of the peasant economy is different from that proffered by Hyden (1980) and his 'economy of affection'.[5] Hyden's construct attempts to explain how and why peasant economies work rather than their morality (although when morality is talked about it is done so in relation to the ethics of local political economies)[6] as he says 'the economy of affection has nothing to do with fond emotions per se' (Hyden, 1983:8). There are many similarities in both interpretations because they are essentially describing the same phenomena. Hyden (1986) comments that this type of economy (of affection), which springs from the needs and dynamics of micro- rather than macro-structures, becomes important in any society where the producer has not yet been cut off from his land, i.e. the rural peasantry.

Both Scott (1976) and Hyden (1986) agree that the peasantry operate within a type of economy which must be conceptualised independently from either capitalism or socialism. In most parts of the world, the economy of affection has been reduced to an historical artefact; the moral economy that Scott described in Southeast Asia has been effectively overpowered by other economic forms but this is generally not the case in Africa (Hyden, 1986). This is because of the resilience of peasants as producers coupled with a weakness of the state that cannot actuate development.

---

4 In a similar vein, Platteau (1991:155) has interpreted the moral economy as a 'social-security' economy and says that people belonging to these communities find collective methods to protect themselves against major contingencies and production hazards. Platteau also points out that Scott made the mistake of confusing social-security arrangements with altruistic behaviour.
5 The economy of affection (Hyden, 1980:18) has its basis in the intimate connection between the local resources and technologies and a kin-based mode of production (Anon, 1990:7). It is an economy where all aspects of the community's livelihood (resource base, exchange system, family duties, social relations, religious/cultural activities, etc.) are internalised and carry equal relative worth. It is not a cash economy, nor is it a formal economy and, as such, has been little understood by western modes of thinking. Economic analyses of African social systems concerned with capital flows alone (and this includes classical sustainable development approaches) miss the centrality of symbolic forms of capital in everyday life: the complexities of gift giving, duties and other practices associated with the maintenance and accumulation of prestige and status (Bourdieu, 1977:173).
6 'Rights and obligations are still defined primarily in relation to precapitalist structures associated with a system of smallholder peasant production' (Hyden, 1986:25).

As long as Africa's leaders do not effectively control the means of production, they can sustain their own power and influence only by following the rules of the economy of affection. Although such measures as price incentives may have effects, the most important step is manifestation of direct support for the relevant communal realm. (Hyden, 1986:25–26)

Peasant Adaptation

The African farmer will adapt his or her farming system in response to household needs, regardless of the availability of new technologies or extension messages. Boserup (1972) was critical to the arguments of agricultural intensification in response to demographic change. She provided a crucial balance to Malthusian interpretations of the carrying capacity of land and the inelasticity of agricultural production. Boserup said that population, not agricultural production, is the independent variable that will dictate growth in subsistence economies.

Boserup (1972:15–16) identified five agricultural systems of increasing intensity: forest-fallow, bush-fallow, short-fallow, annual cropping and multicropping. The crucial variable in all these systems is the presence of fallow as a method of fertility management. With low population densities land can be cultivated for short periods (one or two years) while the fertility remains high, then left fallow for up to 40 years. As populations increase and the need for agricultural land increases, fallow periods will decrease because of competition for land. This does not mean that all the land in a given area will be farmed; some land in that area may be devoted to other land uses such as gathering, pasture, gardening or for future farmland. In this situation the agricultural period (i.e. frequency of cropping) is too long to simply utilise the soil's natural fertility and fallow period is not long enough to completely restore soil fertility. Thus, additional techniques need to be used, such as crop rotations, mulching and other techniques of soil fertility management. As the frequency of cropping increases (and the agricultural land available decreases) so do the inputs that the farmer must use. This may culminate in annual cropping where the land is only left uncultivated for several months or in mixed cropping where the land is continually cropped. Boserup (1972:13) comments on this process,

> By contrast, when the analysis is based upon the concept of frequency of cropping, there can be no temptation to regard soil fertility exclusively as a gift of nature, bestowed upon certain lands once and for all. Thus, soil fertility, instead of being treated as an exogenous or even unchangeable 'initial condition' of the analysis, takes its place as a variable, closely associated with changes in population density and related changes in agricultural methods.

Fairhead and Leach (1996) identified in Kissidougou, in Guinea, that local communities value their soils according to how long they have been cropped, i.e. the longer they have been cultivated, the longer the process of soil fertility management and the more fertile the soils (called 'the feminisation' of the soil in relation to intensive home-gardening carried out by women).

Intensification of the agricultural system has more to do with an intensive system of soil fertility management, which largely consists of reducing the natural role of fallow. This is in contrast to increased mechanisation of the agricultural system or the increasing productivity of labour.

Family Dynamics and the Farm

In order to understand the production system, we must understand the unit of consumption, i.e. the household unit. The system of consumption organises the use of production and the modalities of production. It is not sufficient to simply talk about the 'farm family' because of its implication of a single unit composed of husbands, wives and children, although these do exist. In southern Burkina Faso, and in many parts of Africa, the household is composed of several family units from the same lineage, with each member having his or her own duties, responsibilities and obligations to ensure the social reproduction of the household.

Single family units do exist and they represent breakaway factions from a larger 'family unit' (or household) of the same lineage. These, let us call them young families, often still have links to the larger compound they have left; i.e. obligations of work, remittances or social duties, and, in return, receive support from the larger unit. It is a gradual process of gaining total independence that is linked with the growth of the young family into a mature family that has the ability to support itself in terms of agricultural production. Independence brings forth interdependence, in the sense that once a conjugal unit has broken away from the parental home, its survival still depends on the remittances and reciprocity of its parental source. Parallels here can be drawn in the province of Sissili, on the breakaway village of Saboué from Pissai (see chapter six). However, unlike the young family unit whose main priority is to gain independence in material terms, i.e. food production to ensure its own social reproduction, it has taken many years for Saboué to gain its self sufficiency in spiritual and 'legal'[7] terms from Pissai. The breakaway family still relies to a large extent on the paternal home for spiritual and legal guidance.

To return to the universality of peasant modes of production,[8] it is

---

7 Legal in this sense relates to the customary law and management arrangements.
8 Shanin (1975:240) says that 'peasantry appears to be a type without localization'; it would seem from the proceeding lines that they are 'a type without localization' in time as well as space.

pointed out that 'the head of the family appears as the manager rather than the proprietor of family land' (Thomas and Znaniecki, 1918:92). This is coupled with the observation, in 1888, by Mukhin that the family head's function has the role of the manager of the common family property. These dated observations remain true today in Africa.

In the province of Sissili, within the sedentary ethnic groups the organisation of the production unit, i.e. the family farm, is organised through and within the household. The head of the household, the most senior male member, allocates land to the smaller production units within the same household. All of these production units, including that of the household head, contribute to overall household food security and the social reproduction of the families. The household in Sissili is usually made up of more than one (from one to four) conjugal units with the most senior, i.e. oldest, of the lineage being the head. The size of the household, i.e. the number of working members, will dictate the size of the land surface that is farmed. In Sissili, the Land Chief will assess the individual household's need in terms of land surface area for food production. The chief will then apportion land accordingly. For example, he would not allow a single family household to have ten hectares even if sufficient labour was available.

Vierich (1986:163) in her study of peasant households in Burkina Faso correctly interprets the household leader's duties:

> The compound head represents the interests of the whole group in the larger field of lineage and village politics. Furthermore, he had the authority and responsibility to request land from the lineage head [i.e. the Village or Land Chief] and to arrange, and often to finance the marriages, baptisms, funerals and group labour invitations that took place within the compound group, even when these were for the benefit of an ordinary household within the group.

In this way, the household head has to ensure the welfare of all household members and responsibilities are great. The household head must ensure the survival of his household which means: ensuring enough food (grain) for all household members even in famine years; providing for visitors and lodgers; caring for the infirm, handicapped and aged of the household (and often those external to the household) and ensuring visiting group workers are fed or remunerated appropriately. This means that the production unit (i.e. farm) of the household head is likely to be proportionally bigger in size than those of the separate household units, whose purpose is only to provide subsistence for the respective units. In other words, the household head must strive to produce a surplus that can be used to fulfil social and political obligations as household leader. Vierich (1986) notes that compound leaders may even raise their annual cereal requirements in anticipation of a certain frequency of failure, because of illness or other misfortune, within the smaller production units sharing their compound. This welfare system is highly sophisticated and goes a long way to guarantee subsistence to all members; like all welfare systems, there are contributions from the beneficiaries.

The household head does not have all these obligations and responsibilities without material support; there are also privileges that come with the position. Firstly, the household head has the best agricultural land and ensures its higher productivity through the labour contributions of other family members. Thus, in addition to working on their land, the conjugal units must work on the larger farm of the household head. In addition to this, the household leader, because of political and senior lineage position, can secure labour from other sub-units from other households in the community. This not only reduces labour bottlenecks but also ensures reciprocity from one household to another in times of need, such as hungry periods. The household head also has access to the resources, both monetary and physical, of the other household members in times of need. This 'commandeering' of vital resources is recognised as necessary by the household members and is not contested. In the words of the Mossi proverb, 'The snake gets whatever is in the belly of the frog' (Skinner, 1964:115).

The position of 'leader' in relation to other deferential household members is not a relationship open to abuse. If he were to abuse this position, he would lose the support of his juniors and with it, his access to extra labour, land and capital (Duval, 1985). It is an unspoken rule in households that if the leader invests in his own material wealth or physical well being then he must also do the same for the other members of the household. His wealth or development must be at a pace with the entire household and not at its expense.

This 'living under the umbrella' has certain advantages for the smaller production units within the larger household. Because they are more-or-less assured of their subsistence, they have the relative freedom to pursue other activities, often of an economic nature. These activities include wage labour, trade and craft production which may have been prohibited by the requirements of crop work. This leads to a diversification of household activities and spreads risk. Vierich (1986:163) traces the development of the position of the household head and his rationality.

> If one considers the special rights and obligations of the compound head, one can better understand the economic performance of the production units that they lead. The compound leaders ...were at one time simple [family] heads within the compounds of their elder kinsmen. With their ascent to compound leadership, the pressures and privileges of their position pushed, and permitted, them to invest more in agriculture and to produce at surplus intensities.

Thus, there is a linear hierarchy in peasant society in Burkina Faso that allows all to enjoy the privileges and punishments of being at any one particular stage.

Lifescapes

The term 'lifescape' was first introduced by Salibo Somé and Kevin McSweeney (1996) while carrying out research and development in the north of Burkina Faso. They defined it as the social, cultural and economic interactions that occur across the landscape. It is appropriate that the term was used in relation to West African communities because of regional characteristics of movement and adaptation. Lifescapes are more than physical landscapes. It implies a livelihood or production system which is linked, but not tied, to place; lifescapes are dynamic in both time and place.

People create landscapes, they produce nature and it is the people/people relationship in a local place which is the critical variable. To understand environmental phenomena in the context of a social environment, it is less appropriate to calculate carrying capacity as the followers of Malthus did, and more appropriate to examine human agency, as Boserup has done, to examine people's ability to create lifescapes.

Lifescapes are necessarily interactive. In this study, three groups are analysed in three different villages which have contrasting resource and population dynamics. A general summary of these three groups would be:

- the Nuni, who are the indigenous, sedentary group. The Nuni were once the majority but now only make up 22 per cent of the population in the province of Sissili;
- the Mossi, who are sedentary immigrants coming from the Mossi plateau in the north of the country. The Mossi now make up the majority (almost 50 per cent) of the provincial population; and
- the Fulani, who are agro-pastoralist immigrants. The Fulani came from the northern regions of Burkina Faso with their cattle and now make up 11 per cent of the population in the province.

In chapter two, the context for the lifescapes is provided with a description of the province of Sissili and an examination of the major influences on provincial production patterns, including Islamic influences.

Chapter three culturally locates the lifescapes and their respective production patterns. The three ethnic groups with their major characteristics are presented which illustrates the diversity of practices in the province of Sissili.

Chapter four, five and six present the three village case studies where the different ethnic groups are located in three villages providing a range of very different lifescapes. While the differences are explicit, it is also apparent that there is a variety of similarities between the ethnic groups and in the ways they have negotiated their positions in the lifescapes.

Finally, chapter seven concludes the study and discusses how Western thought differs from rural African thought and then examines local environmental management and the new emerging natural resource paradigm.

2 The Province of Sissili

Introduction

This chapter introduces the province of Sissili, where the research for this book was carried out. It serves to contextualise the case study villages in terms of the provincial economy and its physical and socio-cultural characteristics. The discussion then progresses to issues of resource use and an analysis of the recent introduction of pastoralism in the province. There follows an introduction to the three case study villages that form the basis for this book. There is also an examination of the influence of Islam on local communities. It is demonstrated in this that the complex physical and social conditions in the province are not static but are in the process of constant change as new problems or opportunities arise. However, it is important to know what these physical and social conditions are in order to understand local production and management practices.

Physical Environment

Location, Climate and Geography

The province of Sissili lies to the south of Burkina Faso (see Figure 2.1) between the latitudes 10°59' and 12°0' North (corresponding to the Ghanaian frontier to the south) and between 1°18' and 2°53' West. It is bordered on its western limit by the Mouhoun valley, the Nazinon river runs along the north-eastern border and the Sissili river limits the province to the south-east. Its total land surface covers 13,211 km^2 which makes it 5 per cent of the total land surface of Burkina Faso. The land surface is divided up into 13 administrative departments[1] and 533 villages.

Sissili's climate is classified as sudano-guinean in the southern region, with a rainfall of 900 to 1200 mm per year, and sudano-sahelian in the

---

[1] The case study villages of Lon, Boutiourou and Saboué are located in the departments of Cassou, Léo and Biéha respectively.

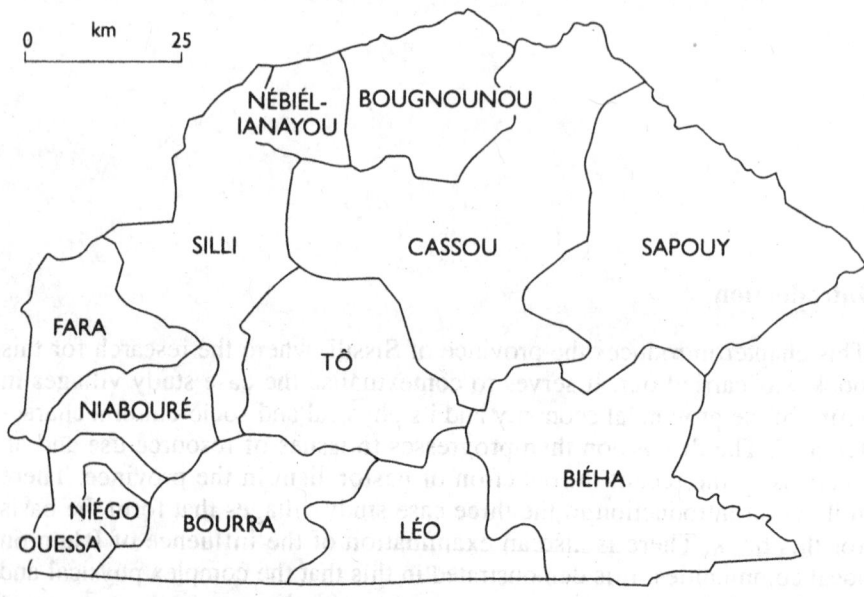

Figure 2.1 The province of Sissili

Table 2.1 The departments of Sissili and their land surface

Department	Area km²
Biéha	1,669
Bougnounou	819
Bourra	1,102
Cassou	2,338
Fara	698
Léo	932
Tô	1,215
Nébiélianayou	400
Niabouri	519
Niégo	146
Ouessa	183
Sapouy	2,034
Silli	1,156
Total Province	13,211

Source: IBS, 1993.

northern zone, with a rainfall of 750 to 900 mm per year. The transition between these two different climatic zones is seen in cropping patterns, with cotton production dominating the northern areas and tuber production in the south. There is not a severe change in natural vegetation cover, although a rough division can be made between the boundaries of the departments of Tô and Cassou.

Rainfall comes over 130 and 150 days between May and October, with the past 15 years having medium to poor rainfall. Mean temperature varies between 27°C and 34°C, with the hottest months being March and April. Annual rainfall (see Figure 2.2) has been erratic. The potential average annual evapo-transpiration rate is 1744 mm (de Boer and Kessler, 1994).

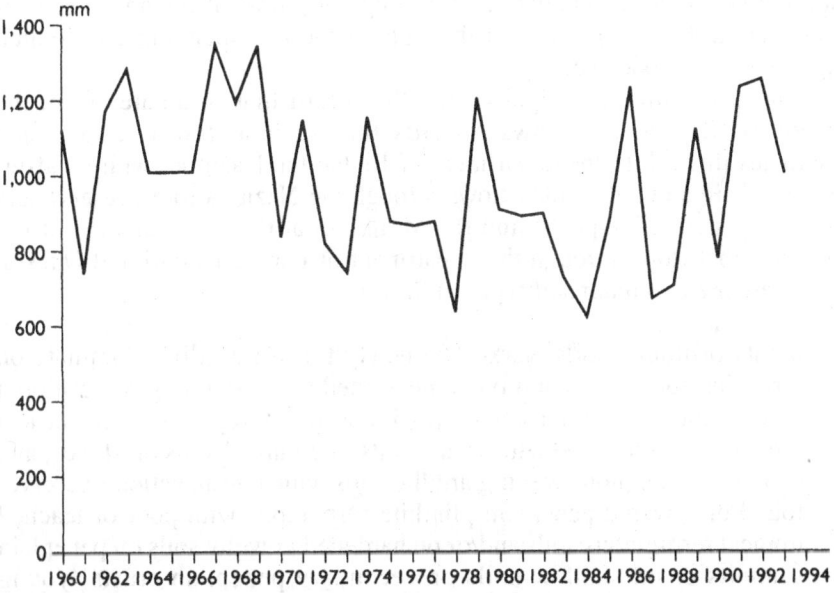

Source: Data from de Boer and Kessler, 1994 (for data between 1960 – 1991) and SPA, Léo (for data for 1992 and 1993).

Figure 2.2 Total annual rainfall in the province of Sissili, 1960 to 1993

The natural vegetation in Sissili varies between savanna and wooded savanna. The term 'wooded savanna' in this context is understood to mean a savanna made up of low and tall woody species (i.e. bushes and trees) associated with a more or less continuous grassy layer. This grassy layer is frequently destroyed by bush fire at the start or in the middle of the dry season which lasts from October to April (for bush fire distribution patterns in this region, see Millington *et al*, 1994).

The indigenous fauna of the province principally consists of bird species, wild pigs (*Phacochoerus aethiopicus*), antelope (*Hippotragus equinus*) and vervet (savanna) monkeys (*Cercopithecus aethiops*). However, in the Nazinga game reserve (part of which lies in Sissili) there are buffalo (*Synceros caffer*), elephant (*Loxodonta africana*), oribi (*Ourebia ourebi*), common duiker (*Sylvicapra grimmia*), red-flanked duiker (*Cephalophus rufilatus*), western hartebeest (*Alcelaphus buselaphus*), kob (*Kobus kob*), bush buck (*Tragelaphus scriptus*), waterbuck (*Kobus elipispirymnus*), bohar reedbuck (*Redunca redunca*), and olive baboon (*Paio anubis*) (Agrotechnik, 1991). There is little wild fauna outside the game reserve because of over hunting by the local population. Not long ago, most of the above species were found widely distributed throughout the province and contributed significantly to food security.

There are three principal rivers: the Sissili that originates from the region of Beniou and flows towards the Nazinon forest reserve and continues through to the department of Biéha; the Nazinon, with its affluents the Kira and Selé which flows through the Nazinga forest reserve and the department of Sapouy; and the Mouhoun at the extreme west of the province that flows through the department of Fara, Niabouri and Ouessa.

There are two main soil types in Sissili:

- montmorillonite soils marked by newly formed argillics dominate on birrimian formations and on some eroded soils, swelling to develop a strong cation absorption capacity, with brown eutrophic soils or vertical brown soils associated with young soils or colluvial soils on slopes; and
- kaolinitic soils (non swelling argillic soils with a weak cationic reserve) found on covered peneplain plinthite formations with poor or leached tropical ferruginous soils and/or on hardened gravelly soils on peneplain summits or on shallow soils on secondary peneplain crusts (young eroded soils) (IBS, 1993).

Weakly hydromorphic tropical ferruginous soils are found in the valleys on colluvial/alluvial embankments (Bunasol, 1990). Mineral hydromorphic soils are found in some blocked valley bottoms, slightly gley and medium deep (Bunasol, 1990).

The agricultural potential of the soils is medium for the most part of the province, with medium deep tropical ferruginous soils being the soil type most commonly farmed. They are suitable for most crops where water availability is sufficient. Certain brown eutrophic soils have a higher agricultural potential but are often found in the more hilly areas or they are found in limited areas in association with very poor soils (lithosols and young soils) (IBS, 1993). The Mouhoun has little irrigation potential (ferruginous soils with vertical tendencies with limited extension), like most secondary valleys in the province with the exception of some rice producing valley bottoms.

The natural relief in Sissili is monotonous and homogenous characterized by a regular topographic sequence, having the following characteristics:

- uncultivated laterite or granite capped mounds;
- soils on the slopes; gravelly ferruginous, sandy-limonitic, shallow, limited fertility, plinthic evolution, easily exhausted and eroded by agriculture;
- soils on slope bottoms; limonitic-sandy, medium fertility, deeper, much agricultural activity; and
- valley bottoms with heavy, sandy soil.

The sandy-limonitic structure of the soils is linked to the low organic content, which makes the soils easily compacted, erodible and susceptible to run-off the longer it is farmed (Bunasol, 1990).

An important aspect to note, in Table 2.3, is the low surface area of farmed land in relation to the total overall land surface and the dominance of long fallows over short fallows (715,000 ha compared to 107,000 ha). It should be noted that 1990 was a poor year for agricultural production having only approximately 700 mm of rainfall, but, in spite of this, there was still a 19 per cent cereal surplus.

Natural vegetation and land use

The province of Sissili contains a wealth of woody biomass, with total woody savanna covering around 60 per cent of the province. The estimations of different land classes give roughly similar results:

Table 2.2 shows that there is a high wooded area to farmland ratio and much of the wooded area is high quality forested savanna. In addition to the unprotected woody biomass, there also exists four areas of protected forest land in Sissili:

- Nazinon forest (previously called the *Volta Rouge* forest) which covers 66,500 ha, of which 35,700 ha are in Pô national park;
- Pô national park (the majority of which is in Sissili) with an area of 41,000 ha, 35,700 ha of which are in Nazinon forest, with 5,700 ha outside the province;
- Sissili forest park covering 37,000 ha, of which 15,600 ha make up the Yalé pasture zone; and

Table 2.2 A classification of land cover: Burkina Faso and Sissili

Land Classes	Burkina Faso[a] (ha)	Sissili[a] (ha)	Sissili[b] (ha)
• Forested/woody savanna	4,578,000	643,514	644,000
• Bush/shrub savanna (and burned areas)	10,184,000	178,420	178,000
• Gallery forest	270,000	13,400	13,400
• Thickets	387,000	24,200	24,200
• Agricultural land and fallows	11,980,000	382,225	445,550
• Unproductive agricultural land	no data	105,961	42,600
Total	27,399,000	1,321,100	1,321,100

Source: a FAO, 1983; b Gouvernement du Burkina Faso, 1986.

- Nazinga game ranch which covers 94,000 ha.

In 1993, the IBS classified local vegetation types in Sissili as a part of a provincial study on land use and vegetation patterns, largely based around the interpretation of satellite imagery. The IBS calculated surface areas under specific vegetation configurations. These can be used to measure the impact of human activity and vegetation recovery rates (i.e. fallows) in specific areas of the province. In the study, IBS give figures for the vegetation units corresponding to their occupation of the land space in Sissili as a whole and by department. From the figures, we see there are two dominant uses: firstly the medium density wooded savanna which occupies almost 63 per cent of the province and, secondly, the deforested areas which take up almost 21 per cent of the province. As an illustration and for future reference, the detailed occupation of space is given in Table 2.4 for the departments of Cassou, Léo and Biéha (which contain the case study villages).

As can be seen from Table 2.4, there remains significant portions of homogenous woody savanna, with Biéha having 30 per cent of its area covered with dense savanna and almost 50 per cent under medium dense homogenous savanna. The departments of Léo and Cassou, which are two densely populated departments, both have almost 70 per cent medium dense homogenous savanna. These figures represent a province, not experiencing an environmental crisis, but under significant woody biomass cover.

Table 2.3 General overview of the environmental and human situation in Sissili

	Unit of measurement	1990 situation
TOTAL SURFACE AREA	km²	13,211
Unproductive land area (village, road, rock outcrops, etc.)	km²	2,540
Managed forest area (sylvo-pastoral and village woodlands)	km²	1,210
Land available for agriculture	km²	9,461
POPULATION	persons	300,000
Density	per/km²	22
Natural growth rate	percent	2.5
Permanent managed forest	ha	121,000
Land available for agriculture	ha	946,100
Cultivated area/person/yr	ha	0.5
Cultivated area/family	ha	5
Cultivated area/year	ha	137,000
Fallow	ha	809,050
Relationship between cultivated area and fallow area	coeff	5.5
Duration of cultivation	yr	7
Duration of fallow	yr	38
Fallow area (with a duration > 5 years)	ha	715,000
Fallow area (with a duration < 5 years)	ha	107,000
Natural wood production (0.83 m³/ha/yr)		
Grands massifs	m³	100,000
Fallow (> 5 years)	m³	593,000
Total	m³	693,000
Fuelwood needs (0.5 m³/per/yr)	m³	150,000
Fuelwood surplus	m³	543,000
	percent	360
Agricultural production (expressed in sorghum equivalent)	t/ha	0.5
Yield	t	75,000
Annual production	kg	210
Cereal need/per/yr	t	63,000
Cereal needs of the population/yr	t	12,000
Cereal surplus	percent	19

Source: Agrotechnik, 1991.

Table 2.4 The detailed occupation of space (in per cent) for the departments of Cassou, Léo and Biéha and for the province of Sissili

Department	C	B	A	S	I	UNIT N	H	R	M	Water	Urban	Total
Cassou	27.6	0.1	68.5	3.5	0.0	0.2	0.0	0.1	0.0	0.0	0.1	100
Léo	27.1	0.0	66.5	5.4	0.0	0.0	0.0	0.4	0.0	0.0	0.5	100
Biéha	9.1	30.3	48.1	12.0	0.0	0.2	0.0	0.3	0.0	0.0	0.1	100
Sissili	20.8	7.1	62.9	8.3	0.2	0.2	0.2	0.2	0.1	0.0	0.1	100

Source: IBS, 1993.
Key for Table 2.4
C   Deforested zones
B   Dense wooded savanna, homogenous
A   Medium dense savanna, homogenous
S   Low density wooded or bush savanna, heterogeneous
I   Mixed grass and wooded savanna, very irregular
H   Grassy savanna with rare or absent woody species
N   Bare soil to very sparse savanna
R   Ripicole or rice zones in humid valley bottoms
M   Mixed cover: units N, B and R

Bush Fire

Burning the bush is a traditional agricultural and cultural practice which involves the majority of the population, burning around their villages and fields. There are many reasons behind bush burning (which are all strongly linked to customary practice) and thus there are many different 'types' of fire. These include:

- fires to burn agricultural residues;
- fires to stimulate growth in perennial grasses;
- fires for hunting;
- fires for discouraging vermin (snakes, scorpions, rats, etc.);
- fires for bush burning;
- fires to improve soil fertility; and
- fires to improve tree fruit harvest.

Fires are generally set in the mornings or early evenings, when there is no wind and temperatures are lower, so the fires can be more easily controlled (Schrekenberg, 1996). Usually several people work together, one setting the fire and the others keeping it under control with green branches.

Bush fires start in November when the vegetation begins to dry out and the burned area increases with the duration of the dry season. In many provinces, almost all the surface area is burned at some point in the year. In October to November, fires are classed as early fires or *'feu précoce'* and burn 30 per cent of the total area. In the proceeding months, a maximum of ten per cent is burnt and these are carefully controlled. Fires become more potentially damaging later in the dry season as vegetative matter loses much of its moisture content. The local communities use the early fires to burn vegetation close to sensitive areas (houses, plantations, fields still in cultivation, etc.) which consequently controls the later fires.

Bush fire destroys much of the herbaceous layer and almost all the dry annual grasses. Most of the dry annuals are lost towards February and March. Fire can destroy young trees, depending on when the fires occur, making tree regeneration difficult. Its positive effect is to stimulate growth in perennial grasses, burning dry and dead grasses, reducing soil shading and allowing more favorable conditions to resprouting perennials. De Vries and Djitèye (1982) explain that bush fire is a natural phenomenon and much of the natural vegetation is adapted to fire and indeed needs fire for seed germination. Bush fires are most dangerous when they come late in the season, the fires then attain high temperatures made possible by a build up of combustible material created with the advance of the dry season. The high temperatures kill a wide range of regenerating tree species. Early fires however have positive effects on the seedlings, allowing them, because of the mildness of the fires, to regenerate. The dominance of early fires in this area can lead to an increase of woody species (see Boutrais and Bassett, 1996). A reason for bush fire, often expressed by the local population, is that if the burning is carried out early then this leads to a good harvest of the two most important local fruit trees: the shea nut (*Butyrospermum parkii*) and néré (*Parkia biglobosa*).

Fields and fallows remain less burnt than the surrounding bush. This may indicate a change in soil fertility management. Schreckenberg (1996) notes that cultivated fields that previously were burned after the harvest to clear them of weeds and to enrich the soil, now are left for grazing animals that enrich them with their manure. These fields will, however, be burnt just before the rainy season to clear them of weeds.

Vegetative Production

Vegetative herbaceous production (including annual and perennial grasses but not tree production), measured in kilograms of dry matter per hectare per year (kg DM/ha/yr), varies greatly, depending on the quality of the soils and the availability of water. The least productive unit is found on

Table 2.5 Vegetative production of the herbaceous layer in kilograms of dry matter per hectare per year in Sissili (kg dm/ha/yr)

Unit	Production kg dm/ha/yr
S	500
D	2750
Sb	3500
A	3300
R	4000
F	4000
P	9000
C – fallow	3500
H – fallow	3000
b – fallow	4000
B	4000
N	0

Source: de Boer 1992 based on Toutain, 1974.

rocky outcrops or shallow soils and the most productive area is found in the humid prairies and swamps where production reaches 9000 kg DM/ha/yr (de Boer, 1992). The level of vegetative production of the different vegetation zones, to a large extent, dictates the herding patterns of the local Fulani. For example, the IBS land units, C, H and b (fields, young fallows on slopes, on hill tops, and valley bottoms) are considered pasture zones. Their production is estimated at 3500, 3000 and 4000 kg DM/ha/yr respectively (de Boer, 1992). The figures on Table 2.5 are an estimation of production rates related to the land classification units of de Boer (1992). (See Appendix 1.)

De Boer (1992) calculated a considerable amount of dry matter production in the department of Tô, which is one of the most densely populated departments of Sissili, at 370 x 106 kg. Dry matter production in the woody biomass is higher in the valley bottoms or where tree density is high or where the soils are more fertile. It is interesting to note that woody vegetative production in young fallows (of 3–5 years) constitutes an important percentage of dry matter production, with primary regeneration by *Dichrostachys cinerea, Piliostigma thonningii* and some *Mimosaceae*. Very young fallows (of 1–2 years) have a lower dry matter production as they are in the early stages of regeneration.

Table 2.6 Vegetative production of the woody layer in kilograms of dry matter per hectare per year in Sissili (kg dm/ha/yr)

Unit	Production kg dm/ha/yr
S	296
D	425
Sb	436
A	556
R	608
F	608
P	0
C – fallow	250
H – fallow	250
b – fallow	250
B	608
N	0

Source: Egging, 1990 (except for units C, H and b, estimated by de Boer 1992).

Human Resources and Human Systems

Population and ethnic groups

The population of Sissili is extremely young, almost 60 per cent being under 20 years old. The majority of the under twenties are also men (63.7 per cent). But the mature population shows a greater percentage of females than males, largely due to male migration for labour outside Sissili.

There are eight ethnic groups in Sissili which can be divided into primary, secondary and tertiary groups. The primary ethnic groups include, the immigrant Mossi (46 per cent of the population), the indigenous Nuni (22 per cent) and the immigrant Fulani (11 per cent). The secondary group include, the Dagari (8 per cent) and the Sissala (3 per cent), and the tertiary group holds the Lyele (2 per cent), the Bobo (2 per cent) and the Bwamu (2 per cent). The remaining 3 per cent are made up of other miscellaneous tribes. The various ethnic groups have very distinct social characteristics which will be examined later in chapter three.

Table 2.7 gives an idea of principal areas of 'employment' or occupation in the active population (of ten years or older). An aspect of employment that the above table does not show is the dominance of the Mossi ethnic group in the informal commerce and trading sector. Most *commerçants*, or traders, are Mossi and they are traditionally seen as the entrepreneurs, much like the Kikuyu of Kenya. They are seen by the Nuni

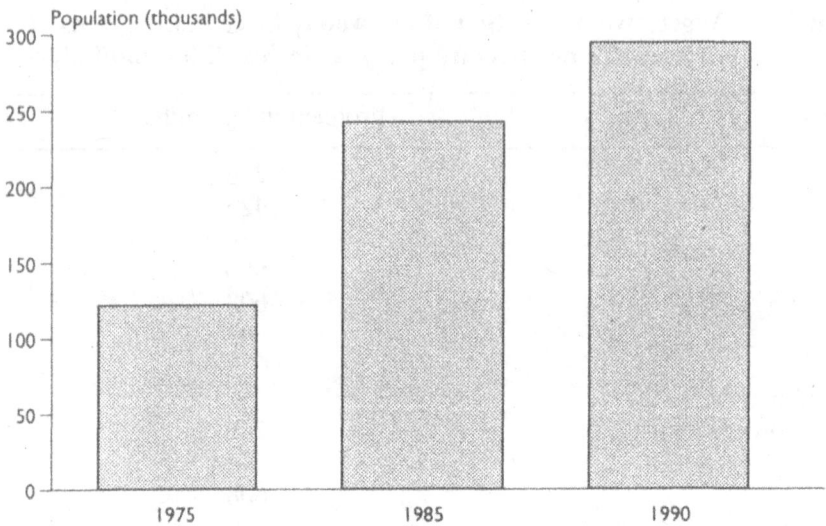

Source: Official census 1975 and 1985; Agrotechnik (1991) for 1990 figures.

Figure 2.3 Population growth in Sissili, 1975 to 1990

Table 2.7 Areas of employment in the resident, active population of Sissili (of 10 years old or older) by sex, 1985

Profession	Men	Women
All professions	64,978	65,909
Agriculture (including animal husbandry and fishing)	63,093	64,001
Higher administration, superior state civil servants	44	4
Lower administration	223	33
Manual labour, manual employees	256	51
Commerce	368	2,533
Craftsmen, artisans	3,222	135
Domestic services	253	52
Armed forces and security	328	–
Miscellaneous	–	7
Non-declared professions	64	63

Source: INSD, 1985 Census.

as agents of economic prosperity rather than heartless exploiters of cheap labour (as are the Lebanese merchants in the major towns of Burkina Faso).

Table 2.8　Village size and frequency in Sissili, 1985

Population	Village size frequency (%)
0–199	13.9
200–499	27.8
500–749	19.5
750–999	13.2
1000–1499	12.8
1500–1999	4.37
2000–5000	6.96
Total	100.00

Source: Berger Sarl, 1989.

In Burkina Faso, 51 per cent of the population are engaged in 'active work', i.e. make up the labour force, the remaining are either too old or too young. In an average family size of 11 (one man, two women, four boys and four girls), six people make up the labour force. The INSD indicates that the working age starts at ten years for boys and girls. Burkina Faso is a country of low levels of education and is dominated by traditional agriculture, where child labour makes up an important part of the total. Village size where 41.7% of villages have fewer than 500 people, Table 2.8 reflects this pattern of agricultural work.

Immigration

Large scale immigration began in the 1970s with the onset of the Sahelian droughts and continued up until the late 1980s. It has, however, almost ceased owing to the good rains throughout the country in recent years. The immigrants come almost exclusively from the northern Mossi plateau and are mostly Mossi and Fulani. Figure 2.4 provides an example from the department of Cassou which shows a significant drop in the population growth from 1985, which was the peak of immigration, to 1991 when immigration had almost stopped.

There are no figures on the actual numbers of immigrants who have entered the province, though indications can be found. For example, the population growth rate from 1975 to 1985 was 7.8 per cent while normally it is between 2.5 to 3.5 per cent. The Mossi are now the majority, making up roughly 50 per cent of the total population, in a province previously dominated by the Nuni ethnic groups. Table 2.9 shows the population growth for the department of Tô and is indicative of growth rates in parts of the province which have been heavily affected by immigration.

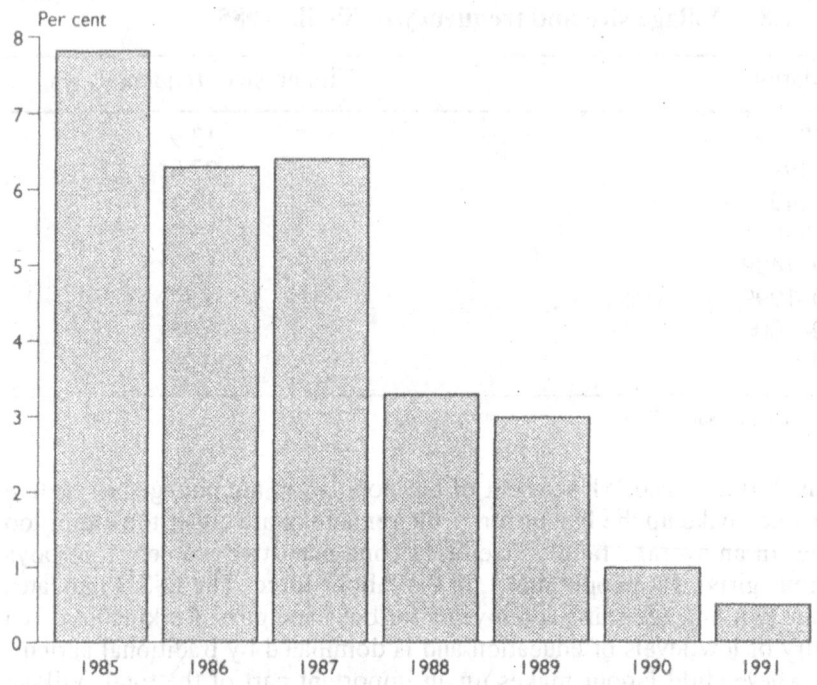

Source: Data from Burkina Faso census, 1985, Berger-Sarl, 1989 and PDR (Sixiéme FED) for 1990 and 1991.

Figure 2.4 Population growth in the department of Cassou, 1985 to 1991

Table 2.9 Population growth by ethnic group in the department of Tô, 1985 to 1991

Year	Nuni	Mossi	Fulani	Total	Annual Growth Rate (%)
1985	9,741	17,111	2,066	29,518	7.8
1986	10,033	19,150	2,664	31,847	6.5
1987	10,334	20,708	2,879	33,921	6.6
1988	10,644	22,388	3,120	36,152	3.4
1989	10,964	23,135	3,266	37,365	3.0
1990	11,292	23,829	3,363	38,484	3.0
1991	11,631	24,544	3,464	39,638	3.0

Source: Bassolet et al, 1989.

Table 2.10 Population growth by department, 1975 to 1985

Department	Population Growth, 1975 to 1985 (percent)
Tô	200.35
Cassou	197.80
Sapouy	168.52
Léo	114.30
Biéha	133.90
Niabouri	103.07
Ouessa	80.90
Silly	79.54
Bougnounou	75.80
Bourra	55.17
Fara	38.87
Nébiélianayou	26.74
Niégo	18.76
Average Provincial Growth	104.56

Source: Bassolet *et al*, 1989

The highest concentration of immigrants is found along the central north-south axis and in southwest Sissili, with the highest populations around Tô and Cassou. Sapouy also has high concentrations of immigrants but has traditionally been a point of arrival for Mossi settlers stretching back to the years before the droughts. Léo, being the provincial capital, has attracted many of the more wealthy Mossi, including artisans and traders. The departments of Biéha and Niabouri have attracted northern immigrant farmers because of their good soils. Table 2.10 gives a breakdown of population growth in Sissili by department.

Immigration has been caused by a series of environmental push factors brought on by a succession of serious drought periods in the north of Burkina Faso. The zones of departure fall into the sahelian and sudano-sahelian climatic regions which, in Burkina Faso, are characterised by low rainfall (400/500 mm per year), high population densities, poor soils, low harvests and degraded land areas. Since the 1970s, these areas have seen a steady decline in both the agricultural and prevailing economic systems. For example, in Yatenga province in the north (one of the major departure zones for immigrants into Sissili) the normal yearly rainfall is around 735 mm, but from 1970 to 1980 it fell to an average of 575 mm and further still to 491 mm in the period 1980 to 1988 (see Table 2.11).

Table 2.11 Climatological data from the province of Yatenga, 1979 to 1988

	1979	1980	1981	1982	1983	1984	1985	1986	1987	1988
Temperature (°C)	29.5	29.0	29.1	29.4	29.4	29.0	29.2	28.5	29.7	30.6
Divergence from the mean	0.8	0.3	0.4	0.7	0.7	0.3	0.5	−0.2	1	1.9
Annual Rainfall (mm)	578.6	576.1	576.1	360.1	360.1	393	421	570	456	707
Divergence from the mean (mm)	−54.7	−57.2	−57.2	−273.2	−273.2	−240.3	−212.3	−63.3	−177.3	73.7
Evaporation (mm)	2234.8	2209	2209	2491.4	2491.4	4101	4034	3822	3874	3681.6

Source: INSD, 1993.

Harvests in the northern areas have been insufficient to sustain populations in the context of successive years of poor rainfall. The national figure for basic cereal consumption in 1988/89 was 237 kg per person. Cereal production in the northern region at the same time varied from 125 kg/per person to 180 kg/per person, showing a cereal deficit. Land shortage has also become a major problem in the emigration zones, with people only having access to approximately 1.5 hectares of land (Bassolet et al, 1991).

Bassolet et al (1991) examine migration characteristics and point out that the decision to migrate is complex and dependent on many different factors. Although the immigrants are motivated mainly by economic incentives, (e.g. the thought of higher agricultural production, the search for work, search for money and to heighten their social position), they are also psychologically motivated by aspects such as family conflicts, lack of freedom experienced by youths, lack of marriageable women and the need to gain access to better physical, and by implication, social facilities. The decision to migrate can be divided into a collective decision or an individual decision. In Bassolet's study, more than 50 per cent of the immigrants took a collective decision with the support of their family. This decision was based on the agreement that immigrants, once settled, will support their family in the emigration zone, by sending money or food back (migrant remittance). In reality, however, this rarely happens with around 80 per cent of immigrants, who initially thought they would send money or food, sending no remuneration back to their 'homes' despite being considerably better off in their new 'homes' (89 per cent of immigrants said they have better living conditions in Sissili (Bassolet *et al*, 1991)). Immigration was also facilitated if the immigrant had family, friends or ethnic ties already in the province.

On arrival the first immigrants experienced few problems, most had no trouble finding 'employment' in their first month of residence. Figures show that 86.2 per cent had found agricultural work (i.e. they had secured a piece of land to farm), 9.2 per cent were involved with animal husbandry (the Fulani were grazing their cattle) and the remaining 4.2 per cent had found miscellaneous work in artisanal activities, small commerce, etc. (Bassolet *et al*, 1991).

The immigrants have become well established in Sissili, with the majority of immigrants intending to stay. At the present moment, the language of communication in Sissili is Mooré, the language of the Mossi immigrants,

Table 2.12 The positive and negative effects of immigration

Effects on departure zone	Effects on arrival zone
Positive effects: • short term increase in household's food supply; • transfer of money and food from the migrants' destination point; • decreased pressure on land resources.	Positive effects: • increased land productivity; • new expertise and professions; • cultural exchange.
Negative effects: • disruption of the division of labour, increased burden on women, old and very young; • lowered agricultural production; • less diversified economic activities of the household unit; • tension and breakdown of family structure; • decrease in men for marriage (men more migratory	Negative effects: • pressure on land resources; • disruption of social structure; • pressure on local laws and customs; • pressure on local resources – infrastructure, services, goods.

Source: Howorth, 1997.

indicating the numbers installed in the province and the levels of cultural dominance.

As Table 2.12 shows, the departure zones have experienced various negative impacts, including disruption of family structure, the creation of social problems, and most importantly, labour shortage because of imbalance in the sex ratio of men to women. In 1975, in the northern province of Yatenga, there were 98 men to 100 women, in 1985 the figure had fallen to 84 men to 100 women (the national average in 93/100). As a comparison, in the province of Sissili, in 1975 there were 101 men to 100 women, but in 1985, because of increased male migration (to Côte D'Ivoire, Ghana and towns and cities in Burkina Faso), the number had dropped to 95/100. The most critical consequence of immigration on the zones of departure is rural village depopulation.

Table 2.13 shows the difference in the role of migration in the respective provinces. In the north, people migrate to secure agricultural land for a primarily subsistence role. In Sissili, people migrate to supplement agricultural incomes by searching for seasonal paid labour, often in other countries. Agrotechnik (1991) has speculated on the following consequences of further population increases in the province of Sissili:

- a growth in the average household cultivated land area from five to seven hectares;
- a growth of the total cultivated surface from 11 per cent to 36 per cent of the provincial surface area;
- a lowering of soil quality reducing the length of cultivation from seven to three years;
- an expansion of agriculture onto marginal lands;
- an increase of resource conflicts between herders and farmers; and
- a decrease in (sorghum) harvest from 500 kg to 300 kg per hectare (by 2.5 per cent per year).

Table 2.13 Intended destination of people with the intention to migrate in four provinces: Sissili, Namantenga, Yatenga and Soum

Destination	Sissili (%)	Namentenga* (%)	Yatenga* and Soum* (%)
Town in Burkina Faso	13.8	16.2	22.2
Village in Burkina Faso	6.2	60.0	72.2
Another African country	80.0	23.7	5.6

Source: Adapted from Bassolet et al, 1991.
* Northern provinces

A popular and dark future scenario (a 'crisis narrative') for the province, led by analyses such as the one put forward by Agrotechnik, has described the likelihood of: a total disappearance of savanna zones and forested fallows, an upkeep of only delimited forest zones, and the development of a fuelwood deficit for Sissili and its urban centres. The loss of the fallow lands will lead to the loss of organic soil materials especially in the humific horizons, an increase in runoff created by soil compacting especially in cleared and weeded fields and, probably the most worrying, a lowering of the water tables. Agrotechnik suggested that the province can only support 30 persons per km^2 without irreparable damage. This analysis is open to question and will be discussed further.

Administrative and Local Political Structures

The province of Sissili is one of thirty provinces in Burkina Faso and is administered by a high commissioner (*Haute Commisaire*). Within the province there are 13 departments (out of 300 in the country) each of which has a prefect (*préfet*) as the administrative head. The high commissioner and the prefect are selected by the ruling political party, *Le Front Populaire*. The high commissioner is directly under state authority and is the representative of the *Le Front Populaire*, the Government and its ministries. The commissioner coordinates provincial activities and has responsibility for the development of the province. Each province is officially financially self sufficient through the collection of local taxes and operational permits (Engberg-Pedersen, 1995).

The provinces and departments are administrative units that have been decentralized and 'deconcentrated' since the State ordinance of 14 November 1983 under the reorganization of the provincial structures (Berger Sarl, 1989). Despite this decentralization and deconcentration, some ministries have succeeded in gaining a foothold in the provinces; such is the case for Sissili. In Sissili, there exist: the Ministry of Environment and Tourism (*Ministère de l'Environnement et du Tourisme*); the Ministry of Education (*Ministère de l'Education de Base et l'Alphabetisation des Masses*); Ministry of Health (*Ministère de la Santé*); the Social Security (*L'Action Social*); Ministry of Cooperative Peasant Action (*Ministére de l'Action Cooperative Paysanne*); and the public works (*Le Désenclavement – Travaux Public*). Most other ministries, like the Ministry of Planning and Cooperation and the Ministry of Agriculture, are based in Koudougou, the third largest urban conglomeration in Burkina, 160 kilometres from Léo.

Each village is represented by a '*délégé*', a village delegate who has been elected by the whole village. It is the delegate who receives government instructions, attends local government meetings and is charged with carrying out instructions at the village level. Previously, in the time of Thomas Sankara, there existed Revolutionary Committees (*Les Comités Revolutionaires*). These came before the system of the *délégé*, that was introduced after the Sankara administration by his replacement, Blaise Campaoré. The Revolutionary Committees were created by *Le Front Populaire* in order to 'mobilize, conscientize and organize the people at every revolutionary level and action in the domains of politics, economics, society, culture and security' (Berger Sarl, 1989). The Revolutionary Committees were supposed to have existed in every village but some were more operational than others.

A major problem the Government faced was how to make direct contact with the villagers in order to create a democratic platform for investment at the village level. Previously, there had been little or no contact between departmental prefects and the village representatives. This was partly due to the isolation of the village, the illiteracy of the peasants (discussed later) and partly due to the absence of any organizational or institutional structures at the village level that could be used as planning forums. For these reasons, Sankara began a '*Gestion de Terroirs*' (see Box 2.1) programme with the aim of creating local structures thereby giving the peasants a voice in their own development and thus bridging the administrative gap. However, Campaoré stopped all such efforts and '*Gestion de Terroirs*' has now become a land management tool rather than a direct political force.

Issues of Resource Use in Sissili

Background

Previous to the large tide of immigration that resulted from the 1970s droughts, Sissili province was characterised by a small population living in a large land area which was naturally endowed with a significant stock of natural resources, the most critical of which was woody biomass. Today however, the situation is no longer the same; the population has more than doubled in the last 20 years and agricultural activity has not only increased but the agricultural management systems are also changing. These are the obvious results of immigration but there are also other important implications, such as the introduction of other cultures, the penetration of Islam and the adoption of new skills and information. The indigenous populations' cultural identities are often challenged and conflicts of control may possibly arise, the language of communication changes to the language of the immigrant. The previously dominant tribal group now becomes the minority.

Box 2.1   Gestion de Terroirs

The origins of *Gestion de Terroirs* can be traced back to the mid-1980s from the Government of the socialist leader of Burkina Faso, Thomas Sankara. It came from the need for an extra level of governance at the village level. At that time there were four levels of administrative structures: national Government, regional level administration, provincial level administration, and departmental administration. Below this, on the village level, there was no structure that allowed for planning or administrative activities for development purposes.

The Government of Burkina Faso created an institution called *le Programme Sahel Burkinabè* (PSB), which was officially attached to all the ministry offices, with support from international donors to co-ordinate development activities. Sankara and PSB had talks on how the Government could co-ordinate all development projects and develop structures for bottom-up planning. This came from the rationale that, without structures at the village level, there can be no discussions about investment and planning. The concept of *Gestion de Terroirs* was developed to provide community organisational structures to allow for bottom-up planning and project co-ordination.

Gestion de Terroirs originated from a political will to improve national planning and investment from a grassroots base, i.e. the village, through building organisational and institutional structures. Unfortunately, the initiative started by Sankara was not carried through by the present president, Blaise Campaoré. In the last few years, *Gestion de Terroirs* has been revived as a development approach and has been formalised, most recently by the United Nation Sahelian Office (UNSO). In essence, it is a response to land management in areas that have experienced high localised population growth and are consequently undergoing a management crisis, i.e. as local situations change, old management practices are no longer effective for resource management and so new systems need to be developed. It was recognised that there was a need to make village communities responsible and to protect and restore natural resources with specific reference to the water-soil-vegetation complex. The word 'terroir' essentially means 'land' but is defined as a spatial entity traditionally managed by a village community ('the village') which has occupation and exploitation rights founded on accepted responsibility and a competence recognised by all users of the 'terroir' i.e. a land territory under a common property management scheme (UNSO, 1994).

Agricultural Characteristics

The Nuni The Nuni practice a 'gentle' form of agriculture which is exclusively manual with few inputs, relatively low soil usage and cultivate approximately 4.5 hectares per family. Crops grown include: yam, maize, sorghum, millet, groundnut, sweet potato, cowpea, *pois de terre*, black-eyed beans and cotton. Yams are cultivated within large mounds (*buttes*) and other crops with small mounds. This is a very important characteristic of Nuni farming, indicating a very labour intensive farming technique requiring hand work with a small hand hoe (called a **daba** in Nuni, see Figure 2.5).[2] The technique is indicative of bush farming, i.e. farming in the presence of a large number of trees and root systems, and does not cause great disturbance to the local agro-ecological system. Fields are farmed for an average of four to five years with fallows traditionally being 20 to 30 years. The Nuni also include uprooted weeds in their soil turning methods, again adding to soil structure. Women have their own small fields, dominated by groundnut cultivation, which act as a cash crop. They sometimes help their husbands with seeding and some parts of the harvest. No private tenure management is practised, i.e. land cannot be formally owned by an individual.

Agrotechnik (1991) concluded that the Nuni are preoccupied by short term gains, characterised by:

- ensuring enough food for the year and minimum economic gains;
- the diversification of non-agricultural activities or migration to other areas in search of off-season work;
- minimizing time spent on agricultural activities;
- a lack of investment in agricultural infrastructure;
- the priority of social investment;
- an ignorance of the problem or urgency of protection of land resources or the control of agricultural exploitation; and
- a belief that migration is always possible if things get too bad.

The latter two points are contested in this book. The author argues that the Nuni take a leading role in the protection of the resource base and the production of nature. This will be examined in later chapters.

The Mossi The Mossi practice an extensive form of agriculture with almost total field clearing, mainly for cereal production. On average, each family cultivates six hectares. Women participate fully in all aspects of farming, adding a level of 'aggressiveness' (Agrotechnik, 1991).

---

[2] The agricultural tools in this diagram are common to all ethnic groups, the Nuni, Mossi and Fulani.

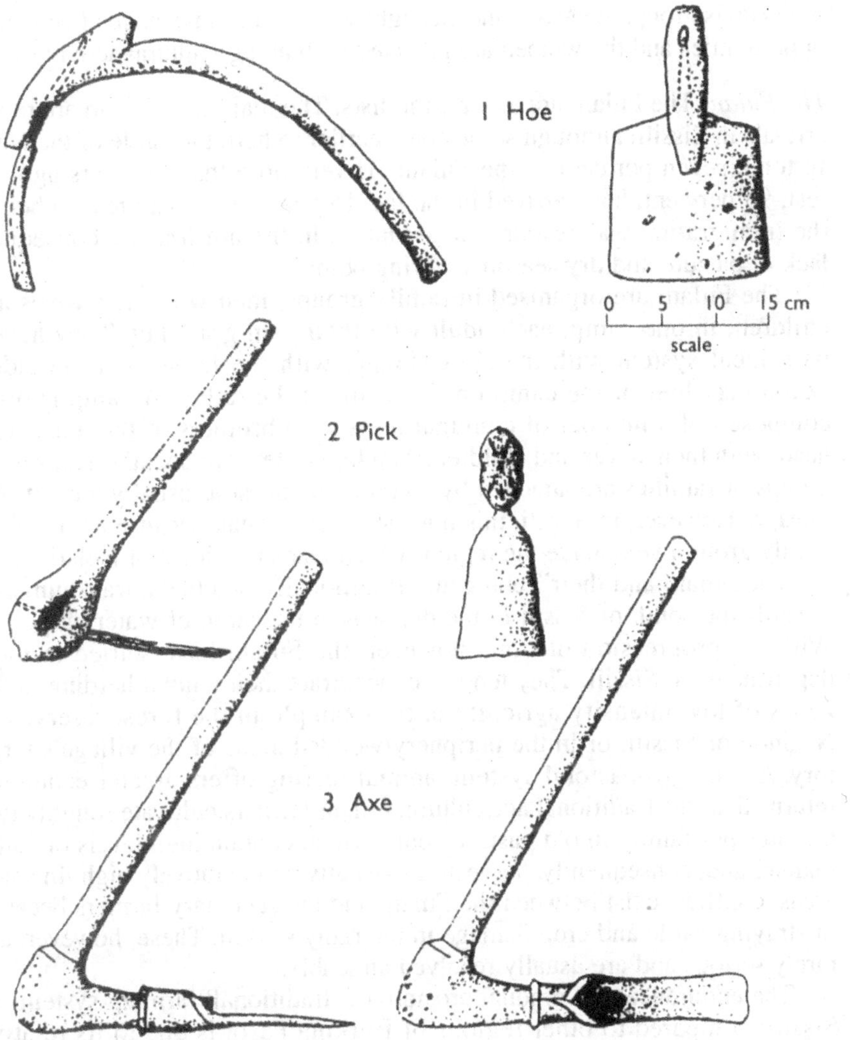

Figure 2.5 Agricultural tools

Source: Savonnet, 1970.

The Mossi arrived in an unknown landscape and imported farming techniques (dominated by the cereal cropping, mainly millet and sorghum) that were taken from generations of farming in a dry Sahelian environment. However, the Mossi have begun to adopt indigenous management practices and started growing crops grown traditionally by the Nuni, but, unlike the indigenous group, the Mossi increasingly seek to take advantage of economic opportunities and the women are involved with all agricultural activities.

The Fulani The Fulani are agropastoralists. The majority of them are recent arrivals in Sissili, although some came earlier to herd the cattle of the Nuni. In total, seven per cent of the Fulani arrived more than 20 years ago, the rest, 93 per cent, have arrived in the last 15 years. The main reason behind the immigration was resource degradation in the north and a consequent lack of pasture and dry season watering points.

The Fulani are organised in family groups, men with their wives and children, in one camp, each adult with their own grass hut. They have a patrilineal system with the sons staying with the father and the eldest becoming chief of the camp on the death of the father. A camp is often composed of a number of conjugal units with brothers of the household head, with their wives and children. At a higher level of social organisation, groups of families are attached by a common ancestor, usually a chief of a lineage. However, in Sissili, this lineage is often weak because many of the family group live outside the region, which leads to a level of isolation.

The Fulani and their Zebu cattle traditionally practice a transhumance towards the south of Sissili in the dry season in search of watering points. With the progression of time, however, the Fulani have settled in most departments in Sissili. They tend to concentrate their animal herding in the zones of low intensity agriculture, for example in the forest reserves of Nazinon or Sissili, or in the periphery/wooded areas of the village's territory. As an agro-pastoral system, animal rearing offers greater economic returns than the traditional agriculture. Fulani farmers cultivate roughly two hectares per family in old pasture zones which contain high levels of cattle manure and, consequently, harvests are usually comparatively high. In some areas, conflicts exist between the Fulani and the sedentary farmers because of straying cattle and crop damage in the rainy season. These, however, are rarely serious and are usually resolved amicably.

The endurance, but gradual erosion, of 'traditional' farming systems in Sissili, compared to other regions of Burkina Faso, is due to its relative isolation. New agricultural crops and techniques (like cotton growing and the introduction of ox-drawn ploughs) have only developed after the advent of the arrival of the immigrants. Farming is very labour intensive: each year roughly 93,000 hectares are farmed in Sissili (Berger Sarl, 1989) needing an estimated 11 million labour days, thus 129 days per hectare per active person (from ten to 60 years old). By comparison, external farm inputs are low, with a total provincial spending of 158 million FCFA on agriculture (e.g. fertiliser, seeds and pesticide), or 1700 FCFA per hectare. The cost of farm labour per person per day in 1994 was 600 FCFA for cereals and 1200 FCFA for tuber fields.

Table 2.14 A summary of some agricultural characteristics of the three main ethnic groups in Sissili

Description	Nuni	Mossi	Fulani
Production system	Farming/ sedentary	Farming/ sedentary	Agropastoralism/ semi-nomadic
Dominant crops grown	Tubers and cereals	Cereals	Cereals
Average cultivated area	4.5 hectares	6 hectares	1.5 hectares
Language	Nuni	Mooré	Fulfulbé

Source: Howorth, 1997.

Land Tenure

Local tenure management in Sissili has developed over many years and exists as a complex and dynamic system. Agrotechnik (1991) has identified certain characteristics within that system:

- the system has been formed over many years in the context of a substantial land surface;
- it has been formed with the traditional Nuni farming systems in mind and with the potential and occurrence of high mobility;
- the land is conceived as a religious entity, permitting the living to keep in touch with their ancestors and spirits, thus certain taboos and sacred points exist;
- the 'middleman' between the individual and the spirits is the Land Chief (*le Chef de Terre*), who gives land to people who need to farm;
- only a serious transgression, either social or religious can lead to a refusal of land;
- the level of land appropriation has various grades according to the type of field; they include the household fields in the habitation zone where appropriation is controlled by the individual families, the fields of the village canton (or neighbourhood), which is under the control of a clan (or family lineage), and bush fields again controlled by the clan but can be 'given' to strangers. The Land Chief, however, controls all decisions and his word is final;
- social standing is accorded at birth and rising up the social ladder is not possible; in the case of breaches in the social code the individual can be excluded from the group or more seriously be condemned to death; and
- private property is not permitted.

These traditional systems act as a very complex set of rules that are further complicated by the administrative structure, which consists of three different types of authority vested in three different persons. These different positions of authority are made up of: the Land Chief (of the local ethnic group), the Village Chief (le *Chef de Village* – the customary chief, a member of the original colonizing clan) and the administrative representative working for the State. This relationship is problematic because there is a high level of illiteracy among elites making direct communication obligatory. Confusion is also created by the existence of allegiances and hierarchies between villages and the existence of pieces of land in the middle of villages governed by old laws from other villages as is the case with the three village case studies.

Agrotechnik (1991) has suggested a number of characteristics that will lead to the development of a breakdown in traditional tenure management systems. They examined the evolution of the breakdown of tenure systems in the Mossi plateau, with a high population density (50 to 100 per/km^2) and give indications of how tenure systems in Sissili may develop under similar population densities. This evolution is thought to be characterised by:

- the 'rigidification' of the system of progressive land appropriation, without title deeds, by a system of land ownership by each clan (or village canton) and, within this, the fixation of land by individual families;
- the desire of young men to reject the customary land tenure management system by farming individually with cash crops;
- the emergence of the notion of land 'exchange value';
- the development of land 'loans' to immigrants in exchange for money or other exchanges without titles or juristic meaning (deeds or knowledge), to the benefit of Village Chiefs or village canton chiefs;
- securing land types outlined above, after having 'paid' thus giving the 'right of entry';
- land shortage, thus giving the need to secure farmed space; and
- the difficulty of access by government agents to villages and their customs and/or rules, to treat tenure problems and conflicts.

It is argued that this interpretation represents a forecast based on a western interpretation of land use change which is not controlled by strictly enforced rules. African tenure systems fall outside conventional or modern views because they deal with both the land and the resources directly linked to it. From a technical and economic point of view, tenure systems determine the management and allocation of a set of productive resources; they also organize access to ground-based natural resources and determine the appropriation mechanisms for these resources and the security of ownership or useage rights over them (Thébaud, 1995). By doing this, such systems help to define a series of economic and institutional incentives relating to the various possible ways of using these resources (Thébaud, 1995).

In terms of state influence, there have been a number of attempts at reducing traditional control over land. The agrarian and tenure bill *'Une Réforme Agraire et Foncière, ordonnance no.84 du 4/8/1984 et décret de 4/8/1985* (a substantial document of 666 articles) gave all land in Burkina Faso to the state, removing cultural or traditional landrights, with the objective of the rational redistribution of land. The bill states it is necessary to destroy the traditional agrarian and tenure laws 'characterised by the mark of the bourgeois and feudal systems and thus used against the labouring masses'. However, because of the weakness of the administrative structure and the impenetrability of the village, the directive has had no effect. In addition, if the directive were to turn into a reality, it would make tenure rights unclear and lead to land insecurity in all aspects.

The Development of the Agricultural Landscape

The rural countryside of Sissili, and its consequent occupation of space, has been defined and created by conscious historical processes based on the different values placed on different resources. The village, and agricultural landscape around those villages, shows a distinct pattern throughout Sissili. The Nuni have deliberately settled in a particular topographical sequence and ecological niche along the local catena. The catena consists of a plateaued hilltop leading down on both sides to a valley bottom with soils ranging from rocky outcrops to alluvial soils, with each section of the landform having specific vegetation configurations, with the soils on the lower slopes being the deepest and most fertile. Throughout the province of Sissili, villages occupy the same space on the lower slopes (here the household fields are found and some village fields, that spread onto the soils on the upper slopes and into valley bottoms).

Figure 2.6 is based on the soils in Cassou but is found throughout the province. It shows the soil catenary sequence, land use and vegetation in Sissili. This has the vegetation classes according to de Boer (1992), elevation, location of agricultural fields and the catenary sequence. A catena consists of three main parts or complexes: an elluvial complex on the upper slopes of the undulations from which solid materials are washed off along the surface and colloidal materials removed downwards by seepage; a colluvial complex on the lower slopes where there is a graded series of deposition down the slope from the coarser materials at the top to the finer at the valley bottom; and an illuvial complex occupying the valley bottom which receives most of its materials by seepage (Hopkins, 1974).

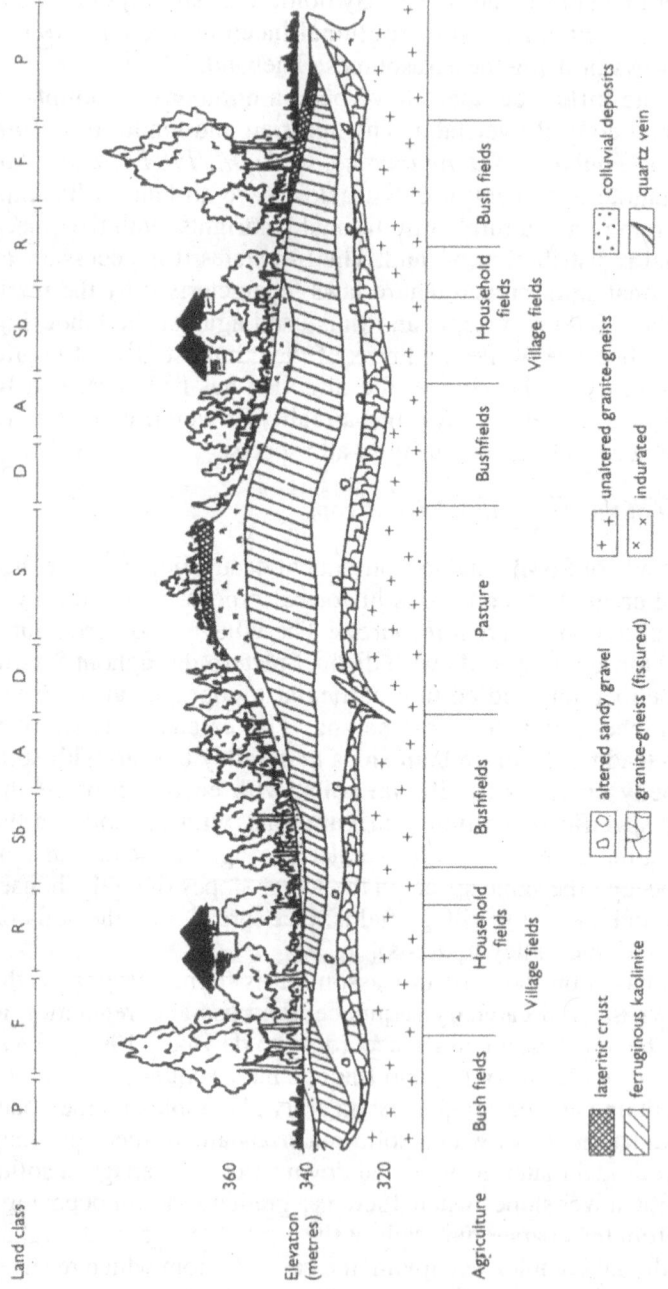

Figure 2.6 The soil catenary sequence and soil profile, land use and vegetation in Sissili

The Nuni villages are located on land according to its potential. Thus, the historic spacing of villages reflects a density of people in equilibrium with the agricultural (and thus soil potential) resources of the province, with the exception of some drainage areas where onchocerosis was rife in the past. When two villages are separated by large distances (from around eight to ten km), it is very likely that there will be a presence of 'tanga' soils, with weak agricultural characteristics (having lateritic crusts and a high gravel content) together with a lack of water points. In all cases, however, the village has its own definite space. The zones far away from the village are not a no-man's-land but exist as a collective resource for pasture or for harvesting wood products. The occupation of space in and around the village is progressive, measured by the growth of the village and the needs of the population.

This is a pre-immigrant landscape where the Nuni were the sole inhabitants. What we see now is a landscape influenced by a new social arrangement. The land or Village Chief has allocated land (old fallows) to the immigrants, both the Mossi and Fulani. In the case of Boutiourou (chapter five), the Mossi have been 'given' a section of the village land to use as their own, to manage and to farm; this is now the 'Mossi's land'.[3] The Fulani prefer the relative solitude of the woodlands in the village's territory. Here the Fulani can guard their cattle away from the village and bush fields of the Nuni and Mossi and also have access to good pasture. The values placed on the resources along the catena by the Nuni chiefs dictate the exploitation patterns, settlement patterns and conservation areas.

The immigrants have generally been given the less fertile areas of the upper slopes. The Mossi, coming from a different environmental background, do not have the same perception of the local environment and the ecological equilibrium as the indigenous Nuni, and they practice an almost total clearing of trees for their agricultural space and leave vast spaces of uncovered soil (Berger Sarl, 1989). The only exception is leaving the *B.parkii* and *P.biglobosa* species which the Nuni reserve the right to harvest usually, however, harvesting rights are passed over to the immigrants.

Women also have different value systems because they use some areas of the territory more frequently than the men. For example, there are certain areas which are almost seen as 'women's areas', such as upper slopes and hilltops because it is here that the majority of forest gathering (including fuelwood) is done. There are even sacred women's sites that only women can exploit, such as sacred streams or groves.

---

[3] Note that all reference to ownership is given in inverted commas because there is no formal private property, only rights of use. All land belongs to the village and is controlled either by the Village Chief (*Chef de Village*), or more usually, the Land Chief (*Chef de Terre*).

Soil Types and Indigenous Soil Classification

The Nuni and Mossi recognise different soil types in relation to where they are found on the catena (Figure 2.6), their texture and their cropping capability. Both the Nuni and the Mossi have different names for the different soils and also for the catenary positions where those soils are found (see Figure 2.7). For example, the Nuni word for the plateau on the catena is **pang**, and the word for the soil types found there are: **pio** for lithosols that have originated from a granite parent material, and **diga** for lithosols that have developed from a laterite material. In Mooré the corresponding names are **tanghin** and **kougouri** respectively. These soils are occupied by bushy savanna and are reserved for pasture, hunting and gathering purposes. These are the most marginal agricultural areas. On the cliffs just below the plateau, depending on aspect, the Nuni identify two areas: **dundulutia** meaning a piece of land which only supports small and stunted undergrowth and bushes; or **petia**, which is a piece of land with rocks that supports abundant undergrowth and is characterised by *Burkea africana* and *Burkea parkii*.

The upper slopes are called **dio** in Nuni. They correspond to the Mossi **zingdongo** or **zinka**. The soils in this part of the catena are principally ferruginous soils on gravelly material. The Nuni call the soil in these areas **kapafounoutia** (the **tia** at the end of the word meaning 'soil'). In Mooré they are called **zinua**. These areas are reserved for pasture, wood harvesting or bush fields (although the latter is a relatively recent occurrence). The ferruginous soils are easier to work although they have a lower fertility than sandy-argillic soils. Ferruginous soils have a low water retention capacity and dry into a very indurated form. This presents problems when preparing the fields at the start of the cropping season (although some farmers add green mulch[4] to their fields after the harvest which improves soil quality).

The lower slopes are called **nédonou** in Nuni and **bissiga** in Mooré. It is here where the Nuni have built their houses and have their household and village fields. The lower slopes have a higher soil fertility but require adequate quantities of water at the beginning of the agricultural season to mobilise soil nutrients and to allow the working of the soil. Nuni farmers distinguish sandy soils (**kasuloutia**) from argillic soils (**bounoutia**). The Mossi distinctions are **bissidagaré** and **dagaré** respectively. The Nuni have another soil type in the lower slope region called **taagatia** which is best suited to tuber cultivation, specifically yams but also sweet potatoes and cassava. **Taaga** is the Nuni word for the tree *Afzelia africana* and the name essentially means where many *A.africana* can be found growing. Therefore where many of these trees can be found growing is where it is good to plant tubers.

---

4 Green mulching is the act of turning green vegetative matter (usually leaves) into the soil to improve soil fertility and structure.

The lowest catenary position is the valley bottom, and is called **vwara** in Nuni (literally meaning 'valley bottom'). Here, the Nuni distinguish two soil types: **ko** which are rich in kaolinite and **tezonou** rich in montmorillonite; both of these are hydromorphic in character. The Mossi call these soils **baongo** and **kossogo** respectively. The Nuni word **bôtia** means 'near the stream' and it is here that dry season gardening takes place. Soils here have an 'A' horizon of approximately 20 cm resting on an argillic 'red' layer; the Nuni call these soils **varatia**. Next to this in the sequence is what the Nuni call **poontia** which translated means 'a piece of land with many trees'. Here are the deepest soils of the catena with a humic horizon of about 30 cm in depth.

The Nuni have additional names for other land units according to their land use capabilities. For example, **suoirè** is the Nuni word for non-exploited or bush land and **cabanô** is used for naming an old field or fallow.

Table 2.15 Nuni soil nomenclature in Lon, Boutiourou and Saboué[5]

Name of soil	Description
Bounoutia	'a sandy argillic soil with many trees and gravely soil'
Diga	'soil on the hills, very poor, grasses and trees'
Dudulutia	'one doesn't find trees here that you can find in other places, undergrowth is stunted, small and limited'
Kapafounoutia	'gravelly soil, found near hills, with few trees and under growth'
Kapataotia	'lots of gravel, found towards Pouri going towards Cassou'
Kasuloutia	'very sandy soil, few trees and grasses, soil becomes infertile very quickly'
Petia	'some rocks, trees, (e.g. *Burkea africana* and *Burkea parkii*) abundant undergrowth'
Tapuana	'a white soil'
Tesien	'a red soil'
Tezonou	'a good, black soil, many trees, almost all species and abundant undergrowth' (in Saboué it is classified as soil that is found around the houses)
Varatia	'a hard argillic soil, found in the valley bottom'

Source: Author's fieldwork, 1993–1995.

---

[5] The soil descriptions come from the Nuni elders and have not been altered.

Tekassoulou, tezounou, varatia, kasuloutia and tagatia are all put under cultivation by the Nuni and are all of medium to high fertility. The Nuni recognise that different soils are suited to different crops. For example **tagatia** is used for tuber production and **tekassoulou** is used for cereal production. They have a range and choice of where and what they cultivate. The land unit preferred by the Nuni is the **poontia** which has the most fertile and productive soils. Cereal cropping dominates on these areas with some cotton cultivation. Sorghum is often planted on the **bôtia** soils because of sorghum's need of water (Konaté, 1995). Groundnuts, cowpeas and bambara nuts can be grown anywhere and are often intercropped.

The Mossi however have less of a choice. The Mossi of Lon cultivate the **bissidagaré** (sandy lower slope soils) and **zinua** (upper slope ferruginous) soils. The Mossi of Boutiourou cultivate on **dagaré** (argillic soils) and baongo (kaolinite, valley bottom soils) and the Mossi of Saboué cultivate on **bissidagaré**, **dagaré** and **baongo** soils. The Mossi have a smaller choice of soils because land is chosen for them by the Nuni chiefs. Added to this, in the case of Boutiourou, a specific area has been designated for the Mossi. The Mossi of Saboué have wide choice of soils because they farm in an area of high land availability. However, in general, because of the poorer soils that the Mossi receive (old fallows), soil fertility management must be employed (i.e. fertiliser inputs) if productivity is not to fall.

Figure 2.7 forms one-half of the catenary sequence (although the two halves are mirror images) and contains Nuni and Mossi soil classifications as well as the FAO soil classification.

Pastoralism

Pastoralism, and its links with overgrazing, is traditionally associated with 'crisis narratives', especially in the Sahelian region. In Sissili, there has been an examination (de Boer, 1992; de Boer and Kessler, 1994; Egging, 1990) of the impact of grazing and the presence of cattle on local vegetation and farming systems. There is little evidence that the presence of cattle in the province is negatively affecting environmental quality. If anything, cattle and the Fulani production system contribute to the strengthening of the local economy and an improvement in environmental management.

Before the arrival of the Fulani, some 20 years ago, there was little, if any, animal herding and animal husbandry was only practised on a very small scale by the indigenous Nuni. For this reason, no rules or regulations exist controlling access to pasture in Sissili, as there are in most of the rest of West Africa (Klintz, 1982). Water access is the most critical aspect of pastoralism in Sissili. At the end of the rainy season, pastoralists dig traditional wells in the valley bottoms, because, towards the end of the dry season, it becomes harder to find water. Visiting or passing herds must first

The Province of Sissili 51

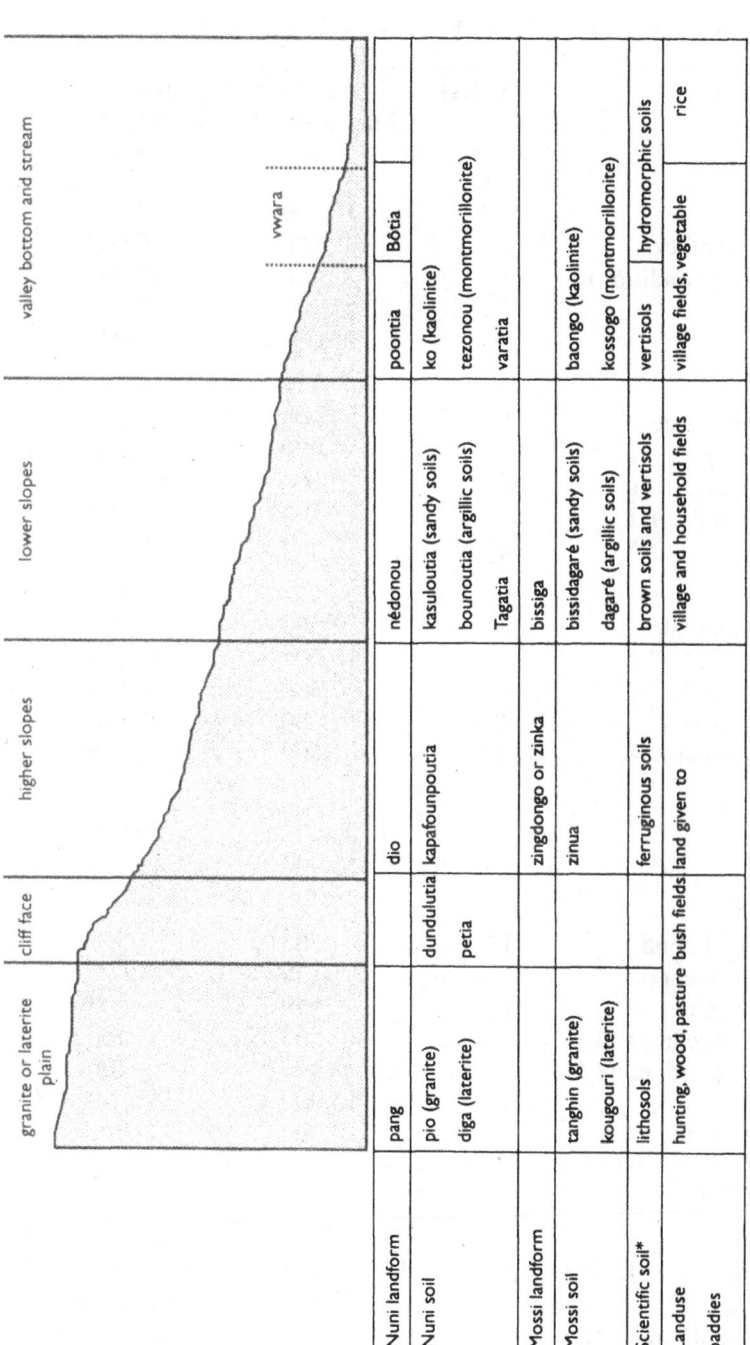

Figure 2.7 Indigenous and scientific soil classification in Sissili

Source: Author's fieldwork, 1994.
* This is the FAO International soil naming system.

Table 2.16 Prices of animals on the market in Léo, 1992

Animal Species	Age (years)	End of Dry Season FCFA	Rainy Season FCFA
CATTLE			
Male calf	<1	15,000	22,000
Bull (good condition)	5	42,000	70,000
Bull (medium condition)	5	32,000	37,000
Female	2	25,000	30,000
Cow	5	25,000	30,000
GOATS			
Young male/female	1	3,000	2,500
Female goat (good cond.)	>2	3,000	3,500
Female goat (med. cond.)	>2	2,000	2,500
Billygoat (good cond.)	>2	5,500	3,500
Billygoat (med. cond.)	>2	2,500	2,000
SHEEP			
Young male/female	1	3,500	4,000
Ewe (good cond.)	>2	10,000	12,500
Ewe (med. cond.)	>2	7,500	8,500
Male (good cond.)	>2	2,000	3,000
Male (med. cond.)	>2	1,500	2,700
DONKEY			
Male	3	20,000	20,000
Female	3	15,000	15,000
OTHERS			
Chicken (good cond.)	1	500	550
Chicken (med. cond.)	1	350	400
Cock (good cond.)	1	650	700
Guinea fowl (good cond.)	1	500	500
Guinea fowl (med. cond.)	1	400	400
Female Pig	3	15,000	15,000
Castrated male pig	3	20,000	20,000

Source: de Boer, 1992.

be given permission before they can drink at these wells from the pastoralists who dug them. In times of water shortage, the well digger can refuse access, although this is rare.

Development programmes that have attempted to carry out pasture delimitation or pasture parcelling to groups of pastoralists have failed. Trying to install restrictive management regimes on previously free systems will take a long time to have any effect. Because grazing routes are dictated for the most part by access to water, the key to controlling grazing patterns must be by regulating access to water points (de Boer, 1992). Table 2.17 outlines the prices of animals on the market and demonstrates the variability of prices according to age of animal and season. The prices in the table show the considerable returns that can be gained from the sale of animals

Pastoralism and the presence of large numbers of cattle in the region have had certain effects on the natural vegetation, over the last 20 years. Pasture is made up of many vegetative components in the pastoral year, with the herbaceous layer the most important pasture in the rainy season, providing 95 per cent of fodder.

De Boer estimates that in the department of Tô there are roughly 20,000 Livestock Units (UBT)[6] which consume 5.8 kg/day/head (Breman and de Ridder, 1991). Assuming this is consumed between May and October (the rainy season) it gives a total consumption in the department of 20 million kg of dry matter (DM) for the six months. Subtracting this from the total vegetative production in the department of 370 million kg/DM/yr, we are left with 350 million kg/DM accessible in the dry season. Bush fires destroys much of the DM available for fodder, thus in November only 85 million kg/DM remains and in April this falls further to leave only 25 million kg/DM (which is still a significant amount).

Table 2.17 illustrates the dominance of the dry herbaceous layer for fodder requirements in the dry season. In the wet season, the new growth in the herbaceous layer provides the vast majority of feed. Despite the small contribution of woody species and tree cutting to fodder requirements they are nonetheless critical in supplementing the animals diet and providing important sources of protein in a critical period of the dry season.

Bush fires destroy about 20 per cent of aerial leaves on the woody species. However, herders will cut branches from certain tree species for fodder, especially *Mimosaceae spp*: *A.africana, Pterocarpus erinaceus, Khaya senegalensis* and *Stereospermum kunthianum*. Approximately 17 per cent of the fodder needs of cattle between January and April comes from cut trees or bushes, contributing 1.4 million kg/DM for the 20,000 Livestock Units per year in the department of Tô (de Boer, 1992).

Regrowth from perennial grasses makes up a very important part of animal dietary requirements. The quality and the quantity of the grasses

---

[6] A UBT is an imaginary animal of 250 kg: 1.5 Zebu, 10 sheep, 12 goats, 2 donkeys, 1 horse and 0.8 camel (Le Houérou and Hoste, 1977, in Breman and de Ridder, 1991); UBT is sometimes refered to as a Tropical Livestock Unit (TLU) in the English literature.

Table 2.17 Vegetative production for different pasture zones in million kilograms of dry matter in Sissili

Pasture Zone	Nov	Dec	Jan	Feb	Mar	April	Total
Dry herbaceous layer	85.00	73.00	61.00	49.00	37.00	25.00	330.00
Woody layer	1.41	1.38	1.35	1.32	1.29	1.26	8.01
Tree cutting	–	–	1.40	1.40	1.40	1.40	5.60
Regrowth in perennial grass	–	–	0.49	0.49	0.49	0.40	1.87
Valley bottoms	0.02	0.04	0.06	0.07	0.08	0.09	0.36
Regrowth in non-burnt pasture	–	–	0.19	0.15	0.12	0.08	0.54
Cereal Residues	–	–	–	0.76	–	–	0.76
Groundnut and black-eyed bean residues	–	–	–	0.43	–	–	0.43

Source: de Boer, 1992.

depend on the quantity of available water and the timing of the bush fire. Regrowth from perennial grasses can be divided into two classes, regrowth from non-burnt land and regrowth from burnt land. The former produces only a half of the production of the latter. A calculation of monthly recovery rates from burnt grasses is based on Geerling (1987): 0 kg/DM for a recovery of 0.2 per cent, 10 kg/DM for a recovery of 2–5 per cent, 25 kg/DM for 5–10 per cent and 50 kg/DM for a recovery of >10 per cent (see Table 2.18 which uses land units from de Boer, 1992). Recovery rates on hill summits are estimated at 1.0 per cent because of excessive drainage. Again here, burnt areas have a higher productivity than non-burnt areas: 1.4 million kg/DM/ha/yr compared to 1.1 million kg/DM/ha/yr (de Boer, 1992).

Another source of vegetative production is found in valley bottoms, not

The Province of Sissili 55

Table 2.18 Recovery of perennial grasses and the percentage of burnt land in Sissili

Land Unit	Recovery percent	Early Burning (percent)	Recovery Production kg DM/ha
S	0.9	40	0
D	7.0	40	0
Sb	10.0	40	25
A	10.3	40	50
R	6.5	40	25
F	6.5	40	25
P	>10.0	17	50
B	7.5	40	25
N	0.0	0	0
C – fallow	5.0	33	10
H – fallow	5.0	33	10
b – fallow	5.0	33	10

Source: Egging, 1990.

from burning, but from the presence of water in the dry season. Crop residues also play an important role in fodder provision and the volume of crop residues varies greatly with different cropping methods. For example, with the addition of compost, one hectare of finger millet gives 3510 kg/DM/ha in residues (leaves, stems and weeds) without compost it gives 2370 kg/DM/ha. With sorghum, there is a yield of 7010 kg/DM/ha with compost and 2790 kg/DM/ha without (Egging, 1990). Fallow land is a very important source of fodder and, depending on availability, can make up 50 per cent of grazing areas.

The quality of forage is also a very important factor in animal health and production. A cow can only ingest 2.5 per cent of its own body weight per day because its stomach capacity can only transform and ferment up to this percentage; this equals 5.8 kg per Livestock Unit (Dahl and Hjort, 1976). The critical factor in fodder quality is its protein content. A nitrogen content of 0.8 per cent is the minimum level to allow growth, 1.0 per cent guarantees growth and production. Between 0.1 per cent and 0.8 per cent the animal will lose weight at 0.1 kg per day, for an animal of 150 kg this represents a loss of 3 kg per month (Breman and de Ridder, 1991).

Table 2.19 illustrates the complexity of the fodder yearly calendar. In the northern areas of Burkina Faso, significant transhumance was required to satisfy all these needs.

Table 2.19 Fodder calendar for Sissili

May to September	Rainy season provides green grasses of good quality.
October	The herbaceous layer becomes dry except in valleys.
November to December	The harvest is finished and the residues become available. During this period the palatability and quality drops and the animals must search for other sources of forage.
January	At this stage the perennial grasses are very important, containing more than 1.0 percent nitrogen, bush fires also stimulate growth and leads, indirectly, to an improvement of forage quality.
February to May	Medium quality forage, many woody species eaten and other poor quality forage of difficult digestibility. At this period nitrogen content drops to 0.8 percent and below, and animals start to lose weight.

Source: de Boer, 1992.

An Introduction to the Three Case Study Villages

The villages are discussed in detail in chapters four, five and six. Oral histories are also provided as an introduction to each of the case study chapters. The three villages (see Figure 2.8) that were chosen for this study provide a continuum in both space and time, from north to south, and from the village which has a very high number of settled immigrants, who have been there a long time, to the village which has a very small recent immigrant population. Three very different case studies are presented all of which, paradoxically, show significant similarities.

Lon

Lon is situated in the department of Cassou and is the most northern of the three villages. It is 43 km north of Léo, the provincial capital, and is situated in one of the most densely populated areas of Sissili. In 1985, according to the INSD census, Lon had a population of 2,978. Lon has the longest history of immigrant settlements of the three villages. Today, the immigrant Mossi and Fulani population outnumber the original Nuni population. It also has the least productive resource base on account of its northerly location,

The Province of Sissili 57

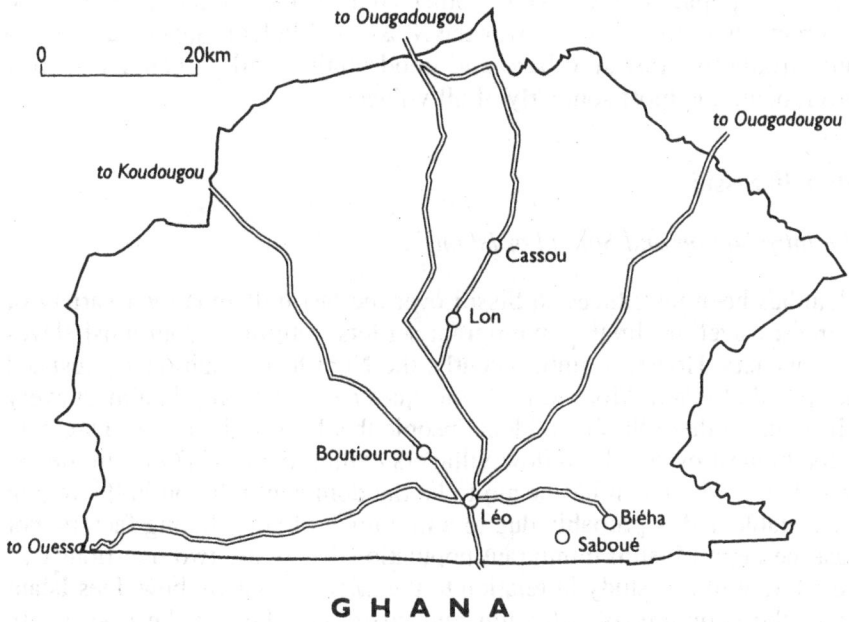

Figure 2.8 The province of Sissili showing Lon, Boutiourou and Saboué

which is compounded by competition for resources by local and immigrant populations alike.

Boutiourou

Boutiourou is situated nine km to the north west of Léo, in the department of Léo. It is the 'middle' village, i.e. after Lon it has the second highest population (903 people in 1985, according to the INSD census), it has the second most productive resource base, again because of its more southerly location and Boutiourou's immigrant population have been resident, longer than in Saboué but a shorter period than in Lon. The immigrant population of Mossi and Fulani slightly outnumbers the original Nuni population.

Saboué

Saboué is situated approximately 34 km south east of Léo in the department of Biéha and five km from the Ghanaian border to the south. It has a very small population of 266 (INSD, 1985) combined with a very low immigrant population. Unlike the other villages, the original Nuni population remains in the majority over the Mossi and Fulani. Saboué also has a very productive resource base and good quality and percentage woody cover, being the most southerly of all villages.

Islam in Sissili

The Introduction and Spread of Islam

Islam has been introduced to Sissili over the last millennia by a variety of sources: travelling Imams, immigrant settlers, returning Gourounsi slaves and invaders. However, until recently, the Nuni have traditionally resisted the spread of Islam. More recently mosques have been built in almost every village in southern Sissili and local people that have visited Mecca are held in the highest esteem by fellow villagers calling them *Al Haji* with deference. Quite why Islam has begun to be the dominant religion in the region is debatable and is probably due to a multitude of contributing factors, not least the large Muslim immigrant population. There are two questions that are relevant to this study in relation to the arrival of Islam: how does Islam affect the economy of affection and customary law in the case study villages? And, if it does, is the impact positive or negative?

West African Islam belongs to a Sunni Islamic typology all of its own, mostly because West Africa's original traditional religions blends into Islamic practices. West African Islam is not the same as is found in the Mahgreb countries and is unlikely ever to resemle Arabic Islam. The reason for this is the strength of the traditional Animist religions and their depth in the cultures of West Africa. Spencer-Trimingham, (1959:9) says that Animism is not an historical religion; its beliefs and rituals are founded upon a timeless mythology. Animism is also one of the central underlying forces of African society. In the absence of a central Government and its laws, Animism offers moral and social codes of behaviour. Opeloye (1996) noted that the indigenous religion lays a premium on the moral order of the society; the activities of man are not left unregulated. In his study of the Yoruba ethnic group in Nigeria, he found that certain norms and codes of conduct are entrenched within society and these facilitate its orderly maintenance. These formed the Yoruba's moral values, or at least contributed to their existence. Thus Animism's strength lay in its provision of the basis for customary social laws and its takeover by Islam is never likely to be complete.

In this sense, religion and society in African Animist communities cannot be separated; they are intrinsic aspects of each other. The reason for this lies in the nature of Animism and its integration of nature, divinities, ancestors (the dead) and the living. Thus all things are connected and the local production systems are as much connected to religious practices as are ceremonies and festivals. Spencer-Trimingham (1959:7) says:

> [Their] world is a world of spirit forces: of the dead, living and nature, among which the living form but a small minority. These forces cannot be classified into categories of good or evil, for power is essentially impersonal and neutral. If harmony is maintained, all is well, but if broken, calamity falls on individual and community.

Islam was brought to Sissili through a mixture of peaceful and violent means, peacefully through traders, travellers and the occasional immigrant from the north who brought the message of Islam and often had the ability to read and write (in Arabic): more violently through the Mossi and Djerma invasions (see chapter three) and also through returned (or escaped) Nuni slaves who took the religions of their masters. In the midst of Nuni villages, the Islamic message dissipated, diluted and disappeared.

Islam is not new in the province despite the fact that generally, in the three case study villages, there was a similar approximate date when the villagers said they had adopted Islam, about 30 years ago. The process of the Islamisation of traditional cultures is protracted, even if respondents say they have been converted 'over-night'. Thus, in Sissili, the contact the population had with Islam over an extended period was a vital part in their conversion to Islam.

Added to this was the ability of the two religions to exist side by side. Today, one is unable to say that 'x' village is exclusively an Islamic village, and likewise it is impossible to say that a village is Animist. Strong Islamic tendencies exist in most villages in Sissili and dominate local religious practices, but there are also surviving Animist practices and beliefs. For example, there is a gradient of Islamisation corresponding to the location of the three villages, with Lon being the most heavily Islamised and Saboué the least (logically corresponding to the duration and level of immigrant contact). In Lon, there are still some old ceremonial sites, the sacred forest towards Tô for example and an 'abandoned' idol on the road to Panassin, but there are few remaining ceremonies.[7] By contrast, in Saboué, it was known that the women of the village continue to make sacrifices in front of water divinities although they profess to be Muslim. Spencer-Trimingham (1959) thought that this situation was an example whereby women, by maintaining old cults (i.e. participating in Animist rites), in contrast to their

---

7 Through the interviews it was impossible to determine whether any Animist ceremonies survived as was possible in the other villages. It was suspected that this was due to the subject's sensitive nature in a predominantly Muslim village.

husbands who are predominantly Muslim, ensured that their families made the best of both worlds, Animism and Islam alike.

The point where a village can call itself an Islamic village is the result of a long process, and is as much a social as an individual matter. For example, it seems that the final determining factor for the conversion of the people of Saboué was the conversion of the chief of Pissai who then ordained that the village was now an Islamic one (and because Saboué was considered a 'suburb' of Pissai, so its inhabitants were converted). Spencer-Trimingham (1959) points out that when a whole family or village becomes Muslim it is not the result of the culmination of an individual's belief but the culmination point of an Islamic movement within the family or village. He goes on to say that a stage is reached which is characterised by the assimilation of significant elements of Islam and the consequent parallel existence of two religions in the community.

This parallel existence of both religions is often hidden or unseen to the observer. In none of the villages, with perhaps the exception of Saboué where some respondents admitted to being half Muslim and others to being Animist, was there an admittance of being half Muslim and half Animist. In Lon and Boutiourou, there was an unwillingness to talk about Animist practices, either old or current. There Islam was synonymous with 'civilized' and their old Animist ceremonial sites were neglected and left to ruin. Opeloye (1996) points out that commonly, the material symbols of the dying cult are not destroyed but simply neglected, for example ancestors' houses gradually disintegrate under the wind and rain, as was the case in Boutiourou where the old Animist village site has been left to decay.

In relation to the impact of Islam on the traditional economy there are some indicators that may either suggest a future weakening of traditional customary law or conversely may lend a religious complementarity. For example, there is now in Lon and Boutiourou a religious leader, who in the case of Lon is a Mossi and Boutiourou a Nuni, of high social standing. Islam may have brought a pacifying influence on the three ethnic groups, being the common religion. The Friday prayers bring the communities together in unity, gathering over a common spiritual goal, as the elders say, *'Maintenant nous prions ensemble'*.[8]

Why Islam Fitted so Well to Nuni Life

The attraction of Islam to West African communities is due, in part, to the complementarity of Islam to Animism and the fact that Islam did not immediately demand a total break from the traditional religion. Also, the two religions share many things in common, or perhaps more accurately,

---

8 'Now, we pray together'.

Islam has the ability to adapt itself in whatever shape or form, so as to incorporate many aspects of the original religion. For example, the process of Islamisation adopts the way of myth and fable, and 'the custom' acquires a new supernatural sanction; no longer is it practised because it was the custom of the ancestors, but because God ordained it (Spencer-Trimingham, 1959). In this way the two religions exist side by side.

The Mossi, Nuni and Fulani join together in the mosque and thus affirm each individual's sense of belonging and communality. Likewise, the Islamic practice of alms giving, complements perfectly the local gift-giving support networks and can be said to fit in to the local economy of affection. Either Islamic alms giving is a guise under which to place existing support practices, or it replaces traditional 'gift giving' and places it in a quasi-religious framework; half Islamic, half traditional. Mauss (1966:16) says 'it [alms] is the old gift morality raised to the position of a principle of justice'.[9] He goes on to say that alms are the result, on the one hand, of a moral idea about gifts and wealth and on the other of an idea about sacrifice. Adams (1993:44) similarly notes; 'Animist practices such as homage paid to ancestral priests for good fortune in farming, coexist with or have even transformed Islamic almsgiving and charity to the destitute'.[10] The two religions blend and complement each other.

Opeloye (1996:85) identifies similar characteristics of Islam which made it favourable to the Yoruba, he says: 'the Islamic institutions of polygyny, impressive Islamic festivals, the [Imam's] use of talismans, charms and divinations to offer protection were liked by the people because these met their social and spiritual needs'. He also identified that Islam, just like Animism, lays down detailed regulations to guide people in all their activities, both spiritual and material; the Islamic superstructure consequently rests on faith, ritual observances and transactions.

However, there were contradictory aspects to Islam that were attractive to local communities. Although Islam is a religion shared by the whole community and as such brings a sense of belonging to the greater population, it is also an individualistic religion. For example, Islamic law is *ad personam*, in opposition to the direction of traditional African law which is communalistic (Spencer-Trimingham, 1959) and, as such, Islam accords the liberty that is so popular, especially amongst the younger age groups in Sissili. Hence the common response of 'under Islam we are more free'. Certainly, in the case study villages, there is a heightened feeling of freedom

---

9 Mauss (1966) noted that originally the Arabic *Sadaka* meant exclusively justice, but it later came to mean alms.
10 Islamic law requires that 10 per cent of annual production or income, be distributed among the old, infirm and the destitute (Adams, 1993). This practice is called *zakkat* in Arabic.

under Islam which can be at least partly attributable to the slackening of the strong social hierarchies that existed under Animism.

There is evidence that it is an astute economic decision to become a Muslim. Animism required high levels of individual contributions to communal events and festivals. In the case of funerals, they lasted three days for a man and four days for a woman. People were buried in a sitting position; corpses in Islamic burials are buried lying down. Each person was expected to bring along animals, grain and beer for the period of mourning. Now funerals only last a day regardless of sex. People were also expected to make regular animal sacrifices before idols on particular days in the agricultural calendar, at field preparation time, seeding and harvest. These were both individual and communal events: communal in the village ceremonial site led by the Land Chief, and individual in home or field. In short, many animals and gift 'tokens' had to be laid out every year. In times of sickness or hardship, again animals would be sacrificed in front of idols. Now, people simply pray to Allah.

Connected to this greater freedom, are the changing agricultural practices. Because Animism is a strong earth religion, it had many codes which were characterized by set rituals in the agricultural calendar. Now however, these ceremonies have disappeared from communal practices. As Spencer-Trimingham notes (1959:38) 'adoption of the Islamic lunar calendar has ... led to changes in the ritual cycle of the agricultural year and the family rites change to Islamic fertility rites'.

Animist Muslims

Neither Islam nor Animism is a religion in the western sense; it is not a weekend religion that can be practised in a definite time and space. It is truly a way of life. Below is a schematic representation of the interrelationships between three parent cultures which qualify, modify and condition each other.

The segment which best describes the situation in southern Burkina Faso is the Muslim Animist. Opeloye (1996) identifies the elements of Animism as existing in Islam as: dynamism, spiritualism, cultism, magico-religious practices, ceremonies associated with the Islamic institutions of circumcision, marriage and death. In these cases it is common for the local customs to hold their ground against the total takeover of Islam and Islamic law.

The reason that there is not a total takeover is because of the foundations that the villages have in communities based on kinship, culture and territory. The communities in Sissili are also not static but they are guaranteed cultural and social stability by the fact that they are essentially agricultural. Therefore, their links with the land provide an anchor which

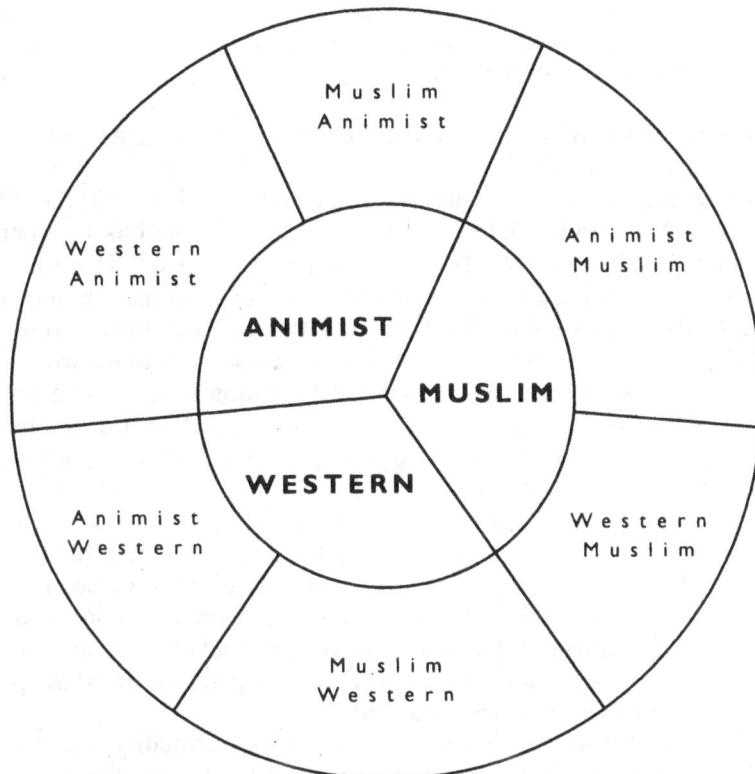

Source: Spencer-Trimingham (1959).

Figure 2.9 The range of religious mixes: Animist, Muslim and Western

can then be attached to a belief system that suits the community at whatever level of mixture that is appropriate. Because of this, when Islam is adopted, the community does not suddenly change its social pattern but remains a unity distinguished by its own pattern of custom (Spencer-Trimingham, 1959:125). Therefore, in Sissili, Islam has become closely entwined with communal life yet without disintegrating its basic structure.

It is clear that people prefer Islam to their old Animist ways. Animism had a very strict code of living with many 'thou shalt nots'. For example, it was forbidden to have sexual relations in the bush or spill blood. Animist laws also decreed certain areas where it was forbidden to fish or farm or burn the bush. Today villagers feel they are free to do whatever they want. One elder said:

Islam arrived 30 years ago and said that God is unique, while Animism considered all idols as Gods. We had to give all the time to the idols before while those who practice Islam live better; they follow the rhythm of civilisation.

Animist traditions still exist and Islam has by no means taken total control of the villagers' 'Animist psyche'. The most obvious untouched traditions are the presence of the Land Chief, Village Chief and (if present) the Village Counsellor. The Land Chief is still considered to be the link between the supernatural and natural world, between men and spirits. There are also sacred sites that still exist where it remains forbidden to fish, farm or hunt, for the Mossi in particular. The Animist fetish has also been given some validity as a 'die-hard' tradition by the Imams, mostly due to the worn fetish (i.e. charm or amulet) occupying a central position in Animist practices. Now instead of putting animal parchment or bones, blood or feathers as charms against evil, bad health and poverty, verses of the Koran are written out on paper and wrapped in leather and worn on the person. However, there are still particular people in particular villages in Sissili who still make 'medicine' (or 'wac' in northern Ghana), i.e. powerful Animist fetishes and charms that are thought to have the ability to curse or kill. In this sense Islam has not 'killed' the belief in Animism, but simply replaced the practice of Animism; there still remains a firm belief in Animist powers as can be seen in the use of Animism in the preparation of homeopathic medicines (see Howorth and Konaté, 1995).

As Animism is an 'earth' religion, in that its spirituality is a result of man's relationship with the natural world, with their fecundity relating to the land's and *vice versa* (e.g. it is best for fertile women to sow the crops), it follows that the Animist yearly ceremonial timetable served the purpose of strengthening management of the land and water. For example, at the appropriate time the Land Chief would begin the 'bush burning' ceremony which calls all people to burn the bush at a particular time, not earlier or later, or the hunting festival which would signal the start of the hunting season. These events were management tools aimed at maximizing production for all and keeping a balance on exploitation levels. The Muslim feels freer than the Animist, at liberty to act as they see fit, free from many of the obligations of gift giving and convinced of their modernity being converts to the 'new religion' of Islam. However, customary law mechanisms still maintain control over issues of resource use and exploitation.

Summary

This chapter has illustrated the complexity of the provincial production systems and its relation to the local environment. There has been a number of critical changes to the indigenous production systems, including new ethnic groups, new languages and new religion, and as such the province will never experience the same conditions that existed before immigration. However, far from experiencing environmental destruction and degradation, the three ethnic groups are in the process of negotiating new resource use patterns and forming new lifescapes. The objective of this current work is to understand this process of change and its implications for local management of natural resources. It is necessary to examine the social, historical and ecological makeup of the local environment, in order to understand how people manage their environments.

3 Culturally Locating Production Patterns

The Nuni

Background

The Nuni (also known as Nuna or Nouna) ethnic group belongs to the larger Gourounsi (also spelt Gurunsi or Grunsi) ethnic group which totals about 230,000 people nation-wide. Duval (1985) estimated the Nuni population to be between 45,000 and 50,000 people in Sissili. The term 'Gourounsi' is used by the neighbouring non-Gourounsi groups and originally was a term of abuse meaning 'savage' or 'barbarian'. The land of the Gourounsi covers approximately 11,125 square kilometres, stretching 200 km north to south and 260 km east to west and its people represent 5.3 per cent of the national population (Atlas du Burkina Faso, 1993). The Gourounsi ethnic group is made up of a number of different groups that speak the same Gourounsi language (coming from the Gour family of Sahelian languages). Even though there are dialectic variations, comprehension between different groups is generally possible. The language of the Nuni is known simply as Nuni.

The Gourounsi (and Nuni) and their territory have been the focus of invasion and attack for many hundreds of years. Invasions, to capture and take back slaves, by the neighbouring Mossi tribes, specifically the Nakomsé (the Mossi nobles), stretch far back into history. In 1740 the Nakomsé invaded and conquered the land of the Nuni. Some of the invading Nakomsé settled, took Nuni wives and also the Nuni language. Some village names in Nuni territory have their roots in Mooré. Duval (1985) points out in his book *Un Totalitarisme Sans Etat* that the name of the Nuni village 'Bouyounou' is likely to have come from the Mooré word **'fuyunugu'** meaning a beautiful robe that transfers its magic to whoever wears it. Many Nuni today will not admit this history out of the shame of the memory of being conquered.

Besides the regular attacks from the neighbouring Mossi, there are two other major invasions in the history of the Nuni; the Djerma invasion and

French colonial conquest. The Djerma, an ethnic group from Niger, southeast of Niamey, came in 1880 to Dagomba, now in Ghana, with their spiritual leader Alfa Hano (Duval, 1985). The Dagomba kingdom used the Djerma, who were excellent horsemen, as mercenaries to capture slaves for trade with the Ashanti kingdom further south. When Alfa Hano died around 1870, the Dagomba king wanted to sever all links with the Djerma mercenaries. Consequently, the Djerma, numbering some 5,000 people (including 1,000 horsemen), moved north through the Gourounsi region, pillaging as they went (Dupperay, 1984). They eventually settled around the villages of Léo and Sati in Sissili. The villages that remained free of Djerma oppression were those that agreed to pay heavy taxes of cowrie shells (currency at that time), cows, horses and slaves. After 1890, certain villages paid a million cowries, more that 100 slaves, young men and girls 'or their value' (Duval, 1985:19).

In 1882 the Djerma attacked Sapouy, in the northeast of the province, with a force of 3,000 horsemen, aided by the Nuni of Cassou. Here they settled for two years, trading slaves as far as the Togo coast. During the invasion certain villages were abandoned and the farmed area considerably diminished. Besides for commercial purposes the Djerma had their own needs for horses, arms, grain and meat. Slaves were the currency for the acquisition of these goods and were necessary to maintain their status quo and for their own progression (Savonnet, 1970).

The Gourounsi (because there were numerous sub-tribes conquered) were partly responsible for their own dominion. They did not unite and it is said that they even sold some of their parents and wives for food (Dahourou, 1994). Certain villages collaborated, like Dalo (historically linked to Cassou) and supplied slaves, millet and maize taken from Bouyounou (Duval, 1985). The Djerma invasion was ended by the invasion of the French in 1896. This period was an important time in Gourounsi politics and represented a centralisation of power. In contrast to the Djerma invasions some of the villages regrouped to resist the French under one leader, the main centres of resistance being Sapouy, Cassou, Silly and Bouyounou which formed an alliance (Duval, 1985). Some other villages remained autonomous. Initially however, the Gourounsi welcomed the French as their liberators from the Djerma. Later the Gourounsi were to experience forced labour, with burning, decapitation, forced farming and public hangings. The tyrannies of the French epoch are still fresh in many of the elders' minds.

The most contemporary invasion to affect the Gourounsi has again been by the Mossi but this time accompanied by a nomadic group, the Fulani. But this time there has been no pillaging or slave trading, it has been an invasion in search of agricultural land.

Power and Governance in Nuni Communities

There are two important positions in Nuni communities, one that governs the land and one that governs village politics. The former is the *Chef de Terre* or Land Chief (**Tiatiu** in Nuni) and the latter is the *Chef de Village* or the Village Chief (**Pio**).

The Land Chief is the descendant of the first family to arrive in the village. It was he that first cleared land to farm under the benevolence of the local divinities (of the land, the bush, stream, rocks or cliffs, etc. (Savonnet, 1970)). Once he has been placed under their divine protection he becomes a master of that land and it is to him that new arrivals must come before touching the land. In some villages the elders believe that the original Land Chief of the village was present at the moment of creation, when God separated the land from the sky. Thus it is implied that God Himself has assured the validity of the Land Chief's lineage. The Land Chief always comes from the same family, if he dies then it is his oldest brother takes charge. If he has no brother his eldest son will inherit the responsibility.

The principal role of the Land Chief is to oversee and supervise everything that has to do with the land, including the bush, the farms and the wildlife. He is seen as the mediator between the human world and the divine world of the ancestors and spirits.[1] He has numerous responsibilities.

If a person would like new land to farm then the Land Chief must be consulted first. He will indicate which piece of land the person can cultivate, what he must do first, i.e. the sacrifices he must offer. If the harvest is a good one then the new farmer must give presents of thanks to the Land Chief, usually, a chicken, a sheep and a pot of millet (De Bolster, 1992). He must also offer a sacrifice to the divinities.

If a person requires a piece of land to build a house upon again it is the Land Chief who will choose the site and then ask the land spirit (**Tia** in Nuni) to bless the new construction. He can also be a rain giver, providing offerings to the spirits to wet the land. He is said to control the fertility of the land and thus female fertility. He is also a war spirit, a priest, a judge and a doctor, healing the land (Duval, 1985). In all cases it is necessary to thank the Tia through sacrifices and offerings.

Thus, the Land Chief has considerable power and responsibility in the life of the community. He is a religious chief of the first order but he is more than that, he watches over the serenity and harmony between the secular world and the supernatural world (Dupperay, 1984). Although he is

---

[1] Religion and spirituality play a crucial part in peasant societies. For example, Dobrowolski in 1958 (pg 289–290) talks about the Polish peasantry, '...they [the holy men] often acted as intermediaries between the world of the super-natural and peasant rank and file, who, feeling helpless, looked for support to these highly influential people'.

probably the most important person in the village he has no power outside his area of influence, his territory. He rarely speaks alone, he has his counsel of village elders of the important lineages who help him decide and govern. The Village Chief (**Pio**) governs everything human. He orders social affairs and has command over all the lineages of the village. The Village Chief is also the descendent of the first or second family to settle in the village and he inherits the title in the same way as the Land Chief does. The Village Chief has the power of decision in the village and he is charged with maintaining order. To reach his decisions he will almost always invite the Land Chief and other elders of important lineages for debate to orient life in the village.

Other positions of power in a Nuni community are chief of the canton and the head of the household, *Chef de Famille*. The canton chief will often be the first member of a new family to settle in the village and set up a new neighbourhood. He will be under total control of the Land and Village Chiefs but will be expected to regulate the minor affairs of his own quarter, with some control over how the land of his canton is distributed, including the village fields, to the members of his canton. The head of the household will control all the family affairs and have ultimate say in all family decisions. The head of the household can distribute his land amongst his family members; this also includes land around the compound.

The Nuni Farming System

In Nuni villages, the compounds are surrounded by household fields or **guédwi**. Varying in distances of between two to seven km away from the households are the bush fields or **karé**. The household fields operate in much the same way as the first ring in the Mossi ring management system (see later). Household field sizes are usually less than half a hectare and are used to grow high value crops, dominated by maize, but also including red sorghum, tobacco, cowpeas, okra, sweet potato, cassava and some vegetables. These are under permanent cultivation, having no fallow period but receiving inputs in the form of organic household rubbish and animal manure from cows, goats, sheep or chickens. Village fields or personal fields (**guedwa**) are found between households in the central area of the village and are mainly used for maize production and serve the purpose of ensuring grain for the hungry period (i.e. they are the first crops to be harvested and fill dietary requirements before the main harvest). Only an elder in a family line can 'own' a **guedwa**. However, the 'owners' of the field are often not those that cultivate the land, it is the youth and the land is often seeded by children of five to six years. Even though the harvest of this field is for the whole family, it is still 'owned' by the particular elder. This serves to keep the hierarchy of governance in place. Women often have personal fields and in these cases all the work is carried out by the women. Women's personal fields are usually given over to groundnuts which are sold to provide cash (Agrotechnik, 1991). Village fields tend to be from half to one hectare. The bush fields are much larger, from two to eight hectares, and are farmed from between four to 15 years after which they are left fallow for ten to 30 years.

The bush fields are a collective possession of the residential household (i.e. the ensemble of relations in one residence: an elder brother, his younger brother, their wives and children, the unmarried girls and the sons' offspring (Dupperay, 1984)). The oldest of the men in the unit does not participate in agricultural work although he may supervise. All farming work is done by men, under the direction of the elders, with the exception of seeding which is done by (fertile) young women (a traditional symbolic fertility rite) and also the transport of the harvest. The latter is carried out by all of the women in the household in the form of headloads,[2] or if available a donkey and cart.

Traditionally women are not meant to farm, except for their field of groundnuts and helping with seeding and harvesting. Presently, however, the socio-economic trends (increase of the need for bought goods, exodus of young men to find paid work, etc.) are forcing women to become involved with more and more agricultural activities and are changing the traditional social norms.

The harvests are then winnowed (removed from the grain stalks and heads) and then put in the granaries. Once in the granary the harvest is only accessible to the women with the permission of the head of the family. It is the family head that distributes the grain every three days which the women ration and cook (Duval, 1985).

In certain fields, because of their bigger size, the farmer needs help to weed, clear or harvest, in which case he can call the group or **kampéné**[3] (a word which has its roots in the English 'company' which is thought to have been introduced by Nuni immigrants that went to work in Ghana) to work in which case the farmer will pay the group in cash or kind. The 'employer' will provide the **kampéné** with food and drink for the work period. The money he pays will go into a central '*caisse*' or kitty and will be used by

---

2 The headloads are carried in head panniers which are symbolically the most important item of a woman's equipment. It contains the food necessary for physical reproduction; it symbolises the fertility that feeds the family. This symbolism is manifested in funerals, where if a woman dies away from her village her pannier will be sent back with the ritual phrase 'nous voulons lui redonner son panier' [we wanted to return her panier] the panier symbolises the wife (Duval 1985:107). This panier can then be buried in place of the body if the latter is irretrievable.
3 The **kampéné** is a work group. It is made up of all the able bodied men in the village. It is called together when there needs to be a large task undertaken that benefits the whole community, e.g. the construction of a well, repairing a road etc. (Dupperay, 1984).

the group at festivals or for group investment. The **kampéné** is controlled by a president, vice president and two 'commanders' who oversee activities but do not participate in the work (Duval, 1985). They regulate the members, fining those who do not turn up for work.

This form of agricultural organisation still exists alongside the more modern form of agricultural organisation; *le groupement villageois* or village group which have been primarily formed as a prerequisite for investment by NGOs and government services in the village.

The collective field (*champ de groupement*), is a field that 'belongs' to the group, the men's group, women's group or youth group. It is worked collectively, normally one day per week in the farming season, and its purpose is to increase the revenue of the group's kitty. The better organised groups use the harvest from the field to create a small cereal bank which serves a commercial or social function depending on the year (i.e. in a good year the extra harvest is sold off, in a bad year, the grain is stored in case of need). Otherwise, as is frequently the case, the proceeds of the harvest are spent on celebrations at the end of the agricultural season. They can also be used for loans, with or without interest.

The Nuni production system reveals a secular *savoir-faire* in relation to soil and water conservation, not only by leaving a significant number of trees in their fields, but also by their practice of *buttage* (mound making around individual plants) and *billonage* (roughening up the soil around the plants to reduce run-off and increase infiltration) and also, through a recognition of the important fallow species (see later). Earth bunds are also built to protect fields against flooding.

The recent appearance (in the late 1980s) of ploughing (mono or dual ox-ploughs are often preferred to donkey ploughs by the Nuni because they tend to cultivate heavy soils, this is reversed for the Mossi) does not seem to have posed too many ecological problems. In spite of this, the Nuni never practice total tree clearance of their fields, even when re-cultivating old fallows that were farmed with a **daba**.

Figure 3.1 shows the Nuni agricultural calendar. It provides information on a range of variables and activities in the Nuni year, including staple foods, times of harvest, seeding, farming activities, labour allocation and rainfall. The preferred food staple is millet which is purchased from the market when harvest supplies dwindle. The most critical time for household food security is between May and June, called the *temps de soudure* or the hungry period. It is at this time when gathered forest fruits and wild foods (see Figure 3.2) are critical for sustaining household food security. Labour requirements are highest in March which coincides with field preparation and seeding times and at harvest time. Labour demand remains high throughout the rainy season.

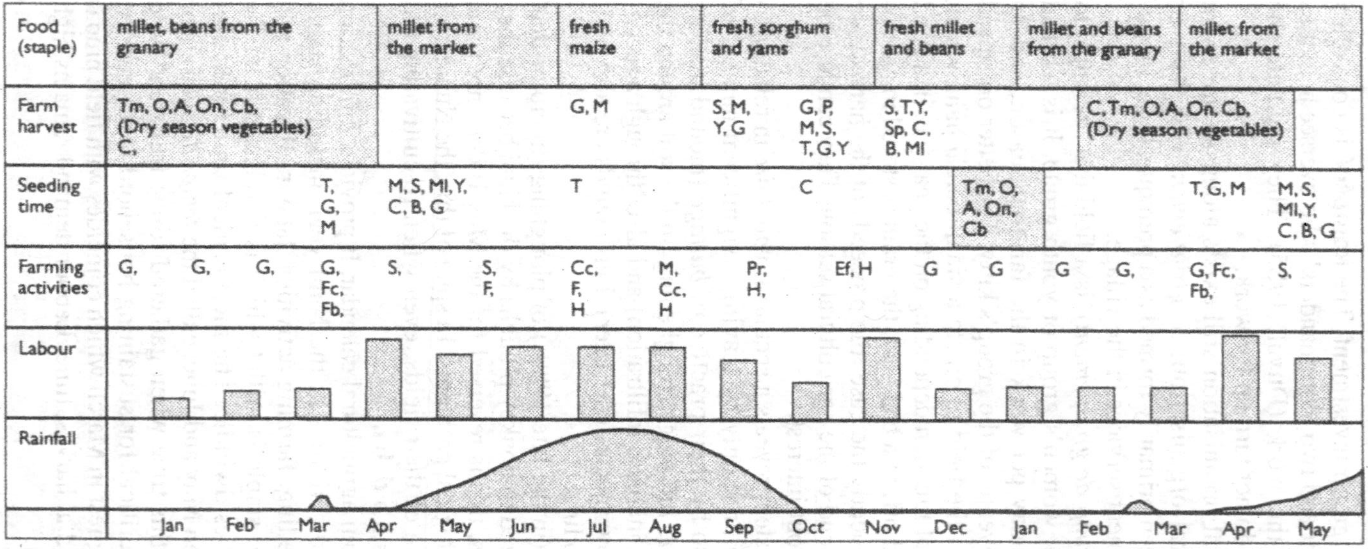

Figure 3.1 The Nuni agricultural calendar

	Jan	Feb	Mar	Apr	May	Jun	Jul	Aug	Sep	Oct	Nov	Dec	Jan	Feb	Mar	Apr	May
Food (staple)	millet, beans from the granary			millet from the market		fresh maize		fresh sorghum and yams		fresh millet and beans		millet and beans from the granary			millet from the market	
Farm harvest	Tm, O, A, On, Cb, C (Dry season vegetables)									G, P, M, S, T, G, Y	S, T, Y, Sp, C, B, Ml	Tm, O, A, On, Cb	G	G	C, Tm, O, A, On, Cb (Dry season vegetables)			M, S, Ml, Y, C, B, G
Seeding time			T, G, M	M, S, Ml, Y, C, B, G	G, M	T			C							T, G, M	M, S, Ml, Y, C, B, G
Farming activities	G,	G,	G,	G, Fc, Fb	S,	S, Fc	Cc, F, H	M, Cc, H	Pr, H,	Ef, H	G	G	G	G	G	G, Fc, Fb	S,
Labour																	
Rainfall																	

Farm harvest
A Aubergine
B Beans
C Cassava
Cb Cabbage
G Groundnut
M Maize
Ml Millet
O Okra
On Onion
P Petits poids
S Sorghum
Sp Sweet potato
T Tobacco
Tm Tomato
Y Yam

Farming activities
Cc Crop care (weeding, thinning, replanting, etc)
Ef Early fires
F Fertilizing
Fb Field burning
Fc Field clearing
G Gardening
H Harvest
M Mound making (around the individual plants)
Pr Preparation of next years fields
S Seeding

Source: Author's fieldwork, 1993–1995.

Hunting and Gathering

Wild fruit trees found on village territory belong to everyone and everyone has a right to their products – they are collective property. Trees in fields, however, belong to the elder who has usufruct rights, even if the field is fallow. Although children may gather fruits as they will, in play or whilst at work, their gathering activities are informal. It is forbidden to harvest all the fruits for personal use at the expense of others' rights to harvest.[4] Gathering, as an activity, is firmly rooted in the domain of women. It is rarely an individual activity and is usually done in groups; women from one compound or family unit group together for forays into the bush to collect plants or fruits for their needs. Gathering, again, sees the operation of a hierarchy with the eldest woman supervising the work, and she eventually may appropriate most of what has been gathered for her own uses and purposes (Duval, 1985). In general, unless some of the gathered product is consumed (or part consumed) in the bush or fields, the gathered product is used for the common good of the residential unit. Figure 3.2 shows the gathering yearly calendar which demonstrates the range, variety and seasonal distribution of gathered tree products (which includes domestic species like grafted mango). The Nuni rely significantly on tree products for household food security throughout the year. Collected tree products include roots, leaves, flowers and fruits and are often highly nutritious. They are mostly used as sauce ingredients that complement the To (the staple carbohydrate made from maize, millet or sorghum flour). Some tree products are also traded, like the *karité*, *néré* and *kapokiér*, and sold to provide an important source of money, especially for women.

In the Sahelian, Sahel-Sudanian and Sudanian (Millington *et al*, 1994:55–57) eco-zones, where limited and variable rainfall makes harvests irregular and uncertain, the products of local woody plants are of primary social and economic importance for rural populations (Guinko and Pasgo, 1992). Guinko and Pasgo, who carried out research in the province of Zitenga, noted that tree products, such as leaves, flowers, fruits, seeds or tubers, are sometimes eaten on the spot (fruits), after cooking (flowers) or after considerable processing and preservation (e.g. shea butter, **soumbala** (see Box 3.1)). They also point out that many products are eaten raw or cooked 'in season'.

Hunting in Nuni society is exclusively a male activity; a woman cannot even touch or hold a bow and arrow. Hunting, however, in Sissili, is on the decline, because of the population increase and the introduction of the gun

---

4 The Nuni have a similar traditional law where a traveller, whilst taking rest, may help himself to a crop (such as yams or sweet potatoes) to feed himself. However it is again 'illegal' to take too much, which would be classed as theft.

Tree product	Am, Af, Bc, Dm,	Af, Dm, D,	D,	Aa, Ba, Lp, Tl, Vl, M,	Al, Aa, Ba, Lp, Lm, Pb, Tl, Vl, M, X,	Al, Bs, Bp, Lm, Pb, Pr, Sb, Tl, C, X, Bf,	Al, As, Bs, Lm, Pr, Sb, Tl, C, Mg, Bf,	As, Bp, Sb, C, Mg,			Tf, Vf, Ms, P,	Am, Bc, Dm, Tf, Vf, P,
Month	Jan	Feb	Mar	Apr	May	Jun	Jul	Aug	Sep	Oct	Nov	Dec

Key
Am	*Acacia macrostachya* (seeds)
Af	*Adansonia digitata* (fruits)
Al	*Adansonia digitata* (leaves)
Aa	*Afzelia africana* (leaves)
As	*Annona senegalensis* (fruits, flowers)
Ba	*Balanites aegyptica* (leaves, flowers)
Bf	*Balanites aegyptica* (fruits)
Bc	*Bombax costatum* (calyx, flowers)
Bs	*Boscia senegalensis* (leaves, fruits)
Bp	*Butyrospernum parkii* (fruits, seeds)
P	*Caricum papaye* (fruits)
C	*Citrus spp.* (fruits)
D	*Detarium microcarpa*
Dm	*Diospyros mespiliformis* (fruits)
Lm	*Lannea microcarpa* (fruits)
Lp	*Leptadenia pyrotechnica* (fruits)
M	*Mangifera indica* (fruits – non-grafted)
Mg	*Mangifera indica* (fruits – grafted)
B	*Musa spp.* (banana)
Pb	*Parkia biglobosa* (fruits, seeds)
Pr	*Piliostigma reticulatum* (leaves)
Sb	*Sclerocarya birrea* (fruits)
Tl	*Tamarindus indica* (leaves)
Tf	*Tamarindus indica* (fruits)
Vl	*Vitex doniana* (leaves)
Vf	*Vitex doniana* (fruits)
X	*Ximenia americana*

Source: Author's fieldwork, 1993–1995.

Figure 3.2 The forest food gathering calendar

which allows a more effective killing capacity. There are (or were) two types of hunting activities; the collective hunt, thought to have disappeared in the region since 1950/55 and individual hunting. Individual hunting is occasional and is practised by almost every peasant, in his fields or in the bush, usually for monkeys, grasscutters (a herbivorous large rat), birds and occasionally bush pig. When a kill is made, it is for the eldest in the household, in the usual hierarchy (Duval, 1985).

The Nuni's land, both field and fallow, is characterised by the important presence of the néré tree (also called the African locust bean). Traditionally this tree is sown in farmers' fields and its use and exploitation is regulated by strict social laws. It is not unusual to count as many as 30 trees per hectare. The néré, a member of the Mimosaceae family, contributes to soil fertility by the constant, year round, shedding of its leaves. The farmers however, attribute a negative value to the tree in cereal fields, and often prune the tree crown to reduce crop shading. Maiga (1987) showed that néré can cause a drop of 32.3 per cent of grain production in plants in close proximity to the tree.

> **Box 3.1 Néré or African locust bean – *Parkia biglobosa (jacq.) Benth*, Mimosaceae family**
>
> The néré is used for many things by Nuni and Mossi alike:
>
> - It is an important food. The seeds are rich in fat and proteins. They are fermented to give a 'vegetable cheese' called soumbala which is used for food seasoning, very much like a stock cube, with a very distinctive taste. Soumbala is the object of local trade throughout Burkina Faso and Mali.
> - The yellow 'pulp' which surrounds the seeds in their pods contains 60 percent sugar and is fermented to give a high energy drink, which is often drunk before going to the fields.
> - The leaves, bark and roots are used as cures for a multitude of ailments including haemorrhoids, guinea worm and sterility.
>
> Source: Author's fieldwork, 1993–1995.

The karité or shea nut (*B.parkii* or *Vitellaria paradoxa*) is equally as important to the Nuni. Karité are usually found on ferruginous soils (**dio**) or vertisols (that have not as yet been exploited – the Nuni prefer to keep the néré in their farmed area because karité are extremely prolific in the bush). Karité are rarely planted by farmers and they predominantly rely on natural regeneration. Their presence in the already exploited bush represents a selective felling on the part of the Nuni rather than a plantation effort (De Bolster, 1992). Karité nuts occupy a very important place in the local women's economy (see Box 3.2) as the preparation and trade of karité butter is solely a female activity. Again, in Maiga's (1987) research, he showed a drop in grain production of 30 per cent in those cereal plants around the karité's crown.

The fallows are often covered by a bush called **tio** in Nuni (*D.cinerea*) from the Mimosaceae family, which is recognised as a plant which reconstitutes soil fertility (both locally and scientifically (see Von Maydell, 1992:229)). This species reproduces very easily by suckers but is not considered an invasive species as it can be cut back very easily. It is also valued for its forage (leaves, fruits and seeds) its wood and bark for rope, baskets and matting, and for local medicine.

The Mossi

Background

The historical invasions by the Mossi apart,[5] there have been two phases to the wave of migration that has taken place over the last 30 years. The first Mossi farmers arrived 30 years ago into an unknown landscape where many of the conditions were different from those in the north. They imported their farming techniques that were learnt from generations of farming in a dry, Sahelian environment. Their first stages of agriculture are almost complete tree and shrub clearance from the fields, removing the protective cover. These were the original Mossi that were given land by the Land Chief.

The Mossi are effectively confined to their own 'territories' within the Nuni village territory. The new Mossi settlement functions the way any 'new' traditional village would. The first family to arrive becomes the family of the chief. It is this family that regulates internal Mossi affairs and their farming activities. It is he that new immigrants must see first, if the Mossi chief accepts the new immigrant (usually kin to another member of the existing Mossi community), then he will send him to see the Nuni chief to seek his approval. Minor Mossi affairs are handled by the Mossi chief, grave misdemeanours or serious issues are dealt with by the Nuni chief who has the right to expel any member of his community, immigrant or not (though this rarely happens).

After the original Mossi immigrants, the next wave of immigrants regrouped around the Mossi that had already settled in villages in the province. Mathieu (1994) noted that the Mossi consequently recreated the social and spatial structures that exist in their homelands, i.e. the hierarchical organisation of labour, governance and distribution of space (see later text). This can be seen in the case study villages where the original Mossi regulate the number of immigrants and their activities before sending the new arrivals to see the Nuni land chief. This is based on an understanding between the land chief and the Mossi leader or 'chief' that the Mossi will get no more land and therefore it is the Mossi chief's choice whether or not he allows new settlers to be accommodated on his new land.

The Mossi have a specific system when welcoming a new migrant into their territory that allows the newcomer to have a minimum production level in the first year. As already mentioned, the newcomer must pass through a Mossi who already lives in the area who is prepared to speak out

---

5 Totté (1994) reports that the first major wave of immigration by Mossi farmers came between 1911 and 1947. This was thought to have started because of forced labour recruitment by the French colonialists, rising taxes in the north, droughts, forced cotton cultivation and, until 1946, forced labour for working the Niger Delta or plantations in Côte D'Ivoire.

Box 3.2   Karité or Shea nut – *Butyrospernum parkii (G.Don) Kotschy, Sapotaceae* family[6]

The karité's principal benefit is its butter which plays a crucial role in the local (and national) economy. To make the butter, the ripe fruits are collected in the rainy season. After eating the ripe pulp surrounding the 'nut' or by removing it through stockpiling them and letting the pulp ferment away, the nuts are cleaned and collected. The nuts are then boiled in water then dried, this process separates the inner seed from the hard seed coating. These are then pounded in a pestle and mortar to crack the outer seed coating. The mixture is then winnowed, in a strong wind, to separate the seed from their coatings. To stop the seeds germinating they are dried, leaving only about ten per cent water content so they can then be stored for long periods. To extract the butter the seeds are heated above an open fire until they begin to 'weep', i.e. exude oil. They are then placed in a mortar and are pounded by numerous women at the same time. A paste is then obtained. The temperature must be kept above 40°C so that the oil remains liquid and can be poured out into an iron pot. After it cools down it solidifies and it is then ground between two stones. It is then placed in a container and boiling and cold water are alternately poured onto it. Little by little the butter loses its red colour and begins to whiten. It is shaped into balls, and heated again in an iron pot while keeping the balls constantly damp. A creamy layer then forms on the surface of the balls which is karité butter of the finest quality.

The poorer quality butter can be transformed into soap,[7] candles, preservation grease, magarine or beauty products. It is used industrially for chocolate and lipstick production. Karité butter and its products are imported to Europe, America and Japan. Karités other uses include good quality charcoal wood (although because of its value as a fruit tree this is rarely done) and local medicine.

on behalf of the new migrant. In exchange for this, the new migrant must provide a service to the original Mossi that usually includes days of work in the busiest times of the year, e.g. at weeding time. Added to this, the new migrant must clear his own new parcel of land. Because of the level of work required he is forced to call in external labour to help him if he wants to have an adequate harvest in the first year. In exchange for this 'favour', he

---

6 This box draws on Von Maydell, 1992.
7 The vegetable oil (karité butter) is saponified using potash (potassium hydroxide) derived from the ash of a number of tree species (particularly *P.thonningii*) or sorghum stalks (Schrekenberg, 1996).

must give his labour in exchange in the dry season, making houses and thatching. In this way, the Mossi are embedded in relationships of obligation and reciprocity which some may view as oppressive and others as being a successful part of their livelihood strategy.

The Mossi quarters are a reflection of Mossi settlement structure in their homelands in the north. One family is housed in a **zaka** (a compound). Each **zaka** is separated from its neighbours by an area of agricultural land. Different **zakse** (plural of **zaka**) are grouped together in loose agglomerations according to different cantons (**sakse** in Mooré). The organisation of the agricultural work is arranged in counsel with the whole neighbourhood.

A remarkable difference between Mossi society in Sissili compared with that of their places of origin is, in Sissili, the entire Mossi family works on the farm. In the Mossi homelands, it is not unusual to find large Muslim families with many of their children attending Koranic school. These youth and children provide an important labour source and must cultivate the fields of the Koranic teachers, allowing the teachers and their wives a freedom from agricultural work. Also, in the Mossi plateau, a Mossi farmer will seem less 'courageous' or inventive with his agricultural practices compared to his activities in Sissili. This is because, firstly, the Mossi farmer is free from control and the social constraints of the traditional Mossi society, that interferes with his own development, (e.g. jealousies, slander, sorcery, poisoning), and secondly he suffers an 'inverted' social pressure that pushes him to produce more so that he can to subsidise his larger family in his homeland (De Bolster, 1992).

The Mossi, in the first instance, will occupy fallows left by the Nuni that are in close proximity to the Nuni quarters. This arrangement serves two interests: firstly, the migrants need the use of the local infrastructures (wells, boreholes, markets, etc) and, secondly, the host community is able to survey the migrants, to control and monitor their movements (Totté, 1994). Progressively, after building up a network of relationships the Mossi will attempt securing better land further into the bush (Figure 3.3 illustrates this process of sequence occupation). Mathieu (1994) suggests that the land given to the Mossi at this stage may be 'problematic land', areas where the land ownership is unclear, e.g. between boundaries of village territories, as in the cases of Lon and Boutiourou, or in zones that are traditionally used for grazing.

Totté (1994) carried out research in southwestern Burkina Faso in the *Hauts-Bassins*, an area of extensive cotton production. His study examined the impact of Mossi immigrants on the cotton dominated local production system. Although there are similarities between the *Hauts-Bassins* and Sissili, there are also some important differences to be noted. Firstly, the *Hauts-Bassins* experienced significant immigration long before Sissili;

Culturally Locating Production Patterns 79

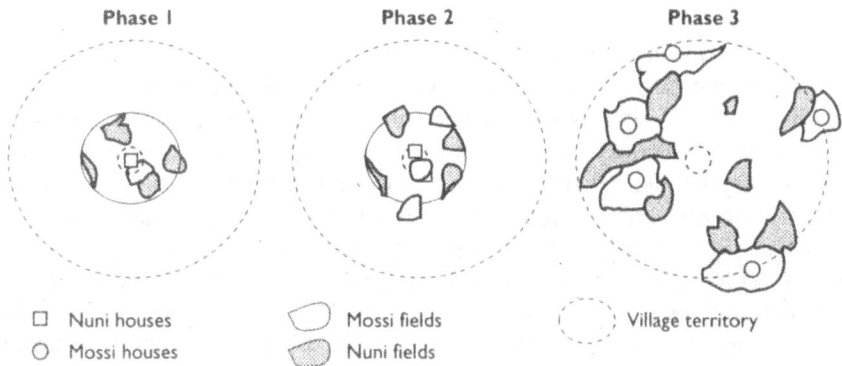

Key
Phase 1: The settlement of the first immigrants very close to the Nuni settlement on the Nuni fallows
Phase 2: The migrants open new fields in the bush
Phase 3: The migrants construct their houses in the bush; the Nuni attempt to surround the Mossi fields for surveillance

Source: Adapted from Totté, 1994:62.

Figure 3.3 The evolution of the occupation of space after the reception of Mossi immigrants

immigration on a large scale started in the early 1960s and was characterised by economic motives. This has implications for the early saturation of space. Secondly, the culture of cotton cultivation in favour of subsistence crops (in Sissili this situation is reversed) means that extensive land areas are needed and which leads to land shortage. Both these factors lead inevitably to out-migration (in Totté's analysis) of the original Mossi when population becomes too high and land too short.

Totté (1994) points out that once the migrants attained sufficient cultural autonomy (which is a result of the Mossi inhabiting land areas which are sufficiently isolated and have the ability to be easily expanded) there begins a process of autodevelopment with a strength of governance. With this semi-autonomy comes a call, from the original Mossi, of welcome to other northern Mossi, usually of the same lineage. It is for this reason that there are concentrated areas in Nuni territories of large Mossi populations, much greater than the indigenous populations. These have, according to Totté (1994) two main implications: firstly a reduction in the cultivated area and secondly a move for new fields, further and further away from their habitation zones. To try to remedy this situation the migrant will move and rebuild his house in his fields in the bush where he will try to create a new settlement. The new free fallows are then available for the new migrants.

80 Rebuilding the Local Landscape

Totté (1994) notes that in the case of land shortage there is a higher mobility, i.e. the Mossi will move to other areas when farmland becomes scarce. The more recent immigrants will only find recent fallows to occupy. This land is their only option as all the other land has been used. After only a few seasons they will have to find new land to compensate for the poor soil fertility of the recent fallows. In the southwest of Burkina where immigration pressure is higher than Sissili, a four stage sequence occurs (see Figure 3.4). Firstly, is the settlement of the first Mossi immigrants who have ample land to farm; secondly is the arrival of new migrants who build their homes close to the original Mossi, some Mossi move more deeply into the bush and the first fallows are left. The third stage sees the newer immigrants acquiring their independence, both economically and spatially. The final stage is the departure of the original immigrants to new areas and the arrival of new migrants who occupy their old fallows.

There are similarities between Totté's analysis in the process of sequence occupation in the *Hauts Bassins* and in present day Sissili (and the case study villages). Figure 3.3, the evolution of the occupation of space after the reception of the Mossi immigrants, echoes the development of the post immigrant landscape in Lon and Boutiourou (although not in Saboué

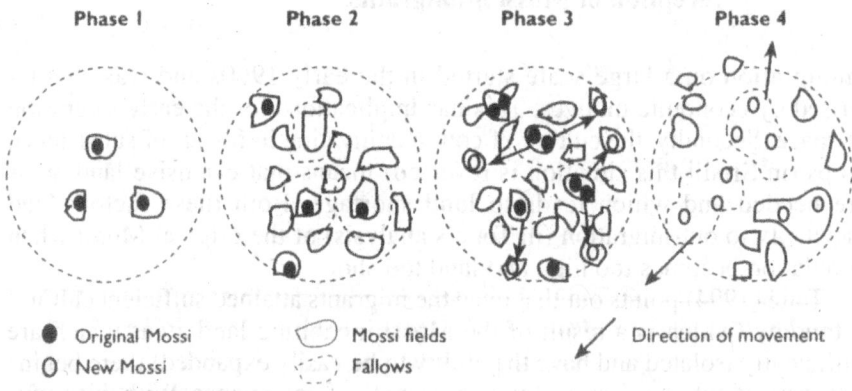

● Original Mossi   ◯ Mossi fields   ↙ Direction of movement
○ New Mossi   ⸰⸰⸰ Fallows

Key
Phase 1: Installation of founding Mossi
Phase 2: Enlargement of Mossi farmed areas and the arrival of new immigrants close to the original settlers
Phase 3: The new immigrants achieve their own economic and spatial independence
Phase 4: The departure of the old families and the arrival of new families which occupy the old fallows

Source: Adapted from Totté, 1994:62.

Figure 3.4 The evolution of the agricultural organisation of the Mossi immigrants

where there is no evidence of surveillance). However, Figure 3.4, the evolution of the agricultural organisation of the Mossi migrants, can only be related to Lon, which is in the cotton producing zone of Sissili. Lon has experienced the three phases seen in the diagram, with the progressive introduction of Mossi from various lineages from different areas and the consequent use, by the newer Mossi, of the fallows that belonged to the original Mossi. Phase four, as seen on the diagram, however has not been experienced and, in the author's opinion, is not likely to occur. This is due to two factors; firstly, immigration has stopped in the village (the Mossi chiefs in conjunction with the Nuni chiefs have decided that there is no more land available for new migrants) and secondly, there is a higher ratio of food crop production than cash crop production.

The Farming System of the Mossi

The Mossi employ a ring management system[8] of crop and soil management which has been imported from their zones of origin into Sissili. In the Mossi ring management system, the fields are located in rings around the compound. It is still apparent that these rings correspond to the household, village and bush fields because of the type and nature of crops grown on them.

There is a distinction in both Nuni and Mossi production systems of household fields, village fields and bush fields. These terms refer to fields which are both spatially different and also fulfil different household needs that correspond to diverse crop types in the different fields. The household field is, as the name suggests, adjacent, or, in close proximity to the compound. Here high value crops are located which require relatively high inputs such as fertiliser, labour and sometimes water (see Table 3.1). The village field is located in the spaces between compounds in the village and is used for staple foods, which require larger surface areas. Again, investment in these fields is still relatively high. The bush fields can be as far as six km away from the compound, but are usually much nearer (normally from 1.5 to four km from the house). Here staple crops are cropped on large land parcels.

In the Mossi ring management system the first ring corresponds to the household field. These fields receive the highest inputs and, in a study by Prudencio[9] (1993), it was shown that nine tonnes of manure per hectare were added to these first fields.

---

8 In this system, different crops and cropping patterns are observed in concentric rings around the village compound, with the frequency of cultivation or intensity of land use declining as one moves away from the compound in a similar manner to Von Thunen's location theory (Prudencio, 1993:237) although the determinant here is labour input not bid rent.
9 Prudencio (1993) carried out research into the Mossi ring management farming system in a Sudanian region of Burkina Faso.

Table 3.1   Crops and their roles in the first ring/household field

Crop	Role	Comments
Maize (*Zea mays*)	To improve food availability in the hungry season	Maize is the first crop to be harvested and has the shortest rotation (60–90 days). The amount of manure available will determine the area planted.
Sauce plants: Niébé (*Hibiscus sabdariffa*), sweet potato leaves (*Ipomea patatas*)*, cowpea leaves (*Vigna sinesis*), okra (*Hibiscus esculentus*), cassava leaves (*Manichot utilissima*)*	Ingredients to complement to, provision of vitamins and minerals	Sauce ingredients are vitally important in the daily diet as they flavour the meals (which are commonly 'meat-less') an absence of sauce would mean an incomplete diet. Grown sauce ingredients are complemented with wild sauce ingredients, e.g. baobab leaves.
Tobacco (*Nicotiana tabacum*)	For smoking and sale or trade	Needs heavy manure application.

* These are principally grown for the sauce but the tubers provide an additional form of nutrients in the hungry period.
Source: Based on Prudencio, 1993.

In the second ring, the village field, manure applications are also common (Prudencio (1993) noted an application of 1.3 tonnes of manure per hectare). Crops typically grown on the village field or second ring include red sorghum, cowpeas, (the major crop) and groundnuts, millet, white sorghum, tubers (used in rotation). In general, these fields make up about 30 per cent of the total cultivated area but provide 40 to 50 per cent or more of the total crop output value per year (Marchal, 1982).

The third ring, the bush fields, is usually devoted to millet which is intercropped either with white sorghum and/or cowpeas. There is no application of manure and other inputs are rare and consequently soil fertility is regenerated through fallowing. Legumes are often planted in rotation, or when soil fertility is very low. These fields tend to maximise the cultivated land area as far as possible in relation to the available labour in the household, i.e. the more excess labour available in the household the larger the bush field, the less labour available the smaller the field. This field is the

Table 3.2 Crops and their roles in the second ring/village field

Crop	Role	Comments
Red sorghum (*Sorghum vulgare*)	Provision of staple crop (least preferred)	There are four reasons for red sorghum to be located here: it responds best to moderate manure application; it has a shorter rotation (90–120 days) than millet or white sorghum (120–180 days); it is the least palatable of the grains for To, so it is consumed less and so lasts longer (i.e. it is a risk minimiser); it is used to make dolo and so has a market value and can be sold in case of problems.
Millet (*Pennisetum typhoides*)	Provision of staple crop (most preferred)	Millet is grown to a lesser degree here because it can grow on poor soils often found in the bush fields.
Cowpeas (*Vigna sinensis*)	Provision of protein crop	Cowpeas form a very important protein source for the household. These are intercropped with sorghum or millet.
Sweet potato (*Ipomea patatas*), bambara nuts (*Voandeia subterranea*)	Cash crop and/or food crop supplement	Sweet potatoes and bambara nuts are grown in rotation with sorghum and millet. Bambara nuts are boiled and used as snacks or can be sold as hot snacks.
Groundnuts (*Arachis hypogoea*)	Cash crop	Most commonly grown on rotation on more impoverished patches.

Source: Based on Prudencio, 1993.

furthest away from the household and thus receives the lowest inputs, in terms of labour, management or fertiliser. If fertiliser is applied, it tends to be chemical fertiliser because of the transportation problems over the

Table 3.3 Crops and their roles in the third ring/bush field

Crop	Role	Comments
Millet (*P. typhoides*)	Provision of households preferred staple carbohydrate	Millet can tolerate poor soils and little management, it is often intercropped with cowpeas.
White sorghum (*Sorghum vulgare*)	Provision of staple cereal	White sorghum is less tolerant of poor soils than millet and so tends to be cropped on the better soils, again intercropped with cowpeas.
Bambara nuts (*V.subterranea*)	Cash crop and/or food crop supplement	Grown on the poorer soils.
Groundnuts (*Arachis hypogoea*)	Cash crop	Grown on the infertile soils in an attempt for a last crop.
Cowpeas (*V.sinensis*)	Provision of protein and base for sauces	Cowpeas can be grown here because of the lower risk of attack by animals (cowpeas are very palatable) if they are hidden in amongst the taller millet or sorghum.

Source: Based on Prudencio, 1993.

distances involved, i.e. manure is too heavy to be carried long distances. The rotation cycles of crops in the third ring are the longest, from 120 to 180 days. Prudencio (1979) shows that the third rings cover approximately 60 to 70 per cent of the total household cultivated area but only provide 30 to 40 per cent of total crop output.

In the Mossi ring management system there is a negative correlation between inputs and proximity to the household, i.e. the further away from the household the less the inputs. More time is spent in the inner ring on activities such as manure application, soil preparation, weeding, harvesting, sometimes fencing, and also the timing of these activities are more precise here compared with the outer rings. For maximum yields with the inner rings it is necessary to have them as near to the compound as possible to ensure ease of access and often frequent surveillance. The closer the field is to the compound the better it can be managed (Marchal, 1982).

The crops that are chosen for each of the rings have different requirements in their sowing, first weedings and harvesting. In this way the farmer plants crops with different rotation times (i.e. from the time of sowing to the time of harvest) to avoid labour bottlenecks and also to ensure a staggered harvest in the agricultural calendar. For example, Prudencio (1993) showed that between planting and first weeding was 18 days in the first ring, 26 days in the second and 35 days in the third ring; all of these lags were due to the differences in the maturity periods. In the same research Prudencio shows that maize in the first ring was harvested on average 66 days after planting, red sorghum in the second ring was harvested 137 days after planting and the millet and white sorghum was harvested on average 161 days after planting. These field level strategies employed by the farmers serve the purpose of ensuring food security at minimum risk and enabling farmers to minimise moisture and labour constraints and to minimise gaps in food availability over time (Kowal and Kassam, 1978). To be able to put into operation the maximisation of food security and availability the farmer must be able to plant a range of food crops that have different rotation cycles.

A vital aspect of this ring management system is that soil fertility is positively related to the intensity of landuse. Far from destroying soil fertility through an over-intensive period of exploitation, the farmers actually improve the condition of the soil through their management techniques. The further the distance the field is from the household, the lower the intensity management regime and the poorer the quality of the soils. Here management relies on fallowing to reconstitute soil fertility.

To end this section it is useful to return to Prudencio (1993:260) who makes two very important conclusions. Firstly, he states that population pressure is shortening the fallow period and this is causing a decline in soil fertility in *the outer* ring or bush field. Secondly, he states that:

> there is little evidence...supporting the conventional argument that traditional farming systems...mine the natural fertility base of soils when they evolve toward more permanent cultivation practices.

The Fulani

The Fulani are the third ethnic group in Sissili whose traditional domain has been in the sahelian zone of Burkina Faso. They are a semi-nomadic group who have always covered large distances with their animals for trade and for grazing. Since the 1970s, they have moved down from the Sahel into the greener southern zones in search of pasture. Pastoralism is new in the province and the management systems remain largely unknown.

The Fulani inhabit a relatively isolated area of each village territory, away from the Mossi and Nuni fields. Their living quarters are referred to as encampments which are geographically distinct clusters of woven straw huts. These encampments are open, i.e. they are not enclosed by a wall like the Mossi or Nuni, but the areas which immediately surround the huts are swept and kept clean and provide the living area.

The Fulani are agro-pastoralists, cultivating cereals on old pasture zones, providing part of the family's cereal needs for the year. The single, circular Fulani fields are always located around their encampments. These are normally situated on old paddocks, i.e. the fields were previously used as cattle corrals which are rich in manure. In the dry season, corrals may frequently be moved around the future farmed area to fertilise as much land as possible and to minimise the labour required to spread manure onto fields. Their harvests do not provide the family with cereals for the entire year because of the small surface area farmed. Food can be provided for anything between six to nine months of the year depending on various factors. For the rest of the year, they buy cereals with money from the sale of cattle. There is a smaller crop variety on Fulani farms (usually dominated by millet), in contrast to Nuni and Mossi crop mixtures. When asked, a Fulani will always value his herd more than cropping, even though the harvest plays an important role in family nutrition. Agriculture is seen as a side issue and is carried out to take pressure off the herd. The Fulani have said that when pasture becomes poor they will go elsewhere; to increase the farmed area and to become more dependent on the harvest is not an option for 'real' herders. Their cattle are kept around the Fulani settlement (in a radius of 20 km) and are only taken for longer distances relatively late into the dry season, from March to May/June (transhumance requires one man to herd from between 15 to 20 cattle (Delgado, 1979)) when grazing is particularly difficult to find (see Table 3.4 for the Fulani yearly activities). For the rest of the year the cattle are held in corrals made from dead thorny branches, around the encampment. Cattle are grazed on unoccupied land during the cropping season, on harvested fields post-harvest, and in the valley bottoms during the hot dry period from March to June (Egging, 1989). Table 3.5 gives a detailed outline of the typical Fulani yearly activities.

In addition, the Fulani will guard and herd the animals of the Mossi or Nuni. For this they will receive no formal payment but may receive gifts (for example, cereals, clothes or a calf) and can use or sell the milk from the guarded animals (see Box 3.3). As the sale of milk plays a vital role in the Fulani economy, guarding other peoples' cattle is an important contribution to household security. In addition to the milk other peoples' cows produce, they also produce extra valuable manure which can be used on Fulani fields or exchanged to manure the dry season gardens of the Nuni and Mossi. Cows from other people can contribute up to a third of a Fulani's herd. It is often Fulani who have recently lost a portion of their herd or who only have a few animals that will guard the animals of others. A Fulani

Table 3.4 The Fulani yearly activities

Fulfulbé name and period	Activities
Dungu – late June to mid-September (rainy season)	The herd is grazed near the encampment but away from cultivated fields. Forage and water are abundant but substantial work must be spent tending crops and moving the corral to control parasites. This is the best time for milk production.
Yamde – after the harvest to cold period beginning in December **Nyaile** is the end of this period when livestock graze on crop stubble on nearby fields	This is the time of plenty as the harvest is in and the cattle are fattened after grazing on the rainy season grasses.
Dabunde – the cold dry season from December to February	Cereals are threshed with the help of the dry harmattan winds from the northeast. Cattle may be taken on to the Mossi or Nuni fields as crop stubble becomes scarcer. Manure from the corrals is spread over Fulani fields. There is no longer surplus milk for consumption by the household.
Cheedu – hot dry season from February to April	Surface water is gone so wells must be dug in the valley bottoms. Around March, most of the herds have left on transhumance to distances of up to 60 or 70 km.
Seeto – after the '*pluits des mangues*' in April to the beginning of the rains in May/June	All the herds are away in search of water and pasture and the cattle mortality is at its peak due to heat stress and lack of forage. The herds then return to the village for the first shoots of the rains. This is the reason why Fulani will plant later than their sedentary neighbours.

Source: Adapted from Delgado, 1979:35–36

without cattle or few cattle is not considered a 'real' Fulani. Richer or older Fulani may pay guardians to herd their cattle, the price for a six month period being 2,500 FCFA (about the price of a Taurin calf of six months). Some exchange takes place at the village level, of milk for cereals for example, or the use of village materials (e.g. mortar and pestle and grinding stones).

Table 3.5   The Fulani seasonal calendar

	Jan	Feb	Mar	Apr	May	Jun	Jul	Aug	Sep	Oct	Nov	Dec
Labour:												
sorghum				▭								
maize						▭						
Seeding:												
sorghum				▭▭								
maize					▭▭							
millet					▭							
Weeding:												
sorghum					▭▭▭							
maize					▭▭▭▭							
millet					▭▭▭							
Harvest:												
sorghum									▭▭			
maize									▭▭			
millet									▭▭			
Herding:												
intensive					▭▭▭▭▭▭▭▭							
extensive	▭▭▭▭▭									▭▭▭		
Transhumance	▭▭											
Milk Production:												
intensive	▭▭▭▭▭▭▭▭▭											
extensive					▭▭▭▭▭▭▭▭							

Source: de Boer, 1992.

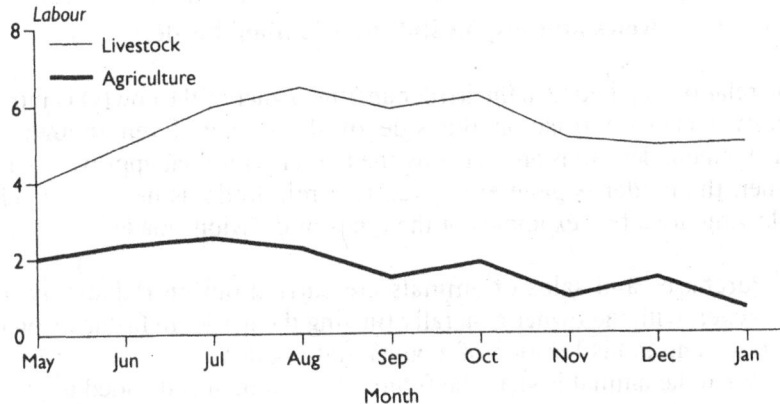

Source: Based on Delgado, 1979.

Figure 3.5 Relative labour allocation for livestock and agriculture amongst the Fulani

Figure 3.5 illustrates the differences in labour requirements of the Fulani herding/livestock activities and the agricultural activities.

There are two types of cattle, the Zebu and the Taurin (or N'Dama) which is without the hump and smaller, more adapted to humid environments and more resistant to trypanosomiasis. These are found more often with the Nuni and the Mossi. Taurins are more resilient in famine conditions, they give more meat, do not get lost as easily as Zebu (they follow the herd and herder) and do not graze at night so are easier to guard and less demanding, spending the night in stalls. The Taurins however produce less milk and the price per head is lower than for Zebu.

The cattle that do not belong to other proprietors in the corral all belong to the head of the household. However, each member can 'own' cattle within the household herd, in the same way that a car may belong to a teenager, even though it is registered in his parent's name (Delgado, 1979). The head of the household has the power to sell all the cattle of the household if he so wishes, (Dahl and Hjort, 1976) although such an act would cause considerable dissent in his family if it was not in a time of crisis. When children marry, however, whether male or female, they can remove the cattle from the father's corral and take full control over them. Women also can own cattle, given to them by their mother and father. The woman retains the right to sell her cattle, although she must gain permission from her husband first. The son of the mother also has rights to her herd, and the father, in times of need, can ask the son to try to persuade the mother to sell. If there

> **Box 3.3   Roles and responsibilities of Fulani herders**
>
> The relationship between the herder and the owner of the cow(s) is intrinsically based on trust on the side of the owner. Even though all management decisions are made by the herder with final approval by the owner, the herder is generally given free rein to do as he sees fit. The following are a few examples of the types of decisions made.
>
> - Purchases and sales of animals are carried out on request by the owner, with the owner generally trusting the herder in his decision of price and in his location of a buyer and a seller.
> - When the animal is sick, the future of the animal is decided upon by the herder, who may sell the cow (often at one fifth of the normal price) or visit a Vet (and the owner will have to pay fees).
> - When a sick animal dies and is close enough to the owner, the herder will bring the animal's head as proof of death to the owner.
> - The herder can begin milking when he judges fit and can also wean a calf off milk when he likes, without informing the owner.
> - The herder must inform the owner of all births.
> - When herders leave on transhumance, the herd is then under the full control of the herder and management decisions cannot be relayed to the owner. If an animal dies, its head cannot be taken back to the owner.
>
> *Source:* Based on research by Delgado, 1979.

is a divorce, the woman keeps the goods or gifts that she has received from the marriage, for example jewellery[10] which can be worth between 150,000 to 300,000 FCFA, in addition to her herd.

There are five legal ways of acquiring ownership of cattle in Fulani communities (after Delgado, 1979):

- inheritance from a parent;
- gifts from a father or a maternal uncle to a child;
- gifts from a proprietor of cattle for herding services;
- acquisition from a son-in-law as dowry; and
- purchase of young cattle with the proceeds from the sale of old stock.

---

[10] Fulani women wear a considerable amount of jewellery in the form of silver coins, plaited into their hair and silver chains around their necks and thick silver bangles.

The Mossi and the Nuni have different reasons for animal rearing. For the most part they keep animals as a form of 'savings account' and for farm labour. Cattle herds are a good way of investing surplus money for the future. It has occurred in the past that Nuni or Mossi have sold all their animals and then they have reinvested when the threat have passed (de Boer, 1992). A Fulani would never sell all his herd and so risk of complete cattle loss from epidemics is high and consequently Fulani must invest in vaccinations. Small ruminants are kept by all tribes for small spending needs such as weddings, funerals or visitors. Manure from animals is rarely used or collected for compost for bush fields (except for the Fulani who farm on old pasture zones) but manure (household waste and manure) is used on household fields. Many people prefer and collect bat droppings for manure.

The favoured sale animals are male. The place of sale is often in the bush, with traders coming out to meet the Fulani and then returning with the animals to the butcher. There are disadvantages to this method; sellers cannot compare animals and prices and traders can misinform the seller of cattle prices. An advantage to this method is that sellers do not need to travel to the market, tiring their animals and risking a non-sale. Traders will often talk to people in the region asking which Fulani are in financial difficulty in order to secure cattle at cheaper prices, or they will follow Government vaccination programmes, approaching poor Fulani and offering to pay for vaccinations in exchange for cattle (de Boer and Kessler, 1994). Sales can also be carried out through intermediaries.

Because Fulani do not produce enough cereals themselves for the year, they are forced to sell some animals to buy the remainder. Towards the end of the dry season, the crops are at their highest prices (a 100 kg bag of millet costs 14,000 FCFA) and the cattle are in their worst condition and thus lowest price. At the end of the rainy season the crops are at their lowest price, 6,000 to 7,000 FCFA for a 100 kg bag of millet, and the cattle in their best condition and highest price. However, at this time the Fulani have also just harvested their crops and so do not feel the 'need' to buy. They will wait until the end of the season and then will sell two or three times the number of animals for the same amount of cereals. This situation is aggravated in drought years where their harvest is already poor. There is little grazing for their animals which become thin very quickly and crop prices are very high; it is years like this where they risk losing their whole herd or where the majority is lost.

Understanding between the Fulani and the Mossi and Nuni is usually good, except when animals stray onto fields. Agreements often exist between farmers through which the Fulani will graze their herds on the millet stalks after harvest so fertilising the fields.

Table 3.6 The agricultural division of labour in Fulani communities by sex

Men	Women
Planting	Help with: manuring, removing
Weeding	grains from cereal heads.
Field preparation	Maize cultivation
Harvesting	Milking
Threshing	Preparation of milk products
Manuring	
Herding	

Source: Author's fieldwork, 1993-1995.

The Fulani farming system, although much smaller in magnitude than both the Mossi or Nuni, is made more intensive through the application of cattle manure. This allows the Fulani farmer to realise significantly higher yields per unit of land than the other two tribes. However, the Fulani farmer has significantly smaller land parcels. In Figure 3.6, there is a comparison between peasant farmers' and Fulani households' allocation of labour hours to one hectare of land (based on research by Delgado, 1979). Even though it is taken from another area of Burkina Faso, the order of magnitude of difference is very similar.

Occasionally Fulani cattle will wander onto a Mossi or Nuni field (more commonly a Mossi field as they tend to be in closer proximity to Fulani encampments). The outcome of this infringement depends on many factors, the most important being the level of crop damage incurred. An ensuing conflict then only arises if the owner of the cattle in question refuses to accept liability. In this case, the farmer can pursue a line of prosecution. Once the offending herd has been identified, the farmer makes an appeal for the redress of grievances to his village or canton chief. The chief will then send for the Fulani chief who is responsible for producing the offender and then securing the fines that the offender must pay. If the Fulani chief will not, or is unable to arrange this, a tribunal will be arranged in Léo, the provincial capital. In the three case study villages, situations of this nature have always been resolved in village council. In part it reflects the authority of the Fulani chief to regulate and survey all Fulani activities in the village territories where they have been allowed to settle. The penalties for being held responsible in a crop damage case are sufficiently severe to ensure great care by the herdsmen during transhumance (Berger-Sarl, 1989).

In Delgado's research (1979) he compared the capital goods of the Fulani to two other sedentary tribes. He noted that the Fulani had a noticeably smaller average number of hatchets and machetes, but concluded that this was simply due to a smaller number of agricultural workers. He also noted that the number of granaries in a Fulani encampment was proportional to the field area and consequent harvest. Fulani capital also includes corrals, that the Nuni and Mossi do not have, but fundamentally most of Fulani capital is manifested in their livestock.

The Fulani herds are dominated by older animals which are retained because of their proven hardiness to drought and disease. Mature females commonly make up one half of the herd (of the Fulani portion) because of the profitability of breeding animals and their milk production capacity (Amanor, 1995). Household cattle herds grow larger through animal entrances due to births, entrustments or purchases; stock holdings diminish with deaths, losses, theft or sales. Household herds grow significantly in June owing to the large number of births but also include additions by outsiders who have entrusted their cows to the Fulani (de Boer and Kessler, 1994). During October and November the number of animals decreases due to profit taking by peasant proprietors who take advantage of the yearly peak in animal prices at this time (Amanor, 1995). This is precisely the time when the Fulani are net purchasers of cattle (Delgado, 1979). This is because, unlike their sedentary neighbours who are willing to take the risk of buying cattle cheaply at the end of the dry season when mortality is high, they prefer to restock their herd with good quality cattle after the rains so they can be grazed by the owner for at least six months before the hard dry season. They will also sell cattle, at a much diminished price in the middle or end of the dry season (depending on when their grain stores finish), to

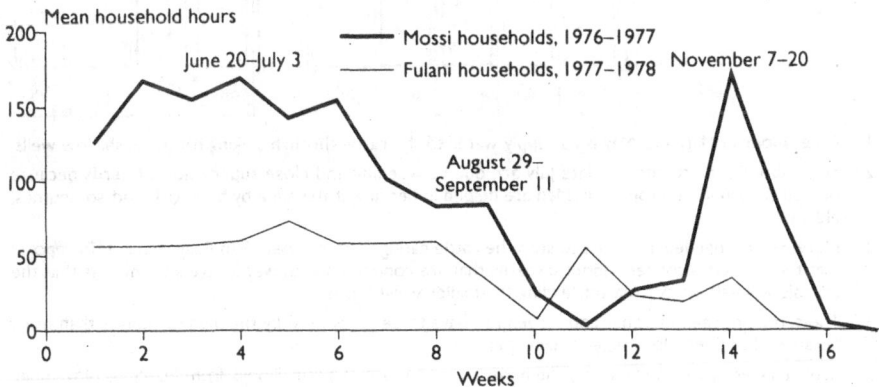

Source: Delgado, 1979.

Figure 3.6 A comparison between farmers' and Fulani labour allocation for agricultural activities

purchase grain to see them through to the next harvest (food items make up one half of the Fulani's annual expenditure).

Delgado (1979) identifies another four areas of economic activity: the sale of milk; the sale of small ruminants (sheep and goats); the sale of eggs and poultry; and miscellaneous payments for herding services or the provision of cattle manure. The consumption of meat (cattle, sheep or goat) for subsistence is rare (as seen in the village case studies) although animals will be slaughtered for Muslim festivals, including Ramadam, Mouloud and Tabaski.

Milk plays an important part of the Fulani household's diet and only the surplus is sold. The collection and marketing of the milk products (sold in callabasses in the form of a yoghurt-like curdled milk which keeps well in the heat) is controlled solely by Fulani women (as is the judgement whether there is a surplus). Surplus milk depends on many things including the number and health of female cattle and the number of consumers in the household.

Small ruminants are a faster maturing and a more accessible form of capital than cattle. Van Raay (1975) concludes through computing forage requirements, that one small ruminant is equivalent to one seventh of a steer, which is the same ratio between the prices of three year old animals of each species. Sheep and goats are used for many cash-oriented purposes such as

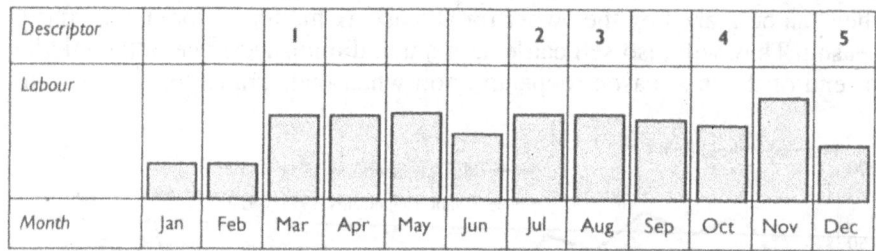

1 Male labour in March to May is to supply water to the cattle through sinking hand dug shallow wells.
2 High labour requirements in late July are due to weeding and close supervision of herds because of their proximity to crop fields. Men are helped in herding at this time by boys, girls and, sometimes, elders.
3 More work is needed in August to stop the cattle eating wetter grasses. Van Raay (1975: 110) reports that this reflects a concern about diseases that are connected with wet forage and the fear that the animals will eat less dry matter, leading to smaller weight gain.
4 The cattle between October and November have to be supervised by the men for longer than usual because of the need for longer grazing periods.
5 Between December and February the herds are taken care of by small boys; from March to November they are in the charge of men.

Source: Howorth, 1997.

Figure 3.7   The Fulani seasonal labour calendar in Sissili

Culturally Locating Production Patterns 95

sale in emergencies; to buy medicine in times of sickness; to buy occasional luxuries such as a radio or new clothes; gifts to in-laws or parents; or for slaughter in ceremonies. Poultry are used for presents or for entertaining visitors, eggs are sold for pocket money or to buy sauce ingredients.

Delgado (1979) concludes that the Fulani household cash income and expenditure reflects a production system which is dependent on the market to convert livestock into food items, principally staple cereals. Figure 3.7 shows the relative distribution of labour throughout the Fulani year. There are descriptions on the figure of critical events in the pastoral and agricultural calendars.

Summary

The Nuni have a strong relationship with their land that has developed over many years. This relationship has developed, not in a static situation, but in a dynamic, forever changing environment. For example, wars, invasions, droughts and epidemics have meant that the Nuni communities have had to be inventive and adaptive in their resource use patterns and survival strategies. The current resource use pattern is the result of generations of adaptation which has again recently evolved to incorporate another two ethnic groups and their production systems. The new resource use pattern is slowly emerging.

The recent history of the Mossi is not significantly removed from their historical background, i.e. the Mossi have always moved. When there is movement, accompanied by settlement, two processes occur. Firstly, they bring the farming systems employed in their zones of departure and, secondly, they adopt local farming practices. In this way their farming systems are always evolving and developing in response to local conditions. Although there are many similarities between Mossi immigrants and their processes in the *Hauts Bassins* and those in Sissili, they are by no means the same because the local socio-economic and ecological conditions are dissimilar. The Mossi are now learning from the Nuni, and vice versa, to develop new resource use patterns that ensure livelihoods for the entire community.

The Fulani have a very different production system from those of the Mossi and Nuni and as a result remain relatively isolated from their neighbours. This is principally because grazing cattle and unprotected crops do not mix (the Fulani fence their own animals in proximity to their own crops). There does exist, however, a significant level of trade and exchange between the Fulani and the other ethnic groups which allows a level of assimilation and integration into the wider social system. Thus, on one hand, the Fulani appear to keep themselves to themselves, but on the other, they are an integral part of the developing tri-cultural framework.

The three cultural profiles illustrate the differences amongst the three ethnic groups. They each have different histories, production patterns and social relations. However, they all now share the same land area and they all share the same production objective; to guarantee subsistence, ensure survival and minimise risk. It is in this context that this book examines the process of local management of the natural resources in Sissili, i.e. the process of the development of production systems in Sissili in the context of three very different ethnic groups. In the following three chapters, three village case studies are presented. In each village there are the three ethnic groups. The complexity of the situation denies the ability to produce blanket commentaries and conclusions on production patterns in the region. Each situation must be looked at in detail in order to understand process and form.

4 Lon

Introduction

Lon is the most densely populated village of the three case study villages and experiences the greatest resource shortages and problems of production. Lon has a territory which covers an area of approximately 26 km^2. It is in the middle of a large settlement network and is surrounded by the villages of Tabou (a medium sized market town and a cross-roads) to the southwest, Tô (a big market town with a high concentration of Mossi) to the east, Poré to the northeast, Tiabouana to the northwest, Panassin to the east and Niéssin to the southeast. The Nuni have links as a result of parentage and marriage to Cassou (the administrative centre for Lon and thus an advantageous town in which to have links), Tabou, Tô, Bonapio, Panassin, Nevri and Pouri. The villagers of Lon, both immigrant and local have a large and complex social network.

As the oral history partly explains (Box 4.1), the village is an amalgamation of two villages: Lon and Badakui. Badakui was the original village which the elders say is 800 years old, and Lon was an offshoot of this. All the political and legal control is held in Badakui. Owing to the large population, the Village Chief has delegated control to the formal administration based in the departmental capital of Cassou for many social problems, petty crimes and grievances. The chief, however, still controls land allocation and still presides over land matters. The traditional leaders of Badakui still oversee social activities when required to but they do not travel out of their way to do so.

Population

The population, according to the most recent population census (INSD, 1985) was 2,978 in 1985, which makes it by far the most highly populated of all the case study villages. The Nuni elders currently estimate that there are approximately 400 to 500 Mossi families and ten Fulani families that arrived 30 years ago and ten years ago respectively. They moved to Sissili

98 *Rebuilding the Local Landscape*

Box 4.1   The oral history of Lon

The village of Lon is named after a type of grass and is said to be 800 years old. The founder of Lon was a great hunter called Boumain Napon and he came from Tassyin near Biéha with his animal herd and arrived at Nevri. Here there was a disagreement between him and the villagers, so Boumain left for the village of Gniga. At Gniga he met Bazao Bénao who became his animal herder and they settled at Badakui which means 'the place of the brave'. Bazao left Badakui and for three days he did not return so Boumain went to look for him and his animals. Boumain found him towards the west and asked him why had he not returned. Bazao said that there was a grass here that the animals like so much that they would not leave the spot. The name of the grass is lon and is the same grass that is used to make the flights of arrows. When it rained the animals would shelter under a large tree called janlon and so Boumain built a grass hut under this tree and gave his permission to Bazao that he could look after his herd and settle there, in the new village of Lon.

Boumain then left for the village of Yillou in the Mossi plateau where he killed an elephant that was stopping the villagers from getting water from the river. When he had killed the elephant he cut off its tail to prove to the chief of Yillou that he had done the deed. The chief had then told the villagers to go and get the meat of the elephant to eat. When the meat was ready Boumain refused to eat. The chief then gave Boumain one of his daughters called Katian that he married and took back to Badakui. Here he had two daughters and he gave one of his daughters for the bride of his animal herder, Bazao, who remained ever grateful. Today, this allegiance continues. When there is a problem at Lon, they come to Badakui to resolve it. Even if someone dies at Lon they will not bury them unless they ask the chief from Badakui first.

Source: Author's fieldwork, 1994.

---

from the northern areas because of drought, poor pasture and poor soils. Lon has 12 cantons: six Mossi cantons, four Nuni and two Fulani camps.

Description of the Landscape

The transect (Figure 4.1) is taken from Badakui to the original site of Lon (the big tree under which Boumain built the grass hut for Bazao). North of the transect is the valley bottom. In contrast to the other transects, it is evident that Lon's local environment has been much more heavily influenced by human activity; habitation occupies much of the transect with the exception of a small band of trees to the right of the figure.

On the left hand side of the transect is the original Nuni settlement of Badakui and the houses seen are those of the Village Chief. Around this habitation zone are found trees and shrubs of high value, both exotics and indigenous species. These include the bamboo for long poles which are used by the women to knock mangoes or karité nuts from the high branches of trees; the neem tree (*Azadirachta indica*) used for 'toothbrushes'; *Parkinsonia aculeata* used for thorny fencing; and *Khaya senegalensis* used for local medicine and shade.

Next to this, on the right, there is a Mossi settlement and its household fields. Again, a number of high value trees including baobab, mango and guava is found. In the household fields red sorghum, millet, maize, niébé and cowpeas are grown. Next to this the Mossi's village fields are cultivated with millet and mixed with fallow. There is a low tree species count but those left are again the high value trees; karité, néré, *kapokiér* and *V. donniana*. There are approximately 30 trees per hectare and some degraded patches where localised soil erosion can be seen. After another small Mossi residential area, there is the forested section. Here is found the most dense and species diverse section of the transect, made up of primarily 'bush' species, i.e. those that local people would not conserve around their compounds (néré are not usually kept around the compound because of their high leaf litter, dirtying the courtyard and providing cover for snakes and scorpions). This section makes up a buffer zone between the Badakui area and the Lon area and provides some pasture and a gathering area.

The adjoining area is another Mossi settlement which leads up to the slope where the original site of Lon is situated.

Evolution of the Farmed Area

The three diagrams (Figure 4.2) show the evolution of occupied space from 1955 to 1983 to 1993. Diagrams one and two are based on aerial photographs taken by the flights; Mission AOF 006 NC 30XXII (1955) and Mission AOF 024 NC 30XXIII (1983). The third is taken from a landuse map (IBS, 1994) that was based on Landsat images from November 1988 and Spot images from December 1993.

Like the other case study villages, the situation in 1955 was characterised by a very small indigenous Nuni population inhabiting a large land area with a high percentage cover of natural savanna bushland. On the 1955 map there are two settlement areas: Lon and Badakui. The fields around Badakui belong to the Badakui Nuni that are based around the Nuni chief's compound (the Napon family) seen on the left hand side of the transect. Likewise the fields around Lon belong to the Nuni of Lon who are members

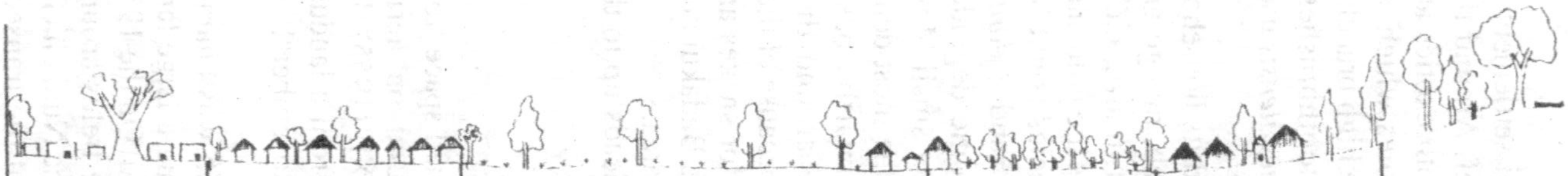

100 Rebuilding the Local Landscape

Trees and Shrubs	Azadirachta indica Adansonia digitata Khaya seuegalensis Cassia siberiana Butyrospermum parkii Bamboo Parkinsonia aculeata Mangifera indica Lannea microcarpa	Parkia biglobosa Butyrospermum parkii Diospyros mespiliformis Combretum glutinosum Afzelia africana Adansonia digitata Mangifera indica Psidium guajava Combretum glutinosum	Parkia biglobosa Butyrospermum parkii Vitex doniana Bombax costatum	Parkia biglobosa Khaya senegalensis Piliostigma reticulatum Lannea microcarpa Pterocarpus erinaceus Prosopis africana Combretum glutinosum Ximenia americana Diospyros mespiliformis Cassia siberiana	Parkia biglobosa Butyrospermum parkii Bombax costatum Diospyros mespiliformis Lannea microcarpa Calotropis procera Mangifera indica Vitex doniana	Acacia albida Diospyros mespiliformis Lannea acida Lannea microcarpa Balanites aegyptica Piliostigma reticulatum Combretum glutinosum Acacia macrostachya Ficus gnaphalocarpa Parkia biglobosa
Remarks	House of the Nuni Village Chief: the original settlement of Badakiri	Mossi settlement and their household fields: maize, millet, sorghum, niébé, cowpeas	Mossi village fields with mixed fallow, millet and finger millet, approximately 30 trees per hectare, including partly degraded patches	Forested section 100/150m	Soils of the valley bottom and Mossi settlements	Road, trees interspersed with bare patches and laterite gravel patches of erosion

Figure 4.1 Village transect of Lon, 1993 to 1995

of the Bénao family. The fields to the west of the map, to the north of the stream on the lower slopes, are fields of families from Tô. The field to the south west belongs to a family from Tabou and the field to the north east is of unknown origin but may belong to a family from Panassin.

By 1985, the picture had radically changed. There had been a significant influx of people from the Mossi plateau and the population had increased far more quickly than the natural population growth rate. As the first immigrants arrived in 1975, the picture of occupation seen in 1983 is a result of 20 years of further immigration and immigrant land exploitation. Even so, the Nuni have preserved much of the southern, eastern and northern zones as forest and land reserves, primarily for themselves and their children. The western, and part of the southwestern area, is a sacred forest reserve which no Mossi are allowed to exploit. Although a Fulani encampment has been permitted to set up camp in the eastern reserve as part of a conscious decision; the Nuni chiefs knowing that no Mossi will cultivate next to Fulani and their animals and also the knowledge that Fulani do not significantly damage the bush. There is another Fulani encampment to the south the occupants of which are from Louga in the north. They remain isolated and fulfil a bush protection role.

There are Mossi from a range of different origins in Lon's territory who have settled in a dispersed pattern. The Mossi of Ouahigouya have settled in Badakui. These are the original Mossi of Lon who arrived in 1969 and consequently this lineage has become the dominant one and contains the Mossi chief. These Mossi are permitted to cultivate around their compounds, but outside of the immediate vicinity they must ask the Nuni chief at Badakui. The Mossi of Ouagadougou have settled in the northeast and the Mossi of Koudougou have settled to the northwest. The Mossi to the centrewest are from mixed origins, some residing in Lon's territory, and other Mossi living on the periphery who are classified as Mossi from Tô. To the northwest there are some fields of the Mossi from Tiabouana.

At present, land continues to be fallowed and there are patches of woodland in amongst the Nuni and Mossi farms, enabling gathering to take place throughout the territory and not just in the forest reserves. It is has recently been shown (Schrekenberg, 1996) that fields and fallows provide most of non timber forest products in the West African Sahel. A significant increase in the number of connecting routes and paths which connect the farms and settlements can be seen together with a marked increase in the size of the neighbouring villages of Pouré and Panassin, illustrating the attraction of the region to Mossi immigrants.

The 1993 map is less detailed and there is likely to be scattered woodlands and bush amongst the farmland shown. However, a number of observations can be made. Firstly, compared with the other villages there

102 *Rebuilding the Local Landscape*

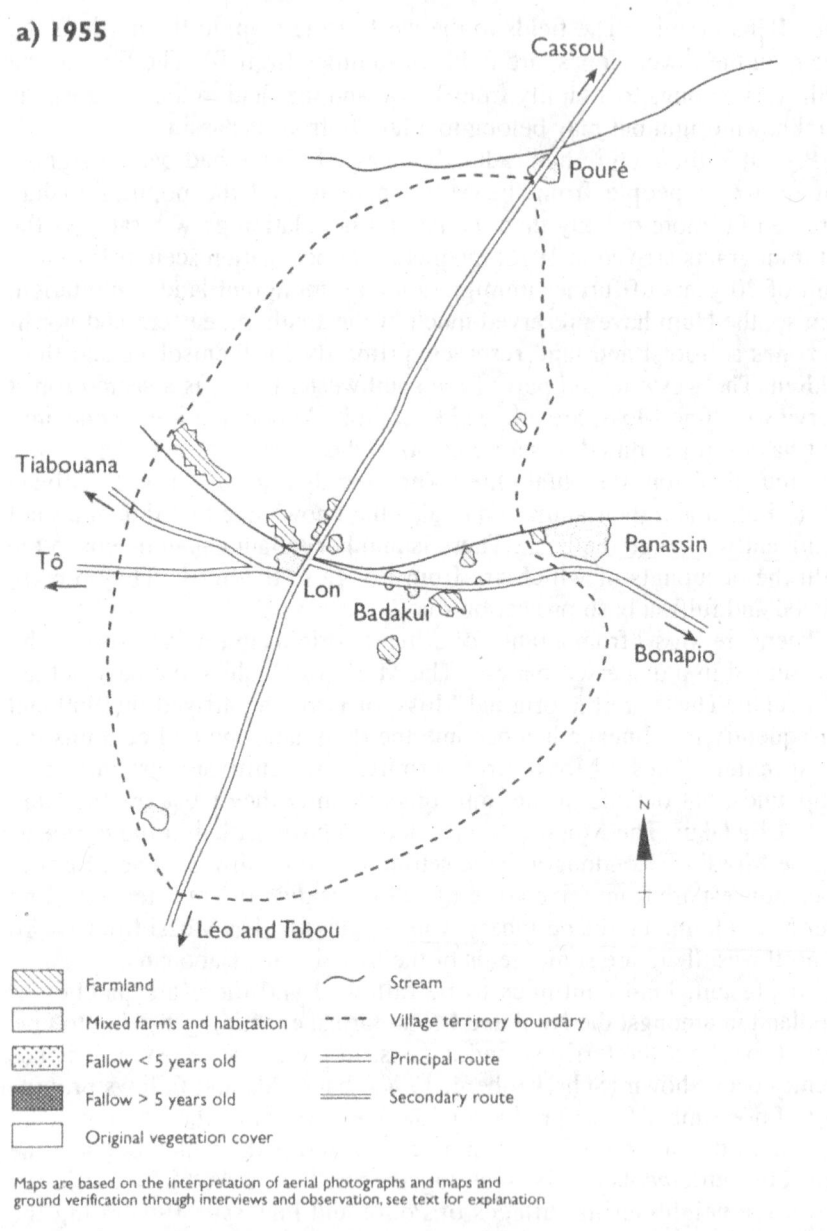

Figure 4.2a The evolution of the landscape in Lon, 1955 to 1993

b) 1985

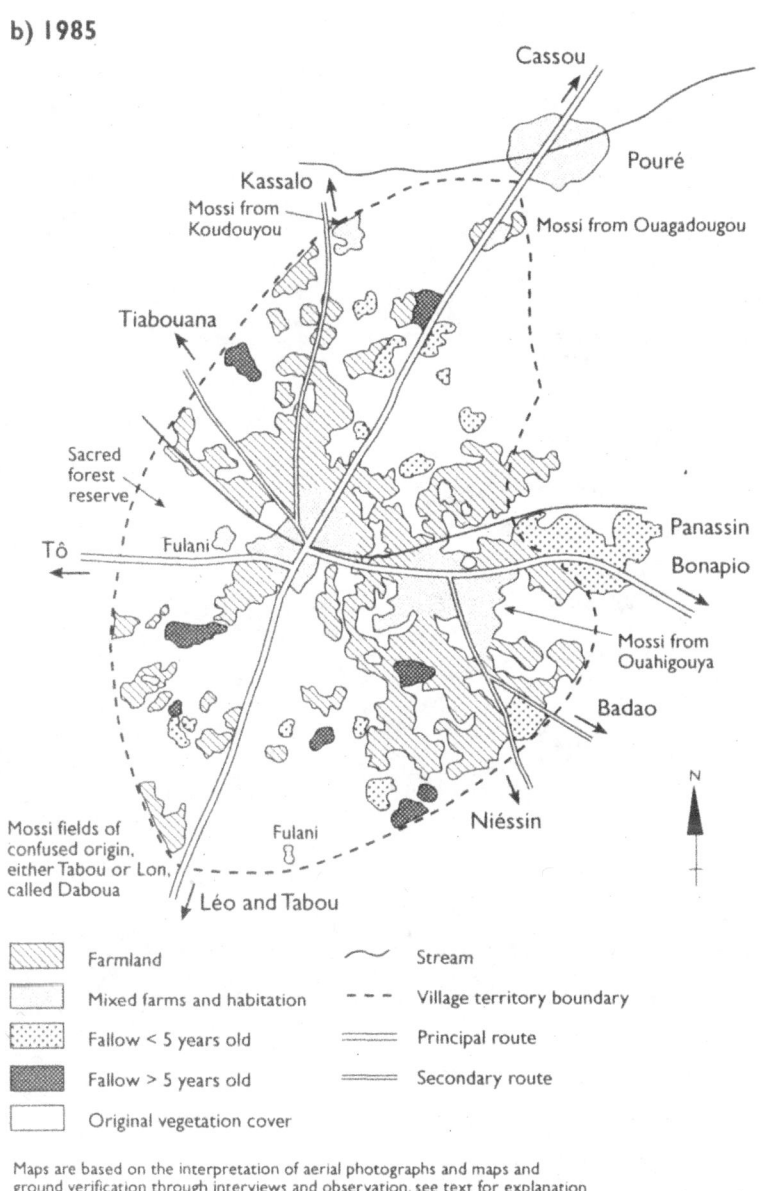

Figure 4.2b The evolution of the landscape in Lon, 1955 to 1993

Note: Map not to scale.
Source: Author's fieldwork, 1993–1995.

104 *Rebuilding the Local Landscape*

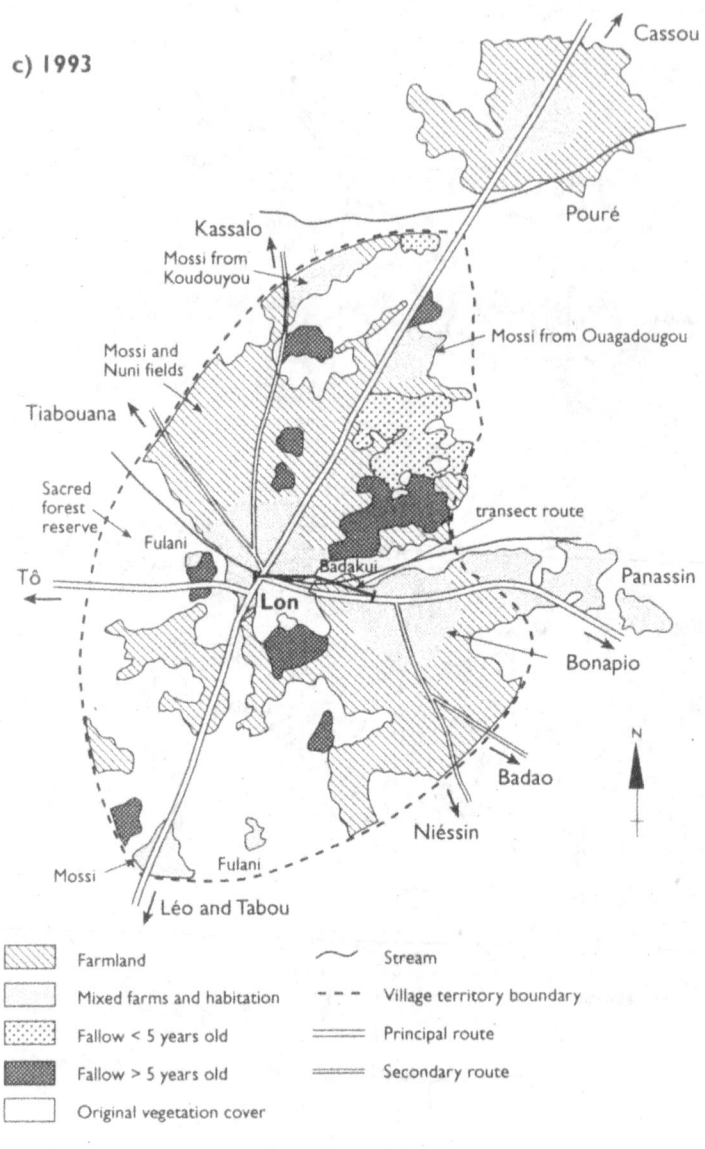

Figure 4.2c The evolution of the landscape in Lon, 1955 to 1993

has only been a minimal expansion of land occupation in Lon; the farmed land has remained relatively static, since 1983. The east, north and southern areas that were reserved for future farming still remain. There is, however, some encroachment, especially in the east where a large part of the reserve has been cultivated although the 'sacred grove' remains intact. The Fulani to the south remain as 'guardians of the bush'. There is some forest regeneration to the east where fallows have been left and the patch of bush that separates Badakui from Lon also remains. It should be noted that the land demarcated as farmland is not devoid of trees, in a Nuni field as many as 40 to 50 trees may remain in one hectare and a Mossi field may count anything from one to 30.

The village of Pouri has grown remarkably due to Mossi immigrants while the land occupation of Panassin seems to have stabilised.

The Future of the Occupation of Space in Lon

Although it is difficult to project future population growth, if immigration has stopped, the occupation and use of the land in Lon will remain limited to the current resident population. With over half of the territory in Lon still covered by woodland it is unlikely that, even with exponential population growth, the village will experience serious resource shortages in the near future. However, the author does not believe that African farmers are natural, even eager, 'soil miners'; rather, they take rational, positive group and individual decisions concerning present and future resource use. As the farmers in Lon know their available resources well it follows that decisions

Table 4.1 The growth in the different categories of land cover in Lon, 1955 to 1993[1]

Total land area – 2,644 hectares	1955 ha	% of area	1983 ha	% of area	1993 ha	% of area
Farmland	65	2.5	797	30	1,200	45.4
Woodland	2,579	97.5	1,736	65.8	1,198	45.2
Fallow <5 years	-	-	60	2.3	93	3.5
Fallow >5 years	-	-	51	1.9	153	5.9
Total	2,644	100	2,644	100	2,644	100

1 Based on the interpretation of the diagrams of the evolution of the occupation of space.

concerning their use will be based on sustainability, i.e. the ability of the land to guarantee subsistence for them, their children and grandchildren.

Networks and Linkages in the Villages

Nuni Networks and linkages between communities tell us something about the security of the villages, their production systems and their kinship networks. These networks, which can be defined as a group of spatially dispersed communities or individuals which are connected in some way, form part of the broader risk-minimisation strategies employed by the village communities. Most of the linkages, which for the networks, are a result of either parentage, i.e. a resident's parent lives in another village which accords bonds between the parent's village and the resident's village, or, as a result of marriage, where a 'child of the village' (usually a girl) is taken as a bride in another village. These linkages have long been recognised as an important aspect of rural communities survival strategies. Adams (1993) notes that 'exogamous marriage alliances facilitate a risk-spreading diversification of social and economic networks beyond the village'. Another important link is that of a member of a village (usually a boy or man, but it can also be a girl or woman) working in another village or country. Additional linkages are administrative linkages, i.e. the connection between the village and its departmental capital, and in the case of Lon skill sharing linkages, where one village exchanges skilled labour with another.

The nature and extent of these linkages differ (if only slightly, as in the case of Lon and Boutiourou) according to the different villages. The differences between the networks are caused by two main factors: the age of the village and the number of founding families.

In Lon links are due either to parentage or marriage and because of relatives working in either Ouagadougou or in Côte D'Ivoire. Not only are relations seasonally migrating to the latter two areas but original members of the village have settled there to become the heads of family and some have not returned for 20 years. The links of such situations, which result from such movements, however, remain strong, with those who have permanently settled in other areas acting as hosts for young men who seasonally migrate to find work.

Lon was formed by two families, the Napon and the Benao, and it is from these that the original links were formed, with their parents (from Nevri) and from the marriage of their daughters in other villages or the migration of their sons. As additional Nuni families arrived they then formed their own networks, thus increasing the overall linkage structure.

Mossi The Mossi of Lon come from three provinces: Yatenga, Kadiogo and Boulkiemdé (see Figure 4.4). This is echoed in the three Mossi settlements

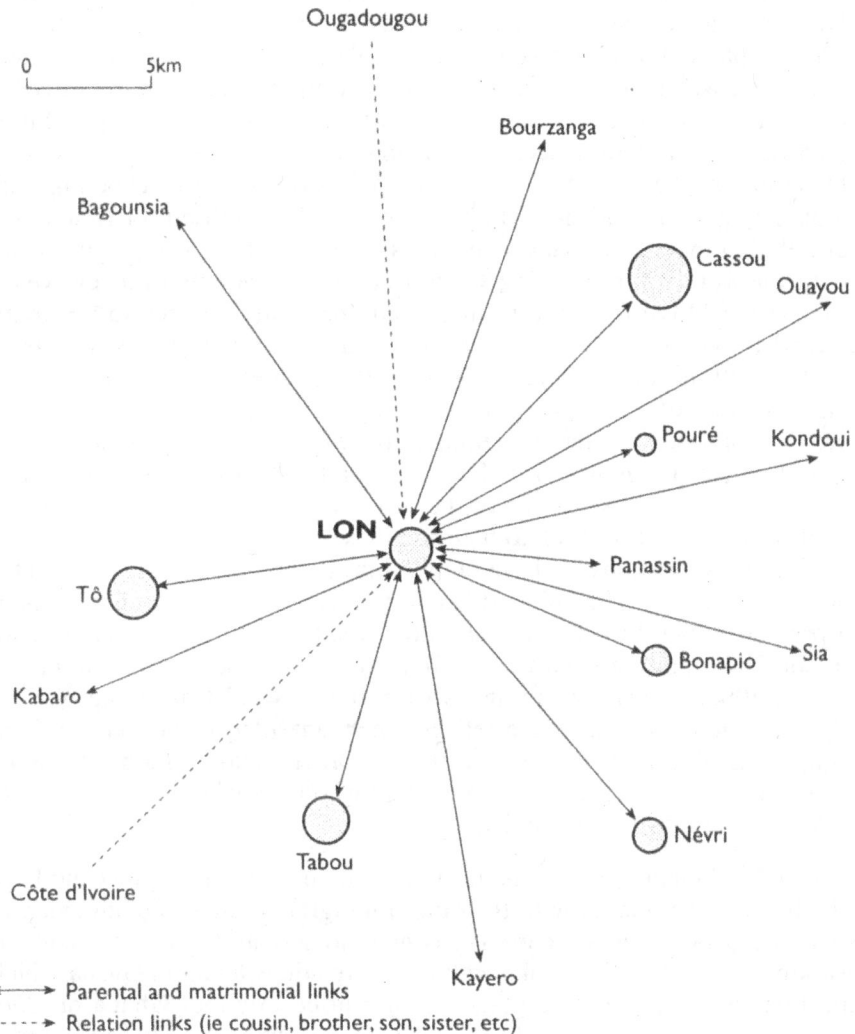

Parental and matrimonial links
Relation links (ie cousin, brother, son, sister, etc)

Source: Author's fieldwork, 1994.

Figure 4.3 Networks and linkages of the Nuni in Lon, 1995[2,3]

---

[2] The links with Cassou has additional administrative links with Lon, being the departmental capital, and Bonapio, which also has additional links through skill sharing artisans.
[3] The size of the circles are proportional to the size of the villages and the village names with no circles indicates that they are situated off the diagram.

in Lon: the Mossi from Koudougou (Boulkiemdé), the Mossi from Ouagadougou (Kadiogo) and the Mossi from Badakui (from Yatenga). These separate lineages have their own links of reciprocity in these respective areas, which are more heavily weighted in the south – north direction (i.e. remittances more strongly expected from those Mossi living in Sissili than vice versa). Remittances, as with all the Mossi in the villages, are more likely to take the form of visitors, marriage partners or for schooling, than monetary or food donations. For example, a Mossi in Lon (or Boutiourou or Saboué) may take younger relations from their places of origin to stay with the family for anything from a couple of months to a few years. Likewise a Mossi from Sissili may send one of his children to a Koranic school in the north. Gifts may be associated with the occasional north-south, south-north visits, but in general these remittances do not provide major sources of food or cash income for either group. Moreover, they will provide 'bonuses' for the remaining northern family, for example a Mossi from Lon (or Boutiourou or Saboué) may, after a good yam harvest, put a portion of that harvest on one of the 'transporters' that service the Sunday market in Léo, to take back to their families.

The Mossi of Lon also have family links in the Côte D'Ivoire and in the province of Houet. The link with the former is by far the more important as it provides a place to stay and an initial point of contact for young males seasonally migrating from Lon to find paid employment. It is common to have quite significant remittances from both the relation living in Côte D'Ivoire (on the arrival of the village inhabitant after the period of migration) in the form of gifts (e.g. a cassette recorder, radio, or food) and, more importantly, the returned seasonal migrant who is duty bound to return with at least some gifts for his family.

Fulani The Fulani in Lon came from the province of Sanmatenga and have few linkages compared with the other immigrants. These Fulani came in their clan groups and are currently content to stay in the southern zone of Burkina Faso. They have links with family relations living in Ghana which are related to trade (cattle gain a higher price in either Ghana or Côte D'Ivoire). 'Living' is a fluid term when it concerns nomads and is more likely to mean that they constantly have some family members in Ghana, but these members are interchangeable with those in Lon. As a large part of their transhumance entails routes through Ghana, family members in place are a necessity. They also have links with other clan members in Bougouriba and another village in Sissili relatively close by. This 'close spreading' is also seen with the Fulani of Boutiourou and is related to herding. Some members of the family will go and 'live' in one area for an unlimited amount of time with their herd, or part of it, while the pasture and water remains

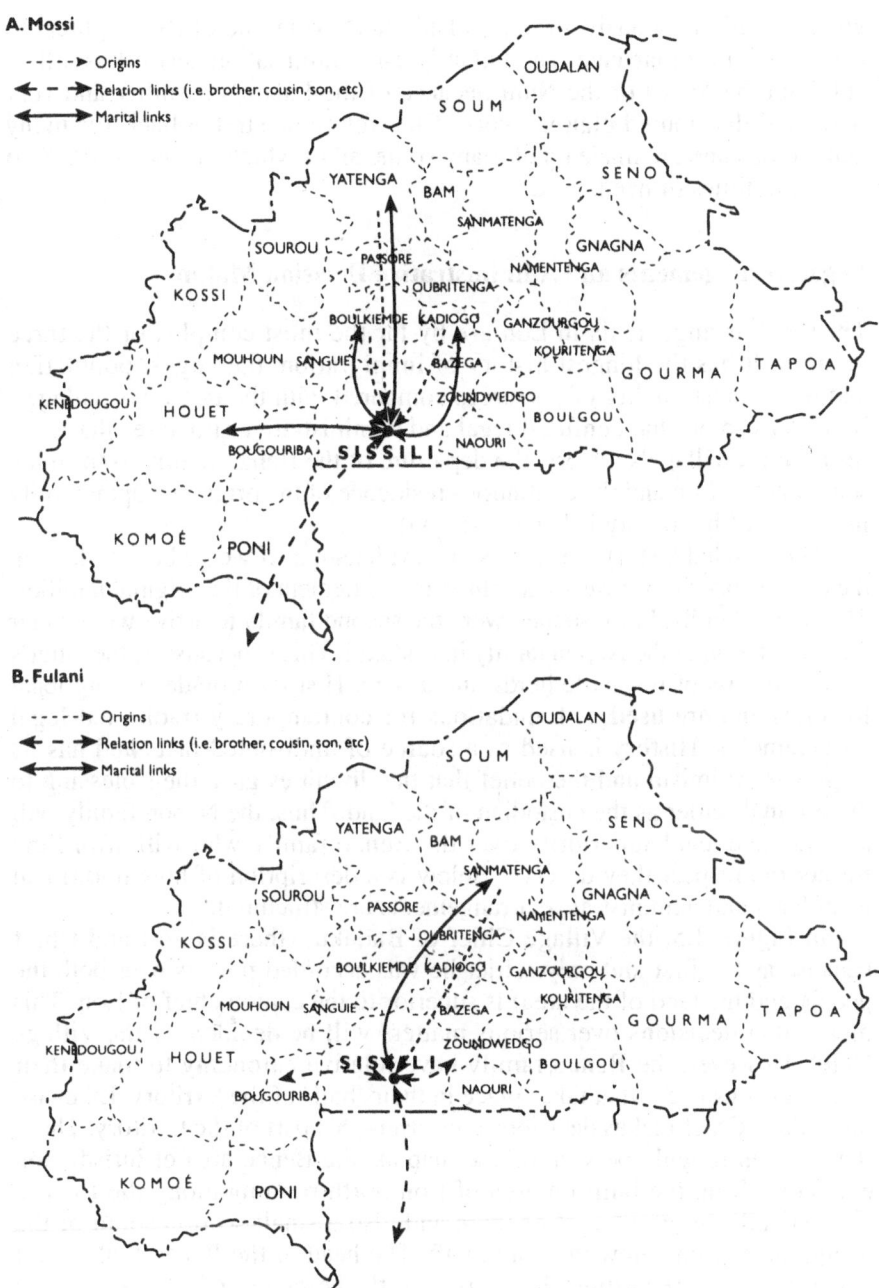

Figure 4.4 The origins and linkages of the immigrants of Lon

good. It will also consist of one Fulani clan giving one of its daughters to another clan for marriage. The Fulani's risk minimisation network is different from the Mossi or the Nuni because of the Fulani's mobility and very wide and distributed clan network. Clan relations stretch back for many generations and are made up of many splits, all of which maybe available to call on in times of need.

Legal Arrangements and Administrative Decision Making

The legal arrangements in Lon are by far the most complex of the three villages. It has the longest history of immigration, the largest population and the poorest quality of resources compared with the two other villages. It also has somewhat confused legal and administrative structures that are a result of the village's history, the departure of the Benao family to form the settlement of Lon and the continuous residence of the original Napon family in Badakui (the totality is known as Lon).

This tangled history warrants some explanation. If we go back to look at the oral history of Lon we see a split in the settlement of the original families. The Benao family, because they were the second family to arrive were under the jurisdiction of the Napon family in Badakui. This is because of the latter's historical gifts of his cattle herds and a wife. History provides strong legal loyalties and are used as foundations for contemporary traditional legal arrangements. History is used as a source of undisputed facts and has its origins in Animism and the belief that the divinities gave their blessing to the original settler as the custodian of the land. Thus, the Napon family will always have legal superiority over the Benao family who will afford the former the respect they deserve. Below is a description of how traditional Nuni legal and administrative arrangements are structured.

In Figure 4.5, the Village Chief of Badakui (there is no Land Chief because as the first and only settler he was accorded powers over both the people and the land of the area) is superior to the canton chief of Lon. This means that decisions over serious matters will be decided by the Village Chief. However, the Benao family have relative autonomy to make their own decisions over what takes place in their 'half' of the territory. Likewise the Village Chief makes decisions concerning his part of the territory. These 'halves' can roughly be seen on the map as: the Benao area of jurisdiction extending from the built up area of Lon north running along the road to Cassou and everything east of there and also a small section south of the habitation of Lon below the road to Tô. The head of the Benao family will make decisions regarding these areas with the elders of his canton and Zioliasan. The Village Chief has control over the remaining territory and he will make decisions with the Nuni elders of Badakui and Nignanliasan. It

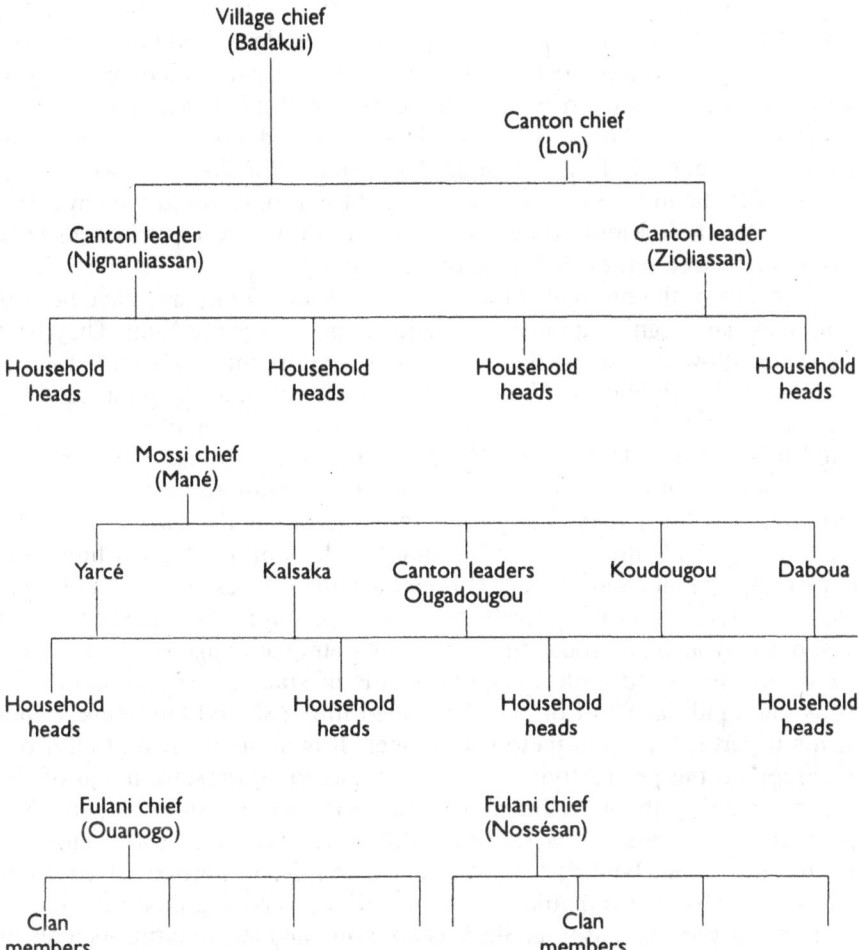

Source: Author's fieldwork, 1993–1995.

Figure 4.5 A diagrammatic representation of the power structures in Lon

should be noted that trust exists between the two families in relation to the good custodianship of the land. However, when misdemeanours occur the Village Chief will intervene and question decisions.

In the preceding paragraph, traditional Nuni law was discussed. However, due to the level of immigration and the immigrant's integration into Nuni society the traditional legal and administrative arrangements have

112 *Rebuilding the Local Landscape*

begun to change. In Figure 4.5, unlike the other village diagrams, there is no confining land area for the immigrants (no circles around the respective immigrant power structures on the diagrams). The immigrants in Lon were never given a definite territory, as in the case of Boutiourou, that they were restricted to. Instead they were only given vaguely defined areas where they could farm, e.g. the first Mossi settled around Badakui and became the Mossi of Badakui where they were allowed to farm. It would not have been possible for these Mossi to farm in the far north, for example, because this would have been out of their area of jurisdiction.

Because of the prolonged time period that the immigrants have been in Lon, they have significant mutual relationships with many Nuni. They have also been allowed to set up their farms in close proximity to Nuni farms and are now their neighbours. The Nuni and Mossi celebrate religious festivals together, births, deaths, prayers and have become extremely well assimilated into the broader society. It follows that this closeness has brought about some sharing of decision making or at least allowed for heavy consultation with Mossi and Nuni alike (and occasionally Fulani). Similar relationships and situations can be found in the anthropological literature. For example, Platteau (1991:122) illustrates that 'access to land and other vital resources is not necessarily predicted upon kinship or descent-based ties, but may also be grounded upon loyalty and patronage relations which are often associated with ascriptive forms of status or social identity'.[4] Thus, the landscape of Lon has developed into a shared landscape rather than a tripartite one as in the other villages. It is in the interest of all tribes to safeguard the productivity of the land and so, at present, much of the decision making about the function of the land, conservation measures and experimentation with new farming techniques, as well as occasionally discussions about land distribution, are taken as an inter-tribal group of elders. The Mossi also regulate their own affairs, advising their relations in the north of Burkina Faso that there is no more land left to farm. As a result immigration has stopped.

The Fulani also play their role in local land management. They have been allowed to settle in the more wooded areas of Lon's territory and, as in Boutiourou, play a protective role, safeguarding the bush for future farming and gathering products. As no farmers will farm next to them, the Nuni chiefs have effectively protected the southern and eastern (sacred forest reserve) areas for the future.

The Mossi have their own power structures with the original Mossi settler acting as the chief to all Mossi in the territory. Although most Mossi disputes

---

4 However, Platteau (1991:122) also says that 'insiders' enjoy more rights and benefits than the stratum of 'outsiders'. This can be seen in all the villages with the Nuni having secured access to the better soils and the upholding of the Nuni traditional rule of law ensures this.

are regulated in the respective groups, in the event of a serious problem, the Mossi chief has the final decision. The Fulani regulate their own affairs within their respective clans and do not have a common Fulani chief.

It is a natural progression that in a territory characterised by a large, relatively integrated population that has lived in the area for a long duration with no major conflicts, that legal and administrative control take on a more consultative and wider ranging nature. Even if the final decision rests with the Nuni there will be a collaborative decision making process which is necessary in an area where questions of resource use and distribution are paramount.

Ethnic Interrelationships in Lon

Lon has the highest degree of tribal integration, i.e. cross-cultural contact. There is significant interaction amongst the three tribes which shows not only cohesion but also a recognition that each contribution is important for the overall production system. The Mossi receive most benefit from the Fulani and Nuni and the latters' contributions are important to the Mossi production system. The Mossi's relationships with the Fulani are strengthened because the two tribes have been cohabiting in the northern areas for a long time. For example, the Fulani visit the Mossi fields more frequently than the Nuni because of the former's increased familiarity with the pastoralist-agriculturalist relationship.

In many instances the presence of more than one tribe has made life a lot easier for local and immigrant alike. For example, cow dung is an important ingredient in plaster for the construction of houses or wall. Farmers will go to the Fulani encampments in search of dung, and in general there is no payment (de Boer and Kessler, 1994). In the past this would have been a long process for the Nuni, as they owned few animals from which to collect the dung. With the advent of the Fulani and their herds, this became much easier, improving this aspect of their production system.

In general it is only the Mossi that intermarry with other ethnic groups. The Mossi may commonly take Nuni wives because of their willingness to assume the language of the Mossi man. (The vast majority of Nuni speak Mooré although it is uncommon to find a Mossi (or Fulani) who can speak fluent Nuni.) It is unusual to find a Mossi woman with a Nuni man, most commonly because of the inability of the Mossi woman to speak Nuni and the unwillingness of the Nuni man to have a foreign tongue used exclusively in his household. However, occasionally there are Mossi woman-Nuni man intermarriages. For example, in the more cosmopolitan surroundings of Léo one of my key informants, a young Nuni farmer, took a Mossi woman for his second wife.

Table 4.2 Ethnic interrelationships in Lon

Direction of transfer	Activities
Fulani ⟶ Mossi	• Cattle guarding • Milk/meat sale • Thatched mat sale • Medical information • Animal sale • Dung • Grazing animals on post-harvest fields
Mossi ⟶ Fulani	• Labour • Sale of cereals, foodstuffs, tools, etc • Dolo
Fulani ⟵⟶ Mossi	• Participation in some decision making in communal village affairs (in village meetings some Fulani will participate, usually the elder males who have had most contact with the Mossi (and Nuni) through sale or guarding of cattle) • Cattle vaccination, either with or without an extension worker • Celebration of religious festivals, marriages, baptisms, etc.
Fulani ⟶ Nuni	• Meat/milk sale • Dung • Animal sale • Cattle guarding • Medicinal information • Gifts
Nuni ⟶ Fulani	• Labour • Sale of cereals, foodstuffs, soumbala, tools, etc • Occasional loan of materials sur place (e.g. pestle and mortar) • Administrative control • Land
Fulani ⟵⟶ Nuni	• Some participation in meetings, more listening that voting or discussing • Participation in religious festivals and celebrations • Some skill sharing • Demonstrations of animal traction, veterinary issues, vaccinations, etc., with extension agent

Table 4.2   Ethnic interrelationships in Lon (continued)

Nuni ⟶ Mossi	• Wives • Labour • Administrative control • Medicinal advice • Land • Sale of cereals, foodstuffs, tools, etc.
Mossi ⟶ Nuni	• Labour • Gifts • Sale of cereals, foodstuffs, some hardwares, etc. • Dolo
Nuni ⟷ Mossi	• Skill sharing • Labour exchange/sharing and knowledge exchange • Equal participation in mens' and womens' agricultural groups • Religious ceremonies • Transport and trade • Participation in decision making concerning, the use of currently (or about to be) used land

Source: Author's fieldwork, 1993–1995.

This closeness of tribal interaction shows a growing maturity in a production system that has recently been interrupted. There is continuity and change within the village where the local production system mirrors entitlement exchanges that were once part of the broader spatial boundary exchange systems. This occurs while each ethnic group maintains its own basic agricultural system. In the following two villages, the levels of interaction are of a different nature, reflecting their respective stages in the development of a new production system.

5 Boutiourou

Introduction

Boutiourou has a territory of approximately 24 km² and is composed of five Nuni cantons, one Mossi and one Fulani. The village territory shares borders with the villages of Dabiou to the south-southeast, Kouri to the northwest, Longa to the west, Taaga to the west-southwest and Mouna to the east-southeast, with which there are good relations. Boutiourou has parental and marital links with the villages of; Sagalo, Silli, Sati and Korobou and also with Kation, Nianon, Dabio, Nadion, Taga, Woro, Longa, Kouri and Beune .

The landscape of Boutiourou is typical of Sissili, consisting of a succession of undulating granite plateaux, that often have hard laterite crusts on their summits and mid-slopes. It is a landscape which is characterised by sandy-silty soils that become more argillic towards the valley bottoms. These soils sustain a range of vegetation types; wooded savanna on the hilltops; bushy savanna on the mid-slopes, riverine forest in the valley bottoms and aquatic prairies in flooded valley bottoms.

The majority of the population is Muslim, with a few Animist and Christian families. The common language of communication in the village is Mooré (the language of the Mossi immigrants).

Population

The population of Boutiourou numbered 77 people in 1975, 903 in 1985 and calculating from the number of homesteads, 1,126 in 1995. The Mossi form the majority of the population, with 71 compounds, followed by the Nuni with 16 compounds, and a small minority of Fulani with two encampments. The Mossi originated from the province of Bulkiemdé and Oubritenga in the Mossi plateau. The Fulani also came from Oubritenga, 17 years ago. The migrants left their regions of origin because of persistent droughts and the need to find fertile farm land. Seasonal out-migration from Boutiourou is common and is mostly composed of young men who look for work to pay for consumer goods such as a radio or a bicycle. There are

> **Box 5.1 The oral history of Boutiourou**
>
> The village of Boutiourou, meaning the *'pancreas of the goat'*, is estimated to be 400 years old. The first family to arrive was the Zio family who came from the village of Diona. One day, two brothers left Diona because they had argued with their third brother and the brothers took their belongings and their animal herd. After travelling some distance they found a green valley bottom where the soil was fertile and the water was constant, and it was here that they decided to settle. After some time another family arrived, the Dahourou family who came from Sati. They were then joined by the Nignan family. All three families, being together, decided to kill a goat for a small feast. The Dahourou and the Nignan family, after killing and cooking the goat, asked the Zio family which part of the goat they would like. The Zio brothers then said, 'even if you were to give me the pancreas of the goat I will eat it and it will taste good'. (The pancreas is traditionally recognised to be the least appetising part of the animal). This signified the bounty and peacefulness of the new village (even the bad parts are good). The Zio family became the Village Chiefs, the Nignan are the Land Chiefs and the Dahourou family are the village counsellors in charge of the streams and water.
>
> *Source:* Author's fieldwork, 1994.

seven cantons in Boutiourou: five Nuni cantons, one Mossi and one Fulani.

Description of the Landscape

The village transect, Figure 5.1, shows a highly managed environment, with the central Nuni village, unusually, on the top of the catena. The village, even though it is seen to be on the top of the catena, is not situated on the laterite or granite outcrop; it is on one of the landscape undulations. Usually, Nuni villages are situated nearer the valley bottom, on the more fertile soils of the lower slopes. Boutiourou is situated on the upper slopes because it moved from its original site, near the valley bottom, on conversion to Islam. The village moved the site of the village up-slope to physically remove themselves from their Animist past.

In the majority of areas along the transect, there has been a change in the natural vegetation, except for those areas near the streams (**poontia**). Here the relatively dense riverine vegetation has remained largely intact, characterised by *P. erinaceus* and *F. platyphylla*. Dry season gardening and riziculture have not developed in Boutiourou and consequently the semi-permanently flooded areas have been left alone.

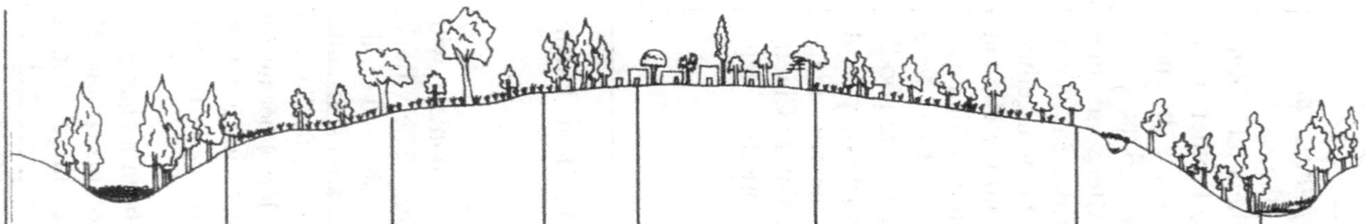

118 Rebuilding the Local Landscape

Trees and Shrubs	Ficus platyphylla Parkia biglobosa Lannea microcarpa Piliostigma reticulatum Acacia polyacantha Combretum spp Diospyros mespiliformis	Butyrospermum parkii Azadirachta indica Parkia biglobosa Lannea microcarpa Ficus gnaphalocarpa	Lannea microcarpa Acacia albida Ficus gnaphalocarpa Parkia biglobosa Azadiracta indica	Piliostigma r. Parkia b. Terminalia m. Combretum g. Velutinom spp. Diospyros m. Calabasse tree	Mangifera indica Lannea microcarpa Butyrospermum parkii Parkia biglobosa Gmelina arborea Vitex doniana Moringa oleifera Carica papaye Eucalyptus camaldulensis Psidium guajava Tectonia grandis Musa spp	Parkia biglobosa Butyrospermum parkii (Adansonia digitata Mangifera indica Anachardium occidentale)* Afzelia africana Detarium microcarpa Terminalia macroptera Gardenia spp Lannea acida Crosopterus febrifuga Combretum spp Landolphea spp Enada africana Diospyros mespiliformis Khaya senegalensis	Butyrospermum parkii Balanites aegyptiaca Lannea acida Combretum spp Pterocarpus erinaceus Piliostigma reticulatum Gardenia spp Parkia biglobosa Sterculia setigera Acacia machrostachya Acacia dudgeoni Khaya senegalensis Mitragyna inermis Grasses
Remarks	Dam, stream	Cotton, groundnuts, sorghum Site of old village	Maize, millet, groundnuts Site of old village	Village green belt	Maize animal rearing: sheep, goats, fowl Nuni village centre: mosque village savings bank, tree nursery, granaries, water pump	Finger millet, groundnuts Millet Sorghum Village chief's house Farmland and fallows – good tree cover Reforestation with Eucalyptus camaldulensis, Cassia siamea, Gmelina arborea * planted by village chief	Two locally made bridges, streams in valleys. Exposed laterite on slopes River bed.

Source: Author's fieldwork, 1993–1995.

Figure 5.1 Village transect of Boutiourou, 1993 to 1995

The first crops seen from left to right start after the dense riverine vegetation. These fields, up to the 'village green belt', are the Nuni's village fields where cotton, groundnuts, maize, millet and sorghum are grown. It is at the lower part of the catena that the old village was found. There are six different tree species in these fields with tree density remaining relatively high at about 40 trees per hectare. As yet no introduced species have been planted,[1] although the Nuni will protect and cultivate néré wildings if found in the field. The village 'green belt' is a sacred site and acts as a buffer zone between the cultivated area and the houses. The Nuni habitation zone sees an increase in the diversity of species from seven (in the bush) to 12 because of planted species which include mango (*M. indica*), *Gmelina arborea* (a service tree),[2] *Moringa oleifera* (a food tree), papaya (*C. papaye*), guava (*Psidium guajava*), teak (*Tectona grandis*) and banana (*Musa spp*). Household fields are also located in these areas and are dominated by maize cultivation. Animals and fowl are also kept around the houses, feeding on household wastes. Apart from the houses, the built infrastructure includes a mosque, a village savings bank, a tree nursery, granaries and a water pump. Past the village centre, the number of tree species again increases, which is partly due to a number of species being planted by the Village Chief (baobab, cashew (*Anacardium occidentale*) and mango) in his compound and partly due to the village men's group having planted *Eucalyptus camaldulensis*, *Cassia siamea*, and *G.arborea* for service wood as part of their group activities, as well as the existing natural vegetation. This is another area of village fields where the Nuni cultivate millet, groundnuts and red sorghum. Despite the level of cultivation in these areas there is still good tree cover. Further down the slope there is a patch of exposed laterite near to the main path running through the village which has been caused by excessive sheet erosion and gullying in the heavy showers of the rainy season. Past this area the vegetation becomes dense again with characteristic riverine vegetation. Around the stream there are only grasses as this area is completely inundated in the rainy season.

Evolution of the Farmed Area

The farmed area in 1955, as seen in Figure 5.2, was minimal. Although no population figures exist for 1955, considering in 1975 that there were only

---

1 Neem (*A. indica*) is an exotic species, originally coming from India. It is usually found under *Ficus spp* in dense thickets as a result of birds eating Neem seeds then roosting on large trees. The seeds are passed under the tree canopy with the birds droppings where they self seed.
2 Many types of planted tree can be distinguished on account of their main purpose, e.g. the food and fruit tree; the woodfuel tree and the service tree (whose wood is used for building poles). However, although these trees are planted primarily for their first use, they are always multipurpose trees, being used for medicine, fuelwood, honey production, etc.

120   Rebuilding the Local Landscape

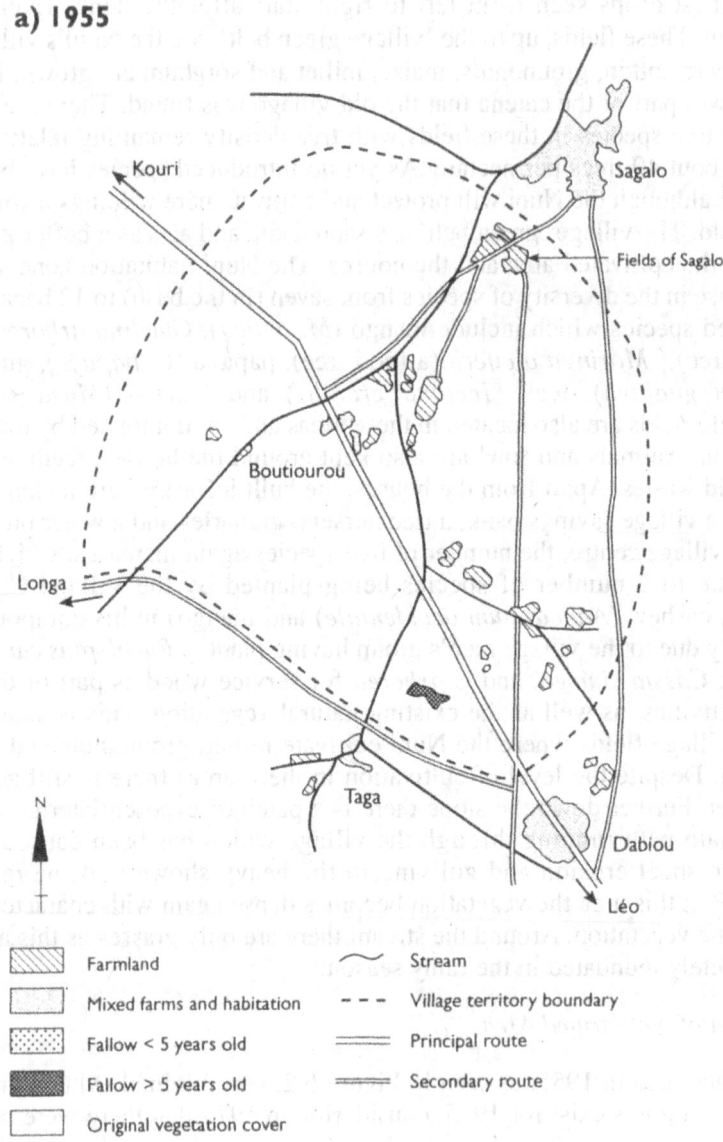

a) 1955

Farmland
Mixed farms and habitation
Fallow < 5 years old
Fallow > 5 years old
Original vegetation cover

Stream
- - - Village territory boundary
══ Principal route
═══ Secondary route

Maps are based on the interpretation of aerial photographs and maps and
ground verification through interviews and observation, see text for explanation

Note: Map not to scale.
Source: Author's fieldwork, 1993–1995.

Figure 5.2a The evolution of the landscape in Boutiourou, 1955 to 1993

b) 1985

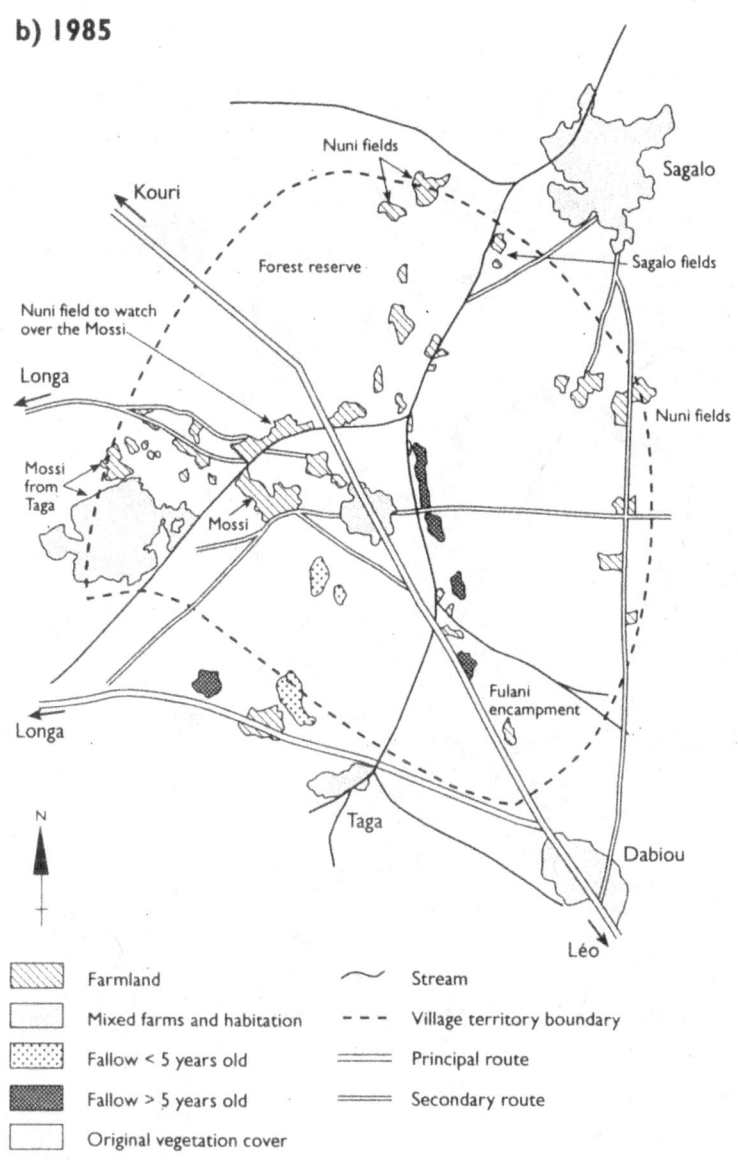

Maps are based on the interpretation of aerial photographs and maps and ground verification through interviews and observation, see text for explanation

Note: Map not to scale.
Source: Author's fieldwork, 1993–1995.

Figure 5.2b The evolution of the landscape in Boutiourou, 1955 to 1993

122 *Rebuilding the Local Landscape*

c) 1993

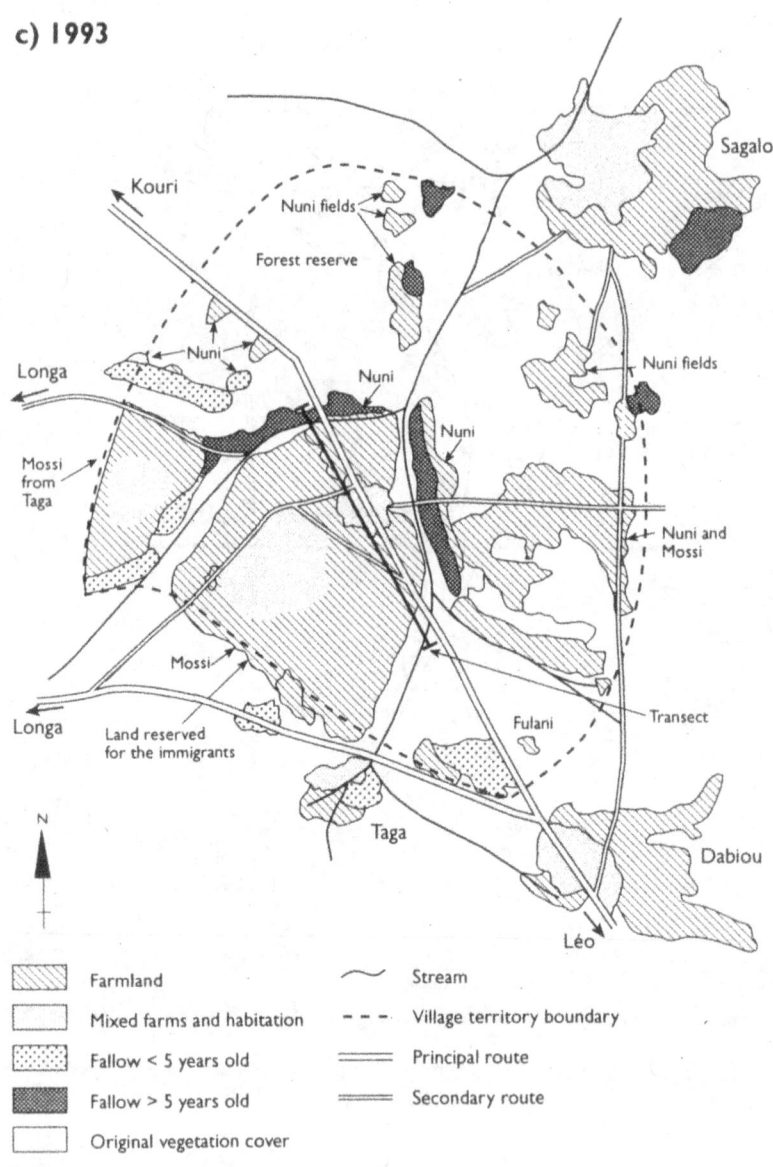

	Farmland	~	Stream
	Mixed farms and habitation	- - -	Village territory boundary
	Fallow < 5 years old	===	Principal route
	Fallow > 5 years old	===	Secondary route
	Original vegetation cover		

Maps are based on the interpretation of aerial photographs and maps and ground verification through interviews and observation, see text for explanation

Note: Map not to scale.
Source: Author's fieldwork, 1993–1995.

Figure 5.2c The evolution of the landscape in Boutiourou, 1955 to 1993

77 inhabitants, the population could not have been bigger than 30 (using the size of the farmed area as a reference). Although the village is just west of centre (where the village fields are found), much of the farmed area is to the southeast of the territory. There is also some farmland to the northeast of the village centre (both these farmed areas are the Nuni bush fields). Most of the farmed area is near the valley bottoms which is the Nuni's preferred farming area and the most fertile land. The fields to the northeast of Boutiourou's territory belong to a family from Sagalo. The presence of other village's fields in others territories is relatively common and the reasons are often lost or forgotten but the agreements hold. Note the position of the village in 1955 and the difference to 1983; this is the village move due to the conversion to Islam.

By 1983, the farmed area had increased significantly and there is the first evidence of the impact of the Mossi immigrants. The Fulani had also arrived by this time and had settled to the southeast of Boutiourou's territory. Two separate Mossi immigrant groups in Boutiourou's territory can be seen; the Mossi from the village of Taga,[3] to the far west of the territory and the Mossi of Boutiourou to the centre west (the two Mossi contingents are separated by a stream). These Mossi came from the north to the village of Taga and asked the Land Chief if they could settle there. Those Mossi then moved, without the knowledge of the Land Chief, onto the territory of Boutiourou. On realising this, the Land Chief from Taga went to see Boutiourou's Land Chief to explain and Boutiourou's Land Chief agreed to let the Mossi stay. Another Mossi group (who became the Mossi of Boutiourou) came to see the Nuni Land Chief from Boutiourou directly and were given land. Progressively as more Mossi immigrants came to see the Nuni chiefs, the Nuni decided to give the Mossi a section of their territory to confine themselves to and to manage. The Nuni chiefs 'gave' the Mossi chief (the head of the first Mossi family to arrive) part of land between the two streams to the southwest. It was made clear that the Mossi would receive no more land. Consequent Mossi arrivals had to see the Mossi chief first to see if there was any available land in the Mossi territory. If there was land for the new migrants, then the Mossi chief would direct the immigrant to the Nuni Land Chief to seek his permission. The Nuni regulated immigration and forced the Mossi to manage affairs on their own land with regard for the other members of the community (both Mossi and Nuni). The Nuni have bush fields close to the Mossi territory (again on the best land near on the lower slopes) to the west. In this way the Nuni could survey and monitor the Mossi activities.

---

3 When a group of Mossi arrived at a Nuni village and asked for permission to settle and farm, these then become the Mossi of that particular village, e.g. the Mossi from Taga, the Mossi from Boutiourou, the Mossi from Tô, etc.

The Fulani have been allowed to settle in an isolated spot to the southwest of the territory. Here they are near to a water source and their cattle are removed from the cultivated areas. They can live in peace and cause minimal damage with their cattle.

The Nuni have left those bush fields on the lower slopes, to the south, fallow and have moved upslope to the east and also to the north. The village fields have remained on the site of the old village on the lower slopes. The Sagalo fields have become smaller, although the village of Sagalo has got noticeably bigger (as have Taga and Dabio).

Although there are fields of three Nuni families in the north of Boutiourou's territory, the Village Chiefs have designated this a forest reserve. This area provides for forest products and more importantly provides their children with farmland. This area was designated a reserve (no immigrants and only a few Nuni are allowed to farm there) through the realisation that population pressure may threaten the future of farming in Boutiourou's territory and thus, there is a need to conserve quality land for the future. There has also been an increase in the number of paths and tracks in the territory. This means both more people and traffic leading to more contact between villages.

By 1993, a radically different picture has emerged with an expanded farmed area, most notably with the Mossi from Boutiourou. This group has almost completely filled up its allotted space with farm land. Some of the Mossi now have their bush fields alongside the Nuni fields to the east. The Nuni have left the lower slopes to the west (the old surveillance fields) fallow and have now returned to some of the fields on the lower slopes next to the streams to the centre east and southeast. Some of these areas remain fallow and have almost regenerated to a natural state. There has also been a large expansion of farmed area to the east by the Nuni and some Mossi farmers. The three Nuni families have kept their fields in the forest reserve, leaving two fields fallow and five Nuni fields have been cleared to the west in the mostly empty area. The Mossi of Taga have remained static and have not invaded elsewhere.

The Fulani have also remained static and are still surrounded by a relatively large expanse of bush, enough to pasture their cattle. The villages of Dabio and Sagalo have grown significantly with Taga growing to a lesser extent.

The Future of the Occupation of Space in Boutiourou

Boutiourou has the second largest population of the case-study villages and has the second largest surface area covered by farmland. The largest expansion of farmland came between 1983 and 1993 which indicates that many of their total immigrants arrived during that period and came to join the

Table 5.1   The growth in the different categories of land cover in Boutiourou, 1955 to 1993[4]

Total land area – 2397 hectares	1955 ha	% of area	1983 ha	% of area	1993 ha	% of area
Farmland	93	3.9	204	8.5	810	34
Woodland	2299	95.9	2171	90.6	1462	60.9
Fallow <5 years	-	-	8	0.3	61	2.5
Fallow >5 years	5	0.2	14	0.6	64	2.6
Total	2397	100	2397	100	2397	100

original (probably their own family members) Mossi. This is unlike Lon which already by 1983 had a significant amount of land under (immigrant) cultivation.[5] However, Boutiourou still has significant woodland stocks, (almost 66 per cent) which includes an indigenous forest reserve. Again with this amount of woodland (i.e. potential farm land) and an emerging coherent social group structure, it is unlikely that resource shortages will become apparent in the near future.

Family Networks and Linkages in the Village

Nuni In Boutiourou, although the village is younger than Lon, it was originally made up of three families. There are 13 links between Boutiourou and other villages because of either parentage or marriage, and two links because of relations living and working in Ghana and Côte D'Ivoire. It is widely held in Boutiourou that Côte D'Ivoire holds the greatest potential for making money. Léo, as it is so close and is a town with good income opportunities is also a favourite place. However, in the case of the latter, it is so close to Boutiourou that people can commute for business.

Both Boutiourou and Lon have significant links with other towns and villages in their areas. In the case of Boutiourou, its catchment of links is relatively close to the village, possibly echoing its more productive southern environment, i.e. people do not have to go too far to making a living and thereby need not spread their living risks through a wide area. In Lon,

---

4 Based on the interpretation of the diagrams of the evolution of the occupation of space.
5 It seems that the more northern the village the earlier it welcomed Mossi and Fulani immigrants. The further south one travels the later the arrival date of the immigrants. This indicates that the later immigrants (coming as a result of the droughts in the late 1980s instead of the late 1970s) found the northern areas of Sissili saturated with immigrants and so were forced to come further south to find land. Therefore the latest arrivals are found in Saboué and earliest Lon, with Boutiourou in the middle.

126 *Rebuilding the Local Landscape*

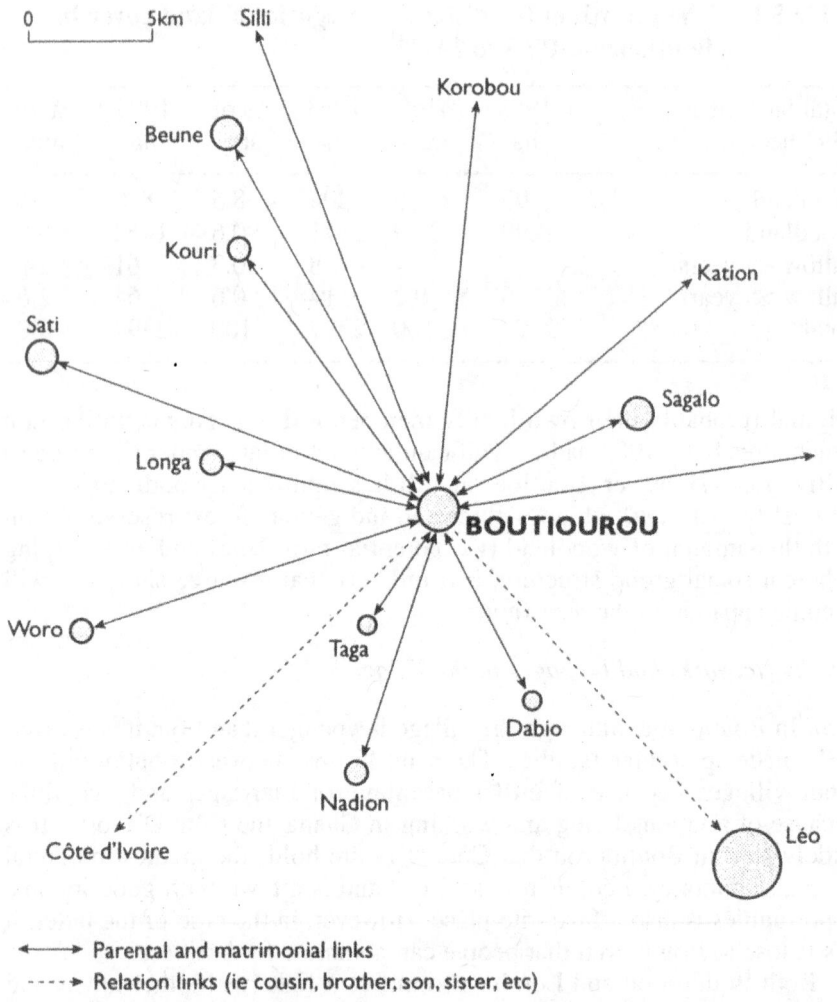

← → Parental and matrimonial links
---- ► Relation links (ie cousin, brother, son, sister, etc)

Source: Author's fieldwork, 1993–1995.

Figure 5.3 Networks and linkages of the Nuni in Boutiourou, 1995[6]

however, eight of the 13 links are more than 25 km from the village. Again, this may show the need to travel further afield in a less productive environment (Lon is just north of the division between the sudano-sahelian (Lon

---

6 All links are of a marital and parental nature with the exception of Léo which has additional administrative links with Boutiourou, being the departmental capital.

Boutiourou

Figure 5.4 The origins and linkages of the immigrants in Boutiourou

and above) and sudano-guinean to the south) to increase the effectivity of the networks in their ability to provide alternate sources of livelihood if the need arises. Meillassoux (1981) says this is a common and obvious way of overcoming risk, i.e. by pooling the risks over a wide geographical area so as to cover ecologically heterogeneous zones and economic activities.

Mossi The Mossi of Boutiourou are from the provinces of Boulkiemdé and Oubritenga and have relations in Sissili (through marriage) and in Côte D'Ivoire through relations (see Figure 5.4). They have no links with Ghana, as it is not a traditional destination for the Mossi (even though that is their country of origin). Côte D'Ivoire has a large number of Mossi already working there so there is an element of safety in choosing that as the host country for seasonal migrant workers. The Mossi network in Boutiourou is very similar to that of Lon.

Fulani The Fulani of Boutiourou have a larger number of linkages than those of Lon. The Fulani are composed of one clan coming from Oubritenga and have links with Passoré province, Ghana (for the same reasons as the Fulani of Lon), Côte D'Ivoire and also with villages in Sissili. In addition to trade through Ghana, they also trade through Côte D'Ivoire, possibly because they are close to established trade routes that pass through the province of Poni into the Côte D'Ivoire. The Fulani of Boutiourou have been residents in the village for 17 years and as such have seen a number of their daughters married and hence the number of their links in the villages of Sissili.

Legal Arrangements and Administrative Decision Making

Boutiourou seems to have the most controlled and regulated legal and administrative system, with each of the immigrant groups being confined to specific areas and the existence of land or woodland 'reserves' that are for '*les enfants*'[7] (i.e. farms for the future). In Figure 5.5 there is a diagrammatic representation of the power structures in Boutiourou, and although it seems very similar to that of Saboué, it is, in reality, very different.

Boutiourou has a significantly larger population, both Nuni and immigrant, and consequently has more land under cultivation (34 per cent of its territory opposed to 13 per cent in the case of Saboué); it also has a smaller area (2,397 hectares opposed to 3,731 hectares). It is perhaps because of this that the Nuni Chiefs of Boutiourou were forced into a tightly controlled system of land distribution and regulation of immigrants in their

---

7 'The children'.

Boutiourou 129

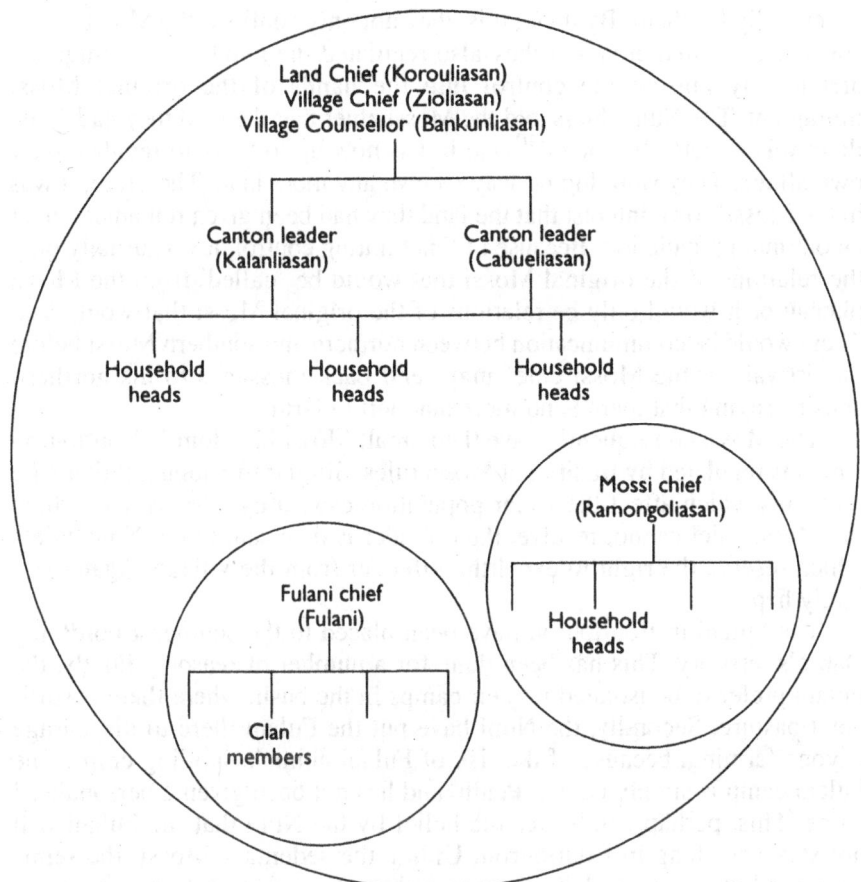

Source: Author's fieldwork, 1993–1995.

Figure 5.5 A diagrammatic representation of the power structures in Boutiourou[8,9]

territory. The chiefs of Boutiourou also had the added factor that there were immigrant Mossi from another village (the Mossi of Taga) that occupied a small but nonetheless important part of their territory.

When the chiefs of Boutiourou realised that the northern Mossi immigrants were continuing to come in significant numbers in the late 1980s they reached the decision that they must reserve a part of their territory

---

8 The circles represent the respective territories.
9 The original Mossi family head acts as the Mossi chief.

specifically for them. By doing this, they not only confined the Mossi to one specific delimited area, but they also regulated the number of immigrants arriving by putting the control into the hands of the original Mossi immigrant. The Nuni chiefs told the Mossi chief that the land they had given them was effectively 'theirs'[10] and it was now up to them to regulate their own affairs. They would in no way receive any more land. Therefore, it was in the Mossi's own interest that the land they had been given remained under an optimum population. Because of this limiting control, it was usually only the relations of the original Mossi that would be 'called' from the Mossi plateau or it would only be relations of the original Mossi that would ask. There would be communication between northern and southern Mossi before the arrivals or the Mossi chief may send back messages to his northern cousins saying that there is no more land left to farm.

The Mossi consequently have their small Mossi kingdom in Boutiourou which is regulated by traditional Mossi rules. Similar to Saboué, if there are problems which affect the wider population caused by a Mossi and which the Mossi chief cannot resolve, the offender is then sent to the Nuni chiefs which reserve the right to expel the offender from the village. Again, this rarely happens.

The Fulani in Boutiourou have been placed to the southeast bordering Dabio's territory. This has been done for a number of reasons. Firstly, the Fulani prefer to be isolated in their camps in the bush, where there is sufficient pasture. Secondly, the Nuni have put the Fulani there to discourage anyone farming, because of the risk of Fulani animals spoiling crops. The Fulani camp is simply called 'Peulh' and has not been given a personalised name. This, perhaps, indicates the belief by the Nuni that the Fulani will not stay very long in Boutiourou. Unlike the sedentary Mossi, the semi-nomadic Fulani always have the possibility of moving on to new pastures and setting up camp.

The three Nuni chiefs (the Land Chief, the Village Chief and the Village Counsellor), commonly hold counsel together along with other elders and notables. The canton leaders are traditionally answerable to them and in turn the heads of household answerable to the canton chiefs.

Despite the apparently strong control and regulation that the Nuni chiefs have over Boutiourou's territory, there are some signs of traditional land use irregularities. For example, to the east of the territory there are now some Mossi fields. The reasons for their presence are the same as for the

---

10 Although all land belongs to the village and only usufruct rights exist, this 'gift' of land will probably never be reclaimed by the Nuni. Thus, in this sense it is lost land. However, returning to support networks, the greatest guarantee of subsistence is to provide another group or person with land, thereby allowing the giver to claim back on the land in times of hardship. It also puts the receiver into a situation of moral obligation with the giver.

Table 5.2 Ethnic interrelationships in Boutiourou

Direction of transfer	Activities
Fulani → Mossi	• Sale of milk and meat • Cattle guarding • Dung • Veterinary advice • Sale of animals • Grazing animals in post-harvest fields
Mossi → Fulani	• Labour • Sale of cereals, foodstuffs, tools, etc. • Dolo
Fulani ←→ Mossi	• Demonstrations of animal traction, veterinary issues, vaccinations, etc., with extension agent • Participation in village meetings
Fulani → Nuni	• Cattle guarding • Sale of milk and meat • Dung • Gifts
Nuni → Fulani	• Labour • Sale of foodstuffs • Administrative control • Land
Fulani ←→ Nuni	• Some participation in meetings, more listening that voting or discussing • Participation in religious festivals and celebrations • Some skill sharing • Demonstrations of animal traction, veterinary issues, vaccinations, etc., with extension agent
Nuni → Mossi	• Wives • Labour • Administrative control • Medicinal advice • Land • Sale of cereals, foodstuffs, tools, etc.
Mossi → Nuni	• Labour • Gifts • Sale of cereals, foodstuffs, some hardwares, etc. • Dolo
Nuni ←→ Mossi	• Skill sharing

Table 5.2   Ethnic interrelationships in Boutiourou (continued)

- Labour exchange/sharing
- Equal participation in mens' and womens' agricultural groups
- Knowledge exchange
- Religious ceremonies
- Transport
- Trade
- Participation in decision making concerning, the use of currently (or about to be) used land e.g. land around the dam, and the division and rationing of tasks, e.g. on the construction of the dam

Source: Author's fieldwork, 1993–1995.

intermingling of Nuni and Mossi fields in Lon; through increasing friendship and closeness the Nuni chiefs are allowing some Mossi (i.e. their friends) to farm alongside them on new land or their old fallows. This may signal a leaking of the Mossi onto new areas or may signal an ample amount of land that can be farmed and, again, through this, the subsistence networks and moral economy is strengthened.

Ethnic Interrelationships in Boutiourou

The level of cross-ethnic contact is, as in Lon, very strong and each production system seems to complement the others. There is however a big difference in the spatial arrangements which reflects both a different approach to land management in the territories and also the duration of the immigrants.

The Nuni and Mossi communities have not merged together to the same extent as Lon, because of the separation of their living spaces. At Lon, the Nuni and Mossi are literally neighbours; in Boutiourou, the cantons are further apart. There is also less intermarriage between Nuni and Mossi, possibly because there still remain distinct groups with discrete identities. However, despite this physical separation, there is strong solidarity and cohesion between the Nuni and Mossi.

The village of Boutiourou has a more 'robust' production system than Lon which is due to a number of factors. A more abundant ecology, strong cohesion and good leadership from the traditional chiefs and a proximity to urban supply centres. Ethnic exchange entitlements are strong and seem to be improving with time. New production techniques (e.g. cotton) have strengthened the farming system and 'learning from each other' seems to complement each separate farming system.

6 Saboué

Introduction

Saboué's territory has an area of approximately 37 km^2 and shares borders with Bétiassan to the west, Yelbouga to the northwest, Pissié to the north and Biéha to the east. It is the smallest of the three case study villages. In 1985 it had a population of 266, at which time, the majority of the immigrants had already settled. The population is thought by the elders not to have altered significantly in the interim period. It has five cantons, three Nuni, one Mossi and one Fulani.

The village of Saboué is an off-shoot of the village of Pissié as can be seen in the oral history of Saboué (see Box 6.1); Saboué began as a neighbourhood (albeit approximately three kilometres away) of Pissié but has now been given village status. It has significant family links and there are numerous Pissié fields in the territory of Saboué. The population of Saboué consider the people of Pissié to be their 'brothers' and will often celebrate feasts or bury their dead in Pissié. Problems may also be resolved in Pissié. As time progresses however, Saboué gains more and more autonomy.

The landscape of Saboué is basically the same as the landscape of Boutiourou, as most villages in Sissili occupy the same position in the landscape. The natural vegetation in Saboué is more diverse than in the territories of the other two villages and there is generally less evidence of a significant human impact relative to Lon and Boutiourou, i.e. there is more 'natural bush'. Saboué also has a larger number of streams and more lower slope surface area and, consequently, more fertile land.

Population

Because it has the smallest population of the case-study villages, there is still a Nuni majority. Also unusually, there is a higher proportion of Fulani than Mossi, reflecting the quality of the bush for pasture, the proximity of Saboué to Ghana (for trade in cattle) and its relative isolation from major markets. (Mossi prefer areas around the centre axis of Sissili which gives them the best access to the markets of Léo, Tô, and further north, Koudougou and Ougadougou and a greater access to other Mossi communities.) However, Biéha holds a weekly market on Wednesdays which attracts a relatively high number of traders, though it is small in comparison to the Sunday market in Léo.

As stated above there are five recognised cantons: three Nuni cantons, one Mossi and one Fulani. There are four Mossi families and six Fulani families. The Fulani arrived 15 years ago and now live to the northwest of the village; the Mossi came 10 years ago and live to the south of Saboué's territory.

Description of the landscape

The transect of Saboué (Figure 6.1) shows two sides to the landscape; one which has been largely untouched by human activity and retains a high species diversity, and the other which has been significantly altered by humankind. Starting from the left of the valley bottom the natural quality of the riverine natural vegetation in southeastern Sissili becomes evident; a high species diversity and density that has remained largely unaltered by human activity. These are the gathering zones that have not been exploited for dry season gardening, paddies or significant pasture. This type of vegetation follows the numerous watercourses throughout Saboué's territory and as such gives Saboué one of the most dense natural vegetation patterns in Sissili.

Box 6.1   The oral history of Saboué

The village of Saboué means 'the bush that has been transformed' and is said to be approximately 200 years old. The first family arrived from the village of Pissié because there was no longer any land for them to farm in the village. Necourou Nacro left his brothers in Pissié and took his animal herd to find pasture. Necourou found a valley bottom where water was plentiful and he drank from the stream using the bark from a baobab tree. The pasture was good and the soil was rich and so he set up camp. After staying there for a while, he returned to Pissié to find his brothers to tell them of the place he had found. He convinced his brothers that the valley bottom he had found would be a good place to settle and farm because of its fertility. His brothers returned with Necourou to help him farm and the village developed and grew from their family. The Nacro family is both the Land Chief and the Village Chief.

Source: Author's fieldwork, 1994.

Saboué 135

Trees and Shrubs	Butyrospermum parkii Parkia biglobosa Diospyros mespiliformis Terminalia macroptera Vitex doniana Combretum spp Crosopteryx febrifuga Detarium microcarpa Lannea microcarpa Khaya senegalensis Landolphea spp Entada africana Annona senegalensis Sterculia setigera Bombax spp Afzelia africana Cassia sieberiana Pterocarpus spp Gardenia erubesens Dichrostachys cinera Lannea spp Erythrina senegelensis		Mitragyna inermis Pterocarpus spp Combretum spp Lannea acida Lannea microcarpa Piliostigma reticulatum Parkia biglobosa Butyrospermum parkii Diospyros mespiliformis Landolphea spp Ficus spp Dichrostachys cinera Vitex doniana Detarium microcarpa	Parkia biglobosa Bombax spp Diospyros mespiliformis Landolphea spp Pterocarpus spp Vitex doniana Detarium microcarpa Combretum spp	Ficus platyphylla Adansonia digitata Citris spp Diospyros mespiliformis Parkia biglobosa Mangifera indica Carica papaye Combretum spp Balanites aegyptica Lannea microcarpa Euphorbia spp	Parkia biglobosa Butyrospermum parkii Pterocarpus spp Piliostigma reticulatum (s) Combretum spp (s) Vitex doniana (s) Detarium microcarpa (s) Cassia siberiana (s) Adansonia digitata Lannea spp (s)	Butyrospermum parkii Parkia biglobosa Adansonia digitata Piliostigma spp (s) Combretum spp (s) Lannea spp (s) Crosopteryx febrifuga
Remarks		Stream valley No trees Sandy soil	Fallow, black soil	Fallow with signs of erosion, concrete well	Household fields, main habitation zone, cemetery	Fallow, poorer soil (s) signifies small trees in process of regeneration	Fallow, poorer soil

Source: Author's fieldwork, 1994.

Figure 6.1 Village transect of Saboué, 1993 to 1995

The stream bed is completely treeless and supports only grasses, which are used for weaving, thatching and dry season pasture. Next to this are the remnants of the riverine woodland that is found to the left, this area has been previously farmed but is now fallow. A high species count still remains (16 species) although not as high as the woodland on the other bank (22 species). Next to this section there is a heavily exploited area which is currently fallow and is showing signs of erosion. This is one of the central exploitation zones of the village and has been periodically farmed since the village was created, making up the village field zone. This area is also fallow at present with only eight tree species and is dominated by the néré which has been encouraged in the Nuni fields. The adjoining area makes up the Nuni zone of habitation and the household fields. Here, there is the first sign of exotic tree species by the resident Nuni. These include the lime, papaya and mango. It should be noted that the number and range of planted species in Saboué compared to the other villages is a lot less due to Saboué's relative isolation and the consequent difficulty in obtaining tree seedlings. The trees that have been preserved around the habitation zone all have important uses, see Table 6.1. Here small household fields exist, kept under permanent cultivation through the application of household waste and compost.

To the right of the habitation zone are the village fields which are currently fallow and in the process of regeneration as seen by the presence of young trees. The results of long term cultivation are evident to the far right of the transect where the number of species has diminished to seven, although there are still a significant number of néré and karité trees. It should

Table 6.1 Trees and their uses in Saboué

F.platyphylla	A shade tree, meeting place, a place of counsel and medicine
A.digitata	Baobab, used for food, medicine, rope making, honey and religious uses (the elders are buried underneath the tree's canopy)
Citris spp.	Fruit, medicine
D.mespiliformis	Fruit, medicine and fuel
P.biglobosa	Fruit, medicine food and money (from the sale of seeds and soumbala)
M.indica	Fruit, medicine
C.papaye	Fruit, medicine
Combretum spp.	Various medicinal and food uses
B.aegyptiaca	Fruit and food
L.microcarpa	Fruit, medicine
Euphorbia spp.	Fencing, medicine

be noted that the karité trees are found further away from the habitation zone and they are less likely to be found in the farmed area. They are more likely to be found in regenerating fallows or in the bush because of their dislike of disturbance or injury, conditions which are tolerated by the néré.

These areas of village fallow have been left to recover and the farmers have moved slightly away from the habitation zone to the east.

Evolution of the Farmed Area

As has already been mentioned, the territory of Saboué began as an extension of the land of Pissié to the northeast of Saboué. Because of this the northern boundary of Saboué, where it attaches to the territory of Pissié is an area of tenurial insecurity. In the past this has never been a problem because of the ample space available for the small population of the area. However, as space becomes a problem there are the beginnings of encroachment into the north of Saboué's territory by Pissié farmers.

In 1955, there was a minimal human population, numbering only a handful of families. The area was in dense bush, much of the southern area covered by dense riverine bush seen in part of the transect, and the northern area would have been covered by almost continuous savanna woodland. The village was situated between two streams that passed either side of the houses and a sacred fishing area was found to the south. The four fields of the original Nuni were situated on the lower slopes and there was one field belonging to a family of Pissié to the far east.

By 1983, there had been an expansion of the farmed area, coincidental with the arrival of the Mossi and the Fulani. The Fulani settled to the west in one camp made up of several families (where the bush is at its most dense), and the Mossi settled to the southeast. The Nuni fields have moved outwards slightly towards the periphery with their old fields lying fallow. Also, there has been the start of exploitation of the northern area by the Nuni in what has become to be recognised as the cereal growing zone, with the southern area being the tuber growing zone. The Pissié field to the east has remained in place although slightly changing orientation and there is the beginning of exploitation in the north by two Pissié families.

There has been no significant influx of immigrants since the first arrived around 15 years ago which makes Saboué unique. The villages of Lon and Boutiourou have continued to receive immigrants up to five years ago. The Nuni of Saboué are also unique because they are a breakaway faction of the Pissié families and as such have a very close relationship, culturally, socially and physically.

By 1993, there had been further expansion of the cultivated area, most notably in the northern area where the Pissié farmers had increased their range. The Mossi remain confined to the southeast, with a slight expansion

138 *Rebuilding the Local Landscape*

a) 1955

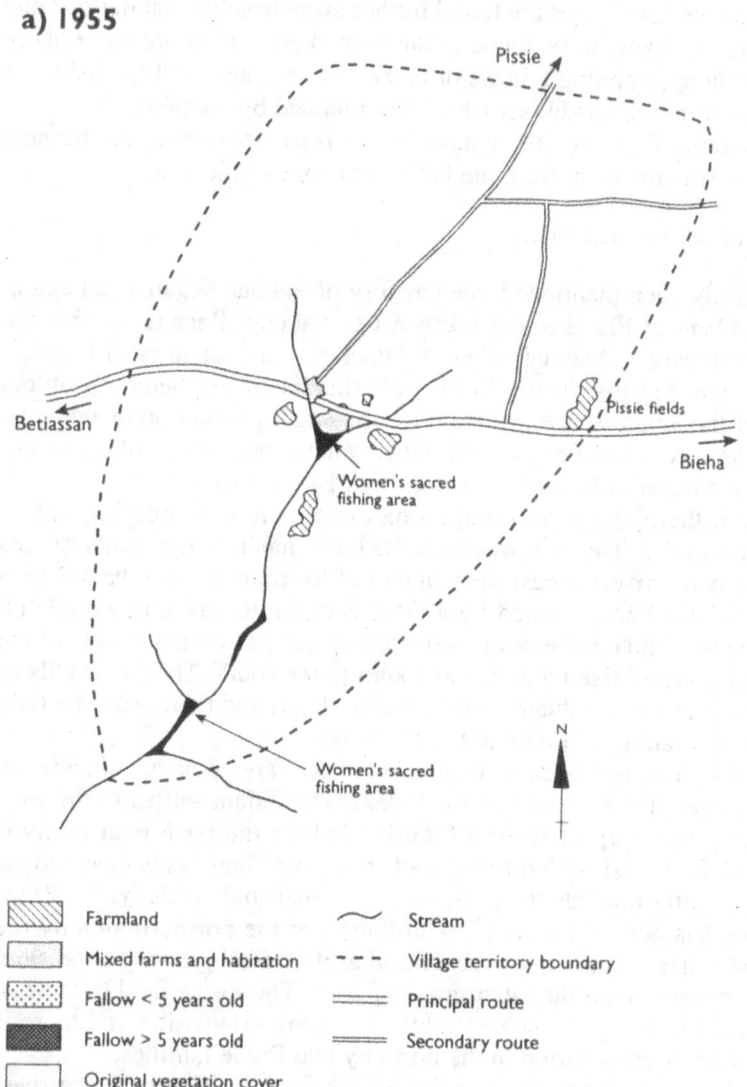

Note: Map not to scale.
Source: Author's fieldwork, 1993–1995.

Figure 6.2a The evolution of the landscape in Saboué, 1955 to 1993

Saboué 139

b) 1985

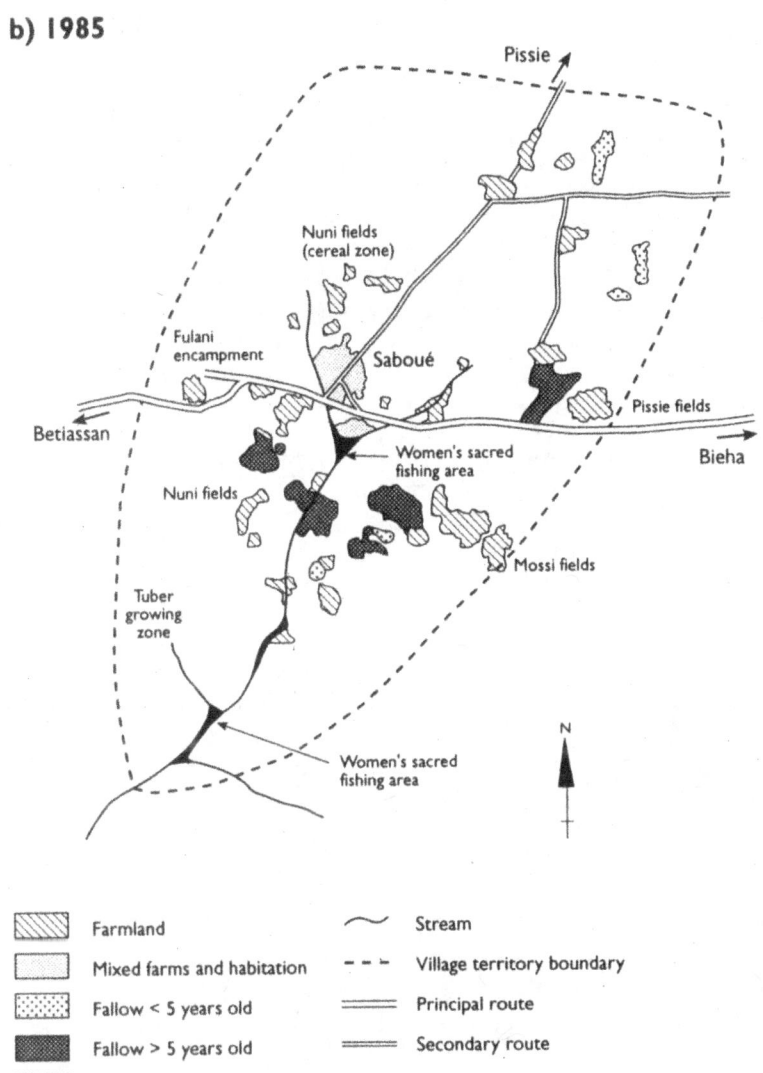

Figure 6.2b The evolution of the landscape in Saboué, 1955 to 1993

Note: Map not to scale.
Source: Author's fieldwork, 1993–1995.

Maps are based on the interpretation of aerial photographs and maps and ground verification through interviews and observation, see text for explanation

140 *Rebuilding the Local Landscape*

c) 1993

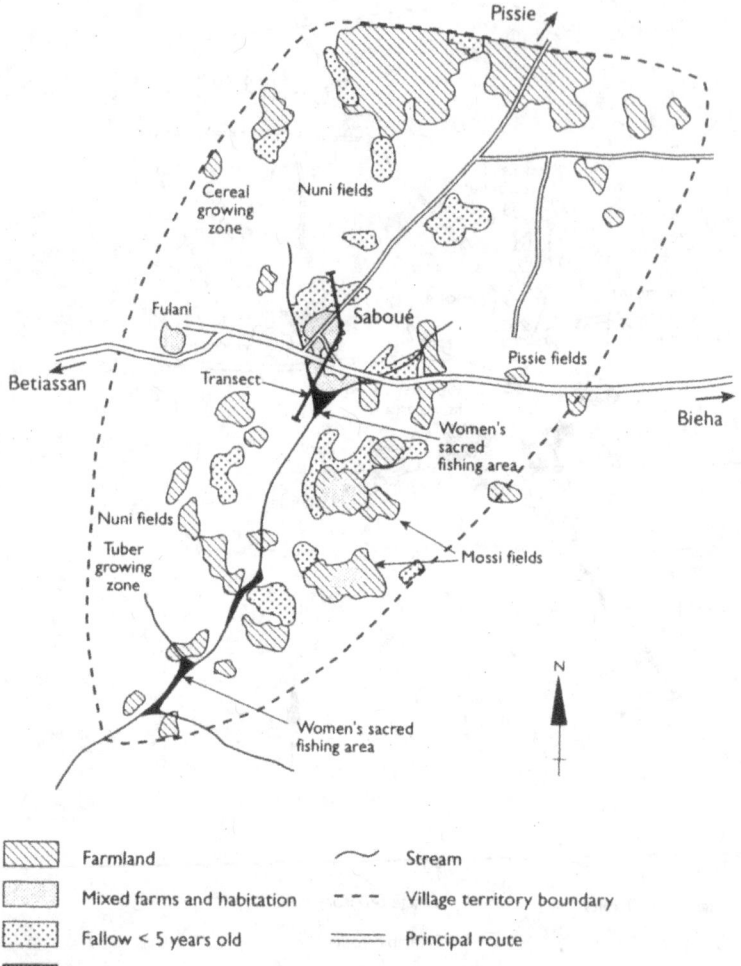

▨	Farmland	〜	Stream
▤	Mixed farms and habitation	- - -	Village territory boundary
▦	Fallow < 5 years old	══	Principal route
▓	Fallow > 5 years old	══	Secondary route
☐	Original vegetation cover		

Maps are based on the interpretation of aerial photographs and maps and ground verification through interviews and observation, see text for explanation

Note: Map not to scale.
Source: Author's fieldwork, 1993–1995.

Figure 6.2c The evolution of the landscape in Saboué, 1955 to 1993

of their farmed area and a movement inwards towards the stream, in virgin bushland. The Nuni had moved their bush fields further south into the tuber growing zone, perhaps as the need for more cash crops arose. The Nuni have also opened up some farms, in the north northwest and the north northeast to supervise the expansion of the Pissié farmed area. The Nuni's sacred fishing sites have also remained, although there is now cultivation on the lower slopes around the sacred area in the south. The Fulani remain in the relative isolation of the east, on the road to Betiassan. This may be a conscious decision by the Nuni chief to discourage any expansion of the farmed area in that region.

The Future of the Occupation of Space in Saboué

Saboué has the lowest proportion of farmland in its territory compared with the other two villages and has the smallest population. The village still has over 80 per cent of natural woodland cover in its territory (and is also located in a department which has one of the smallest populations and highest percentage woodland cover). Saboué, like Boutiourou, experienced the largest expansion of farmland from 1983 to 1993 which again shows the lateness of arrival of the Mossi immigrants as they travelled past or through the densely populated northern and central areas of Sissili.

Networks and Linkages in the Village

Nuni The networks of Saboué are different from the villages of Lon and Boutiourou because of its history and origins. Saboué is the youngest of the villages (as it stands as an autonomous village) but it has links with the old and well established village of Pissié which has its own networks. The village was founded by only one family with which to form links. Saboué

Table 6.2 The growth in the different categories of land cover in Saboué, 1955 to 1993[1]

Total land area – 3,731 hectares	1955 ha	% of area	1983 ha	% of area	1993 ha	% of area
Farmland	53	1.4	188	5	465	13
Woodland	3,678	98.6	3,442	92.4	3,099	82.5
Fallow <5 years	–	–	32	0.8	167	4.5
Fallow >5 years	–	–	69	1.8	–	–
Total	3,731	100	3,731	100	3,731	100

1 Based on the interpretation of the diagrams of the evolution of the occupation of space.

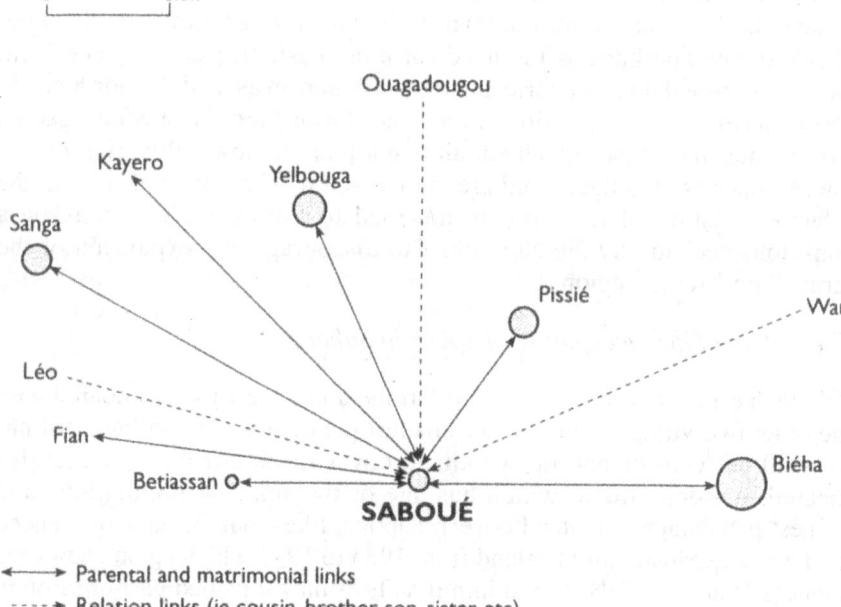

← → Parental and matrimonial links
---▶ Relation links (ie cousin, brother, son, sister, etc)

Source: Author's fieldwork, 1993–1995.

Figure 6.3 Networks and linkages of the Nuni in Saboué, 1995[2,3]

has seven links (see Figure 6.3) by parentage and marriage and three links through relations working in other villages. Its strongest links will be with Pissié because of direct parentage links and it will also share in some of Pissié's links because of common parents. As the age of the village increases, and its population grows the networks will become strengthened.

Mossi and Fulani The Mossi of Saboué have come from Namentenga and Oubritenga and have links only with Côte D'Ivoire through relations working there (see Figure 6.4). It is probable that these links already existed in their place of origin which they brought them with them. Because the Mossi of Saboué have only been in the village for a relatively short time, they have been unable to build up the social networks that other immigrants have built up in other villages. The Fulani, on the other hand, have significant links, because, although they have not been residents of Saboué for long they have

---

2 Biéha which has additional administrative links with Saboué, being the departmental capital.
3 The size of the circles are proportional to the size of the villages.

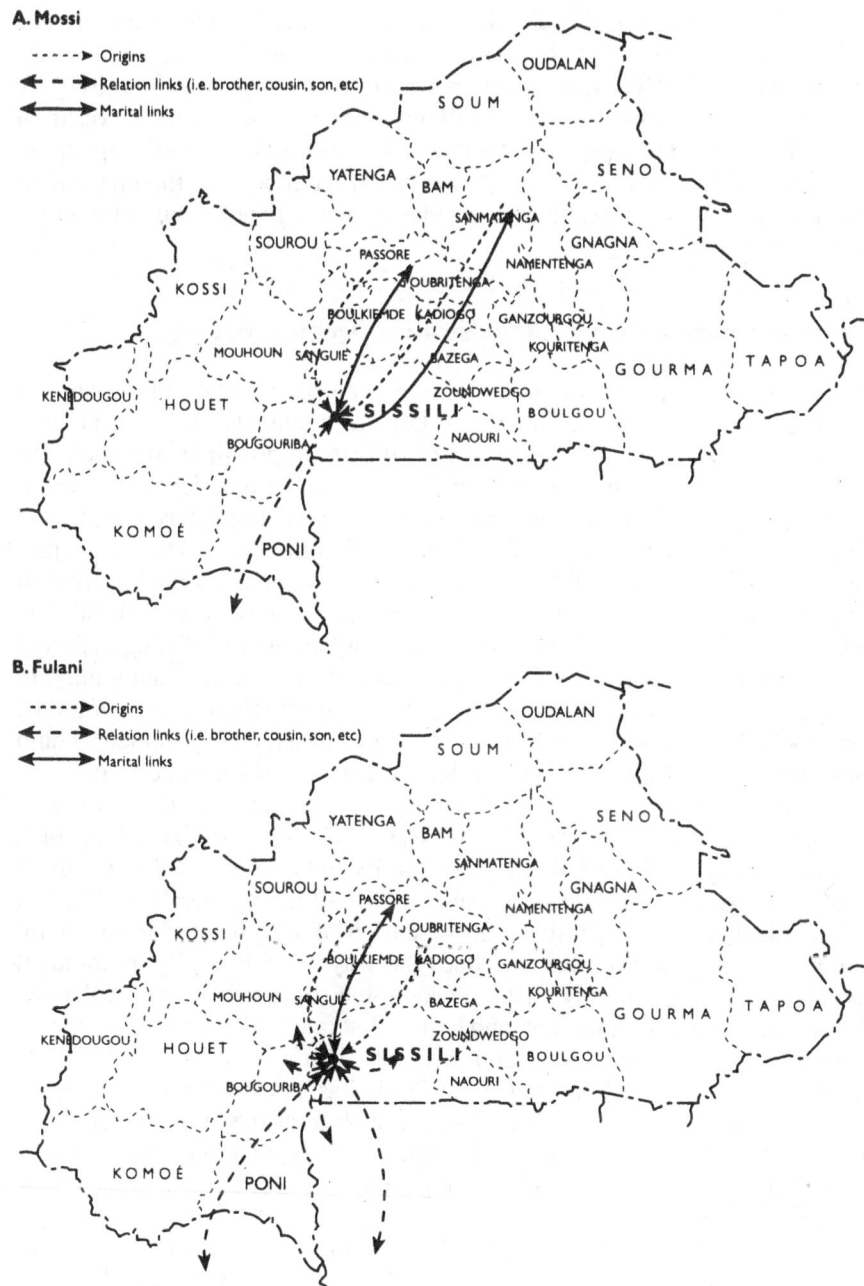

Figure 6.4 The origins and linkages of the immigrants in Saboué

been in Sissili for a considerable time and have moved south for pasture and water. They also have trade links with Ghana and Côte D'Ivoire.

It appears that the Mossi support networks are kept, for the most part, within the confines of the Nuni village, content to concentrate on their immediate surroundings and their neighbours and the building up of relationships therein. The Fulani however, far from being settled have their support networks distributed over a wider area and do not seem to be 'in the bosom' of the village.

Legal Arrangements and Administrative Decision Making

As has already been mentioned, Saboué is an off-shoot of Pissié and, as such, this complicates the customary law arrangements. As migrants to a secondary settlement, the people of Saboué are, in principle still under the control of the Land and Village Chiefs of Pissié. In practice, some major events occur in Pissié. For example, the deaths of important people and their consequent burials, the major Islamic celebrations (at least the representatives of the people of Saboué put in an appearance in Pissié in front of their Imams and chiefs). However, for the day to day affairs of Saboué, which include the allocation of land to the immigrants and the regulation of their affairs, the village chief and counsellor of Saboué have autonomy. In the case of grave misdemeanours or conflicts, the chiefs of Pissié would be approached in a consultative fashion and if no consequent agreements could be made after that, then they would have the power of final decision.

It should be noted that no animosity exists between the people of Saboué, who consider the people of Pissié as *'nos parents'*[4] and the people of Pissié. They are essentially the same family and, as such, share a common responsibility, i.e. that of ensuring survival for all family members. The fact that control resides in Pissié is an indication of who has the most secure production base. In this way it echoes the way a small family or conjugal unit leaves a larger family; it may take some time before the breakaway faction becomes self-sufficient, and before that family does, there are significant flows of resources and labour between the two. By retaining control, the risks are minimised on both sides: Pissié has an extra land reservoir for its larger population, which is seen in Figure 6.2c as the existence of Pissié fields in the north of Saboué's, still relatively unexploited, territory; and in case of hardship or harvest failure the people of Saboué can approach their *'parents'* for aid.

It is not known how the legal control arrangements would develop in case of an ever increasing population, but it is assumed that dialogue

---

4 'Our parents'.

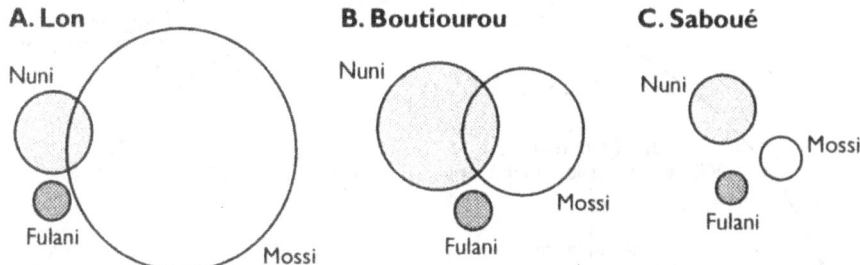

Source: Author's fieldwork, 1993-1995.

Figure 6.5 A diagrammatic representation of the relative integration of the three ethnic groups in Lon, Boutiourou and Saboué

between the chiefs of the two villages would result in decisions that attempt to ensure subsistence for all. Because of the importance of support networks to community survival, it is unlikely that population pressure would result in a *de facto* fencing off of territories. It is in the interest of Saboué and Pissié alike to retain good relations, as it is with parents and children.

Saboué has both the largest territory and the smallest population. It also has the most recent experience of immigration. The Nuni are in the majority which is also unique in relation to the other two villages. The small size of the Nuni community means that dialogue and conflict resolution, in this case, is not difficult. However, in the traditional structure, the Village Chief and the Village Counsellor have decision making control, with the canton leader below them and the consequent household heads below them all. The usual situation for decision making is dialogue between the male village elders. It is very rare for one chief to make an independent decision.

The elders allotted a non-defined area of land to the south of the Nuni canton where the Mossi could farm (see Figure 6.2), close enough to the Nuni so that they could monitor their activities. This is, unlike the Nuni of Boutiourou, who allotted a specific land area to the Mossi where they were confined, but it is similar to the Nuni of Lon. The Mossi in Saboué have their own chief, who was the head of the first household to arrive and ask the Nuni chiefs for permission to farm.

The Mossi then operate much the same as Mossi society functions in their homelands. On their own territory they regulate their own affairs. If however, more serious problems arise which concern the wider population, the dispute is taken before the Nuni. As can be seen in Table 6.2, there is relatively little contact between the three ethnic groups (see Figure 6.5 for a spatial representation of the relative integration between the three groups in the three villages) and, as such, little need for regulation and a small chance

146 *Rebuilding the Local Landscape*

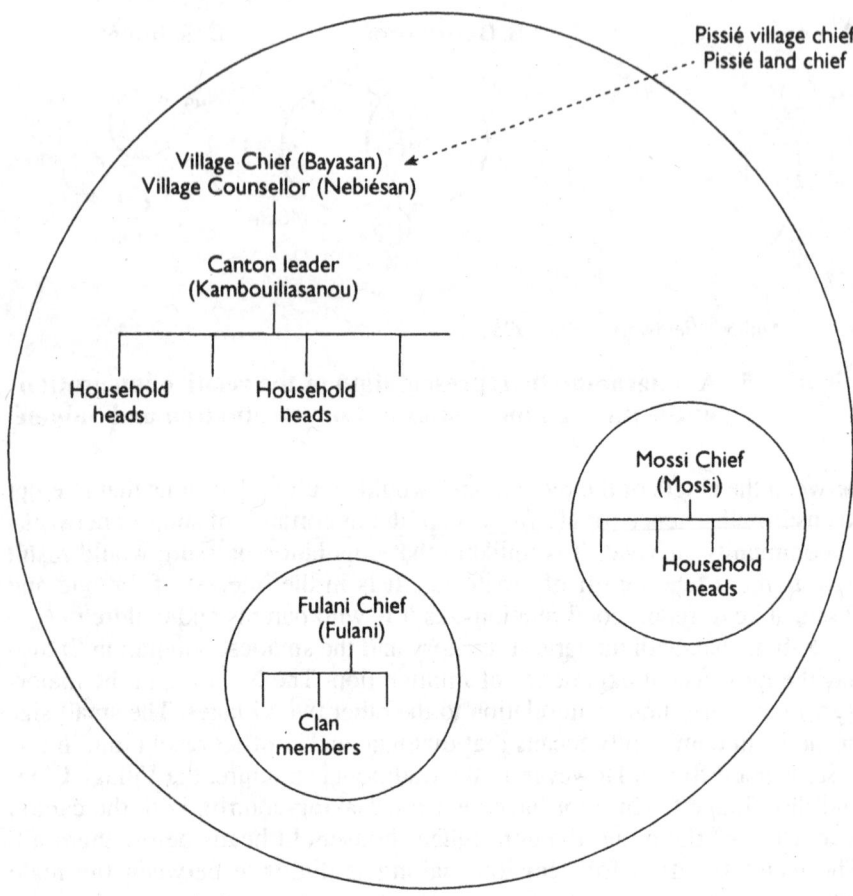

Source: Author's fieldwork, 1993–1995.

Figure 6.6 A spatial representation of the relative interaction of the three ethnic groups in Lon, Boutiourou and Saboué

of problems arising. The immigrants are very much left to themselves. This is the same for the Fulani, with chief who controls the activities of his clan members.

Ethnic Interrelationships in Saboué

The immigrants have been in Saboué for the shortest duration of the three villages and therefore the new, emerging production systems are still relatively immature. The three ethnic groups exist more or less independently of each other and contact is not at the same level as Lon or Boutiourou where ethnic contact is becoming essential for the functioning of the respective production systems, see Table 6.3.

The ethnic groups in Saboué have the least intra-ethnic contact of all the villages. This is because, at present, there is no reason to co-operate: there are no resource shortages, there is ample land available to allow for the large spatial differences in settlement patterns, and the proximity to the large market of Biéha means that intra-village trade is minimal. The proximity of Biéha, its size, its human resources (it contains extension workers from most sub-ministries, health, animal and agriculture) and its Wednesday

Table 6.3 Ethnic interrelationships in Saboué

Direction of transfer	Activities
Fulani ⟶ Mossi	• Milk products
	• Woven mats
	• Dung
	• Trade over Ghanaian frontier
Mossi ⟶ Fulani	• Labour
	• Sale of foodstuffs and cereals
	• Dolo
Fulani ⟷ Mossi	• Animal sale
Fulani ⟶ Nuni	• Milk products
	• Gifts
	• Dung
	• Animal sale
	• Grazing animals on post-harvest fields
	• Trade over Ghanaian frontier
Nuni ⟶ Fulani	• Land
	• Administration
	• Foodstuffs, cereals, tools, etc.
	• Labour
Fulani ⟷ Nuni	• Trade
Nuni ⟶ Mossi	• Land
	• Administration
Mossi ⟶ Nuni	• Dolo
	• Sale of cereals, foodstuffs, etc.
Nuni ⟷ Mossi	• Some exchange of trade and information

Source: Author's fieldwork, 1993–1995.

148 Rebuilding the Local Landscape

market means that any requirements in terms of advice, trade or commerce can be fulfilled. There are also other sizeable Mossi and Fulani communities nearer Biéha that provide points of contact for the Mossi and Fulani of Saboué.

7 Conclusion: African Realities and Western Dreams

Introduction

What becomes clear, from the arguments within this book, is that western professionals, those educated in the 'north' and development 'experts' have had problems in understanding peasant modes of production and African thought systems. In the first part of the conclusion, this substantial stumbling block is examined and pointers are given as to why it is so prevalent.

Western Scientific Thought versus Rural African Thought

> The world does not look the same from down among the millet stalks as it does from a Boeing 747. (Hart, 1982:6)

The quotation above says many things, not least about scale. It implies not only a lack of understanding of many of those who travel in aeroplanes but it also implies an inability to understand and learn. Two different worlds are in existence, worlds that are not stages in a linear development but are two separate kingdoms of existence and comprehension, operating at different levels.

Many of the problems of development come from misconceptions of problems and the inability of development professionals to understand the complex African systems of *modus operandi*. This is our[1] problem and largely stems from the assumption that 'development', as defined by capitalist economics, is a linear process of modernisation that has manifested itself by careful manipulation in western Europe, some parts of Asia and the United States of America. This is our model, our school of thought and our playground and it is this that we try to initiate in the Third World so that we can have more playmates. From this perspective, African

---

[1] In the following text when 'we' or 'us' is referred to it means western professionals who have been trained in the western school of scientific (and all its political connotations) thought.

rural communities are in a stage of development that is comparable to pre-feudal Europe. The notion of this 'stage' of development has been carried over from the colonial period (1850–1950) where the 'natives' were constructed as backward or childlike and the colonisers as rational agents of progress (Gardner and Lewis, 1996). The aim since World War II has been to speed up that process of modernisation using capitalist economics to achieve 'development'. To this end, large sums have been spent and ambitious programmes have been attempted through a global effort (north to south) but, as the Millennium is reached, Africa rural communities remain much the same as they did after World War II. Life expectancy has increased but per capita income has declined over the last 20 years (Chambers, 1997).

It would be wrong to say that the international community has not recognised the minimal impact of development programmes on local African economies and it would also be wrong to say that no efforts have been taken to address the problem. People have blamed the failures on inappropriate technology, on socialist African Governments, on a lack of participation by local people, on corruption, kleptocracies, on poorly trained African development workers and extensionists (the list goes on) while still retaining the central tenet: capitalist modernisation is the aim of all endeavours. There has been a re-examination of approach to look at failures but there has been no examination of the prevailing mode of thought in the development business. Quite simply, the crisis of development stems from the fact that African economies have separate identities and have different agendas to western economies and as a result we have understood very little of their lives and priorities. Hart (1982:126) illustrates this:

> West Africans spent a relatively small number of man-hours per year on acquiring their food, whereas by European standards they may have spent an extraordinary amount of time on funerals. Who is to say that the maintenance of relations between the living and the dead is less important than growing plants?

When we start realising that there are other economic forms, which work in non-monetary ways, then real development initiatives can be started. Why have we not been able to understand African economies?

Why We Have Not Been Able to Understand African Economies

> As captives of the systems we have created for ourselves we are not well placed to appreciate values and rationalities other than those which are modern. (Hyden, 1980:3)

The central assumption of capitalist development theory is that pre-capitalist economies must be transformed into capitalist economies which will

Conclusion: African Realities and Western Dreams 151

bring access to all modern basic needs and more. Pre-capitalist economies (as they have been dubbed by Western professionals) are low down in the linear development scale and need to be pushed up the ladder. It is necessary to put their systems aside, under the table of history, i.e. there can be no complementarity. However, like the persistence of Islam and Animism, things are rarely that cut and dry. Hart (1982:9) argues, it is not particularly useful to talk about the intrusion of 'money' or 'the cash economy' which implies an abrupt confrontation that never took place in modern times. Mauss (1954:86) adds to this point when he says, 'We should not believe that the introduction of a new economic system necessarily kills the old one, or that societies are either "traditional" or "modern" '. Why then do we expect that such things will happen in Africa?

It is necessary as a starting point to understand that African economic processes are rarely linear and are often complex and seemingly confused; African logic is different from Western logic. An example of this difficulty in understanding is African legal and tenurial arrangements that have often been under scrutiny by western observers. This has special reference to customary law and common property resource use arrangements which remain heavily studied in the hope that some classification system can be developed allowing categories to be created and understood. Thébaud (1995:6) says arrangements under common property useage rights can sometimes be disconcerting for modern law. She goes on to say (1995:12) that there is a cleavage between a European view of private property and the complexity of access and useage rights over natural resources in Africa which has always made them very difficult to understand.

The modernisation paradigm dominates mainstream thought (Gardner and Lewis, 1996) and money is the oil that makes the wheels turn. In African societies there are a great many other things which are necessary for the functioning of their economies and societies. Eriksen (1995) says, 'the economy is an integrated part of a social and cultural totality and economic systems and actions can only be fully understood if we look into their interrelationships with other aspects of culture and society'. The 'economy' is at once a universal structure and an isolated sector that cannot be understood in relation to itself alone. For example, Malinowski (1950) noted in the Trobriand Islands there is no word for 'economy' as an institution separated from social life. The complexity of the African economy has ensured its misinterpretation by western researchers who have been unwilling to loosen themselves from preconceived ideas about linear development. In addition to this, western economists have been obsessed by profit margins and the maximisation of resources. Sahlins (1972) says that the concept of the maximising individual is meaningless in societies where the unit of production is the household and not the individual; African families are optimisers, risk minimisers at best, but not maximisers. But, the question must be asked, why have we not been able to understand and accept this? Richards (1985:138) says:

> Part of the answer lies in the widespread acceptance of a model of cultural evolution grounded in the work of the Grand Theorists such as Spencer, Darwin and Marx. The problems faced by many African farmers were thought to be characteristic of a particular 'stage' in societal development. Science belonged to a later stage in this evolutionary process. It was difficult to believe that 'backward farmers might be in the process of working out relevant answers to their own problems, or had anything worth teaching to scientists, the front runners of 'progress'.

It is significant that anthropologists, not economists, have come closest to explaining African economies and they have achieved this because they have spent considerable time with the communities they have studied. They have often dubbed traditional economies as 'exchange economies' or 'gift economies'[2] and words such as 'reciprocity', 'potlatch'[3] and 'obligations' often appear in their monographs. Eriksen (1995) says that, 'A capitalist economy recognises only one form of commodity exchange, namely market exchange based on the laws of supply and demand; non-capitalist economies have many forms of exchange'. If an important part of traditional economies are made up of exchange, then it is not surprising that western economists have problems of comprehension. In their aeroplanes the object exchanged or the gift is the object of scrutiny and valuation, whilst from the millet stalks its importance is primarily in its social and cultural function. Archetti (1991) provides us with a real life scenario: whilst buying a cup of coffee for someone in a European café and bringing it to them, they immediately gave the exact money for the drink. He says that this symbolises an unwillingness to enter into a morally committing relationship with others. Thus, if professionals[4] have lost this in their societies, how can they recognise its presence or function in others?

---

2 Many of the world's economies have been described as 'gift economies', that is to say the distribution of goods takes place with no fixed price (Strathern, 1988).
3 Potlatch is derived from the Chinook American Indians and means 'to nourish' or 'to consume'. Anthropologists have adopted this word to symbolise 'gift-giving societies' (see Mauss, 1966). Anthropologists have however attributed Potlatch with antagonistic, almost aggressive, gift giving rituals, where the giver creates an oppressive bond with the receiver, forcing them to give back more than they received. This is contrary to the view expressed here. Gift giving, that forms part of a wider support network, strengthens moral bonds and obligations through the belief that it forms an effective risk minimisation strategy.
4 Professionals is used instead of society as a whole because there is much evidence of 'moral economies' and support networks in European and American society, especially amongst the poor.

Two definitions of economy have been put forward by Eriksen (1995) which ring true; a system-oriented definition (capitalist) and an actor-oriented definition (non-capitalist). They can be defined respectively as:

- a systemic definition which defines the economy in relation to the production, distribution and consumption of material and non-material goods in society; and
- an actor-centered definition which defines the economy by the ways in which the actors use the available means to maximise value.

Money cannot be used to understand human agency. Mauss (1954) says traditional systems of distribution are multicentric, which is to say that economic resources were distributed according to different principles and did not form a uniform single market (as a unicentric system does, where usually the market completely dominates).

How Can We Better Understand African Economies?

It has predominantly been the anthropologists that have held the monopoly in understanding local African societies and economies. And consequently, it has been the anthropologists that have often spoken out on misinterpretation and misconception by western professionals. One of the most famous anthropologists of modern times says:

> It is difficult to see any intellectual value in a concept of 'development' which defines it as GNP per capita. Analytically, this kind of model is unacceptably evolutionist and reductionist, since it ranks societies on an ethnocentric ladder as well as disregarding local, culturally specific value judgements. (Mauss, 1954:17)

As the years progress, there is an increasing call in the development 'business' for anthropologists because of the recognition that they have an empirical understanding of local economics which is vital for project success. The anthropological school has heavily influenced the revolution in investigative research methods and techniques used in development advocating more participation and longer research periods. This is a very important contribution.

Apart from the anthropologists, there is a range of other people who have increased the understanding of development and the approaches to implementing projects and programmes. These range from moral economists (e.g. Goran Hyden, James C. Scott) to political economists (Lionel Cliffe, E.P. Thompson, K. Hart, Phil O'Keefe) to rural development professionals (Robert Chambers, Ian Scoones, Piers Blaikie). Each of these disciplines has something to say on the prevailing modernisation paradigm and they are making a difference to the debate on development. Peet and Watts (1993) say that there is a need to help uncover the discourses of resistance to received wisdom, put them into a wider circulation and create networks of ideas.

The previous section has discussed the problems development professionals have had in understanding non-western modes of production. The following section examines what this means in the light of environmental management in Africa.

Local Environmental Management and the Emerging Development Paradigm

The difficulty in understanding rural African modes of production has led to misinterpretations of rural resource use and perceptions of environmental degradation and improvement. Indeed, more than this, it has been the fashion to blame environmental destruction on small farmers, particularly their alleged inability to adapt to rising population pressure. When the farmer's ability to adapt is admitted, it is often regarded as insufficient (Brookfield and Padoch, 1994).

These ideas pervade the major development institutions. A good example is a World Bank report (Cleaver and Schreiber, 1992) which implies mutually reinforcing links between demographic growth, poor agricultural performance and environmental degradation. The report states that traditional land use and forest exploitation practices have become the direct causes of environmental degradation and resource depletion. To return to the problems of western thought and science, there exists the basic assumption that 'natural' phenomena exist separately from human society. This distinction does not exist in many African societies, where categories of thought are structured in very different ways and cut across a nature-culture divide (Leach and Mearns, 1996).

Supporting what have been called 'crises narratives' (Blaikie, 1996) are a range of institutions which reinforce the 'received' Western wisdom. These include formal politics, education systems, legal arrangements and mass media and the projection of Africa in a global media which has a western slant. The latter, in particular, show preference for the negative and dramatic and consequently it is especially difficult to feature the positive within environmental reportage (Leach and Mearns, 1996). This cycle of reportage is self-perpetuating, as with more crisis narratives, the more the experts and academics can lay claim to resources in order to solve them, and to peoples' lives who are involved in these crises (Blaikie, 1996). Almost in patriarchal form, the 'business' feeds itself.

However, what is newly emerging is a challenge to the received wisdom or orthodoxy through new people and new forms of investigation. This new trend already has been labelled into different titles, including, neo-populist or post-modern development. What is encouraging however, is that they reject the universal truths of modernism, traditional science and meta-narratives and embrace the diversity of local realities. Brookfield and Padoch (1994:8) highlight this with a practical example:

> The number and variety of farming systems in the world exist because farmers have, over centuries, devised them to fulfil their needs in relation to the physical, biological, social, economic and political environments that they manage. As populations have grown, declined or migrated into new regions, as new crops have become available, as environments have changed through degradation or aggradation, and as the social conditions of production have varied through time, farmers have continually adapted their methods, with greater or lesser success.

Evidence of African success stories, and new ways of recognising lifescapes and how communities interact in them, are being brought forward with increasing frequency. A form of development is being offered or discovered which, according to Blaikie (1996):

- rejects modernisation as an inevitable and convergent direction of social change;
- respects local diversity and local agendas;
- recognises that truth is negotiable and variable;
- is aware of power relations appearing in knowledge construction, development priorities, research agendas and goal setting; and
- encourages local and authentic action so that people can speak and act for themselves.

It is through an approach such as this that allows a discovery of lifescapes. Thus, just as Colombus discovered the Americas (they existed long before he ever arrived!), this study discovers lifescapes in Sissili, through embracing diversity, a recognition of the simultaneity and the multi-use of environments (something which current models do not accommodate). For the purpose of lifescapes it is necessary to talk about places and people. The local ecology leads the household production pattern. In addition to this, the local political system (chefferie), the overall economic[5] atmos-

---

[5] At this juncture I am not talking about the 'penetration of capitalism' and capitalist relations. Markets in West Africa predate capitalism and entitlement exchange has happened throughout West African history through the existence of highly sophisticated non-capitalist economic systems.

phere and the local social relations all combine to create the lifescape. Another important aspect to lifescapes is their changeable natures, and there is continuity in their changing. Lifescapes have a contingency which has a temporal and locational context to it. To back up this point it is only necessary to have a brief look at West African history. Because of this complexity, it is impossible to overgeneralise about population pressure and environmental degradation in the Sahel, as has been done so often in the past.

This study has, hopefully, led to an understanding of an area inhabited by a people that were the subject of a 'crisis narrative' through the idea of a lifescape that is dynamic in space and time. Modern development views did not, or could not, conceptualise the production of nature in this area where, according to northern analysis, desertification should have been taking place.

Appendix: Land Classification Units According to de Boer, 1992

The following classification has been translated from de Boer (1992) who has based his system on studies by Sow and Zombre (1989) and Egging (1990).

S – Low density woody savanna on rocky outcrops

This unit represents rocky outcrops, where one finds granite outcrops and a gravelly surface soil cover. Common features are plateaus with attached cliffs with bare soils and rock outcrops. The soils are very shallow and extremely fragile. Vegetation is made up of small trees and bushes: *C. glutinosum, D. microcarpum, B. africana, S. tormentosa, Stryclinos spinosa*. Tree density is taken at 15–20 trees per hectare and 50–60 bushes/ha. Average tree height is 12–15 m and 0.5–3 m for bushes. The dominant plant species are *Microcloa indica* and *Loudetia togoensis*. There are few perennial grasses present. This land class is rarely farmed.

D – Low density woody savanna

This unit is found in the same general area as unit S but has less rocky outcrops. It is often found on the tops of hills with shallow and gravelly soils with the hard laterite layer found deeper here than in unit S. There are no cliffs present. The low density vegetation is characterised by *D. microcarpum, C. glutinosum, B. africana* and *L. acida*. Tree and bush density is 15–35/ha and 50–80/ha respectively, with heights of 12–15 m and 1–3 m. There are low density grasses, *Andropogon ascinodidis* and *Schyzachyrium domingense* being the most important. This land class is also rarely farmed.

A – Dense woody savanna

This undulating land form is found on the edges of the province on the slopes. The soils are sandy gravel with some agricultural potential. There is a rich vegetation cover with a high pasture potential. Trees include: *I. doka, D. olivera, P. biglobosa, V. paradoxa, B. parkii* and *Gardenia spp*. One finds 25–60 trees/ha, ranging from 12–15 m in height. Bushes number greater than 100 per hectare and are 1–3 m high. Perennial grass cover, predominantly of *A. ascinodis* is good in terms of quality and percentage area cover.

Sb – Bush savanna

The bush savanna covers a large area and is easily recognisable on aerial photos by its spread, regular texture and grey colour. The soils are sandy-limonitic with some gravel and are more fertile than the previous units. It is found on the lower slopes, often in depressions or near to valley bottoms, and has a high agricultural potential. These areas are coming under pressure from agricultural expansion and are disappearing in areas of widespread farming. There is a inverse relationship between bush savanna and the area of the cultivated surface. Dominant species include: *V. paradoxa*, *B. parkii*, *C. glutinosum*, *Gardenia spp* and *P. biglobosa*. Tree density is 20–50 trees/ha at heights of 13–16 m, there are more than 100 bushes/ha with heights from 0.5–2 m. Perennial grasses cover approximately 10 per cent of surface area and include *Andropogonae* and *S. domingense*.

B – Forested savanna

This vegetation class is found on the sides of hills with an undulating relief pattern and sandy-limestone soils. Trees include: *P. biglobosa*, *P. thonningii*, *D. glomerata* and *B. parkii*. There are 30–50 trees/ha at 13–16 m. There are 30–40 bushes/ha at heights of between 1 and 3 m. The dominant perennial grass is *A. ascinodis*.

C – Fields or fallows on slopes

These are the areas where agriculture is concentrated and are found throughout the province on slopes, depressions and often near valley bottoms. The soils are sandy-limestone with no gravel. Cereal production dominates the farming system, mostly sorghum and millet. Trees include *V. paradoxa*, *P. biglobosa* and *B. parkii*. There are many annual grasses, such as *Eragrostis aspera*, *Schyzachirium exile* and *Eragrostis tremula*. Because of the regenerative characteristics over time there are no data available on tree height or density.

R – Low density riparian forest

These are found throughout the province in the valley bottoms and along drainage routes. Relief is flat or undulating. Soils contain more limonite and detrific sedementry rock (fertile) – texture is limonitic-argillic. Tree species include *K. senegalensis, P .thonningii* and *Ficus spp.* There are 10–30 trees/ha with heights of 13–17 m. Bush density is 60–80/ha at 2–5 m. The dominant perennial grass is *A. gayanus.*

F – Dense riparian forest

These are dense forested areas which include gallery forests which are concentrated along the principal drainage routes and the main rivers in Sissili. The soils are heavier compared to low density riparian forests with an argillic-limonitic texture. Species include *K. senegalensis, D. olivera, M. inermis,* A. leiocarpus and *Palmae spp.* There are 70–80 trees/ha at 15–20 m. Bushes have a density of 15–20 per hectare.

P – Humid prairie or swamp

This unit is found in drainage zones which are prone to flooding. They contain heavy, argillic soils and have no trees. Plants include *E. stagina, Hyparrhenia rufa, Panicum spp* and *C. obtusifolia.* The high herbaceous cover gives this unit high pasture potential.

b – Fields or fallows in valley bottoms

There are limonitic and argillic soils. This area is often used for rice production.

N – Bare soil

The bare soils are found in small land parcels, on hilltops near rock outcrops.
The table on page 160 gives a summary of the information in the classification system.

Table A.1 Characteristics of land classification units as described by de Boer (1992)

Unit	Description	Soils	Woody Biomass	A	B	Herbaceous spp	C
S Low density woody savanna on rocky outcrops	rocky outcrop with cliffs	lateritic or granite crust with rocky outcrop	C.glutinosum D.microcarpum B.africana	15–20	50–60	L.togoensis A.ascinodis M.indica	0.9
D Low density woody savanna	hilltops	gravel, granite	D.microcarpum. C.glutinosum. B.africana L.acida	15–35	50–80	A.ascinodis Cochlospermum sp S.domingense M.indica	7.0
H Hilltop fields or fallows	hilltops	sandy	Crops V.paradoxa			Crops (millet, groundnut)	
A Dense woody savanna	undulating higher slopes	sandy-gravel	I.doka D.olivera V.paradoxa Gardenia spp B.parkii	25–60	100+	A.ascinodis	10
Sb Bush savanna	undulating bottom slopes	gravel, sandy limonite	V.paradoxa P.biglobosa Terminalia spp B.parkii	20–50	150+	A.gayanus A.ascinodis S.domingense	10
B Forest savanna	undulating	sandy-limonite	V.paradoxa P.biglobosa B.parkii P.thonningii D.glomerata	30–50	30–40	A.ascinodis	0–10

Appendix   161

Table A.1   Characteristics of land classification units as described by de Boer (1992) (continued)

Unit	Topography	Soil	A	B	C	Species	
C Fields or fallows on slopes	undulating	sandy-limonite				Crops *V.paradoxa*	Crops (sorghum, millet, maize)
R Low density riparian forest	Flat, undulating	alluvial, limonite-argillic	10–30	60–80	6.5	*K.senegalensis* *A.sieberiana* *P.thonningii* *Ficus spp*	*Sporobulus spp* *A.gayanus*
F Dense riparian forest	flat	alluvial, argillic	70–80	30–40	6.5	*K.senegalensis* *Palmae spp* *D.olivera* *M.inermis* *A.leiocarpus*	*A.gayanus*
P Humid prairie or swamp	flat	alluvial, argillic			>10		*Echinochloa sp* *Hyparrhenia sp* *Panicum spp* *C.obtusifolia*
b Field or fallow in valley bottom	flat	alluvial limonitic to argillic				Crops	Crops (rice)
N Bare soil	undulating to flat	varied					

Key: A: trees per hectare; B: bushes per hectare; C: percentage cover by perennial grasses.
Source: Adapted from: Sow & Zombre 1989, Egging 1990, de Boer 1992.

References

Adams, A. (1993), 'Food insecurity in Mali: exploring the role of the moral economy', *IDS Bulletin*. Vol. 24, No. 4.
Adams, W. M. (1996), 'Irrigation, erosion and famine; visions of environmental change in Marakwet, Kenya', In, Leach, M. Mearns, R. (eds). (1996), *The lie of the land: challenging received wisdom on the African environment*. International African Institute.
Agrawal, A. (1995), 'Dismantling the divide between indigenous and scientific knowledge', *Development and change*. Vol. 26, pg. 413–439.
Agrotechnik. (1991), *Etude de protection et valorisation du milieu naturel dans le cadre de programme de développement rural de la province de la Sissili*. Ministère de l'Environnement et du Tourisme, Ouagadougou.
Ahmad, E. and Hussain, A. (1991), 'Social security in China: a historical perspective', In, Drèze, J. Ahmad, E. Hills, J. and Sen, A. (eds). (1991), *Social security in developing countries*, Oxford.
Amanor, K. S. (1995), 'Dynamics of herd structures and herding strategies in West Africa – a study of market integration and ecological adaption', *Africa*, Vol 65, Part 3, pg. 351–394.
Anon. (1990), *Environmental management and local organisation; an example of success – the Naam movement in Burkina Faso*. Ph.D., Harvard, U.S.A.
Archetti, E. P. (1991), 'De l'idéologie du pouvoir; analyse culturelle comparative', In, Klausen, A. M. (ed). (1991), *Le savoir-être Norvegién: regards anthropologiques sur la culture Norvegienne*. Paris, Harmattan.
Atampugre, N. (1994), *Food security and social transformation in Burkina Faso: a case study of Nahouri province*. Ph.D., University of Leeds.
Bassolet, B. Boly, M. and Wetta, C. (1991), 'Diagnostic du phenomene migratoire dans la Sissili, Rapport provisoire', Ministere de l'Action Cooperative Paysanne, Burkina Faso.
Batterbury, S. (1994), *Conservation and community: local organisations and environmental management in Burkina Faso*. West London papers in environmental Studies 2. London.
Beck, T. (1994), *The experience of poverty: fighting for respect and resources in village India*. IT Publications. London
Beets, W. (1990), *Raising and sustaining productivity of smallholder farming systems in the tropics*. AgBé Publishing, Holland.
Berger-Sarl, L. (1989), *Programme de développement et l'amenagement rural – Tome II – rapport definitif*. Sixiéme FED, Ministére du plan et de la coopération, Burkina Faso.
Berry, S. (1983), 'Agrarian crisis in Africa? a review and an interpretation', Paper presented for the Joint African studies committee of the social science research council and the

References

American council of learned societies. Boston, U.S.A.
—. (1986), 'Macro-policy implications of research on rural households and farming systems', In, Moock, J. L. (ed). (1986), *Understanding Africa's rural households and farming systems.* Westview press. London.
Bindlish, V. Evenson, R. and Gbetibouo, M. (1993), *Evaluation of T&V-based extension in Burkina Faso.* The World Bank, U.S.A.
Blaikie, P. (1996), 'New knowledge and rural development: a review of views and practicalities', a paper for *The 28th international geographical congress.* The Hague, Aug 5–10.
Blaikie, P. Brown, K. Stocking, M. Tang, L. Sillitoe, P. and Dixon, P. (1996), 'Understanding local knowledge and the dynamics of technical change in developing countries', Socio-economic methodologies workshop. *ODA natural resources systems programme.* London.
Boserup, E. (1972), *The conditions of agricultural growth; the economics of agrarian change under population pressure.* Unwin University books. London.
Boudet, G. (1984), *Manuel sur les pâturages tropicaux et les cultures fourragères.* La documentation Française, Paris.
Bourdieu, P. (1977), *Outline of a theory of practice.* Cambridge studies in social anthropology 16, Cambridge University Press. Cambridge.
Boutrais, J. and Bassett, T. (1996), 'Cattle and reforestation in the West African Sahel', Paper presented at the Centre For West African Studies workshop Contested terrain, University of Birmingham. 12–13th April, (1996.
Breman, L. and de Ridder, J. (1991), *Manuel sur les pâturages des pays Sahéliens.* Kathala, Paris.
Brookfield, H. and Padoch, C. (1994), 'Appreciating agrodiversity: a look at the dynamism and diversity of indigenous farming practices', *Environment.* Vol. 36, Part 5, pg. 7–11.
Buchan, D. (1994), 'IMF persuades French West Africa to go for growth: the CFA bloc's devaluation will ensure the adjustment needed for revival', *Financial Times* newspaper, 13 January.
Bunasol. (1990), *Caractérisation des sols du centre-sud de la province de la Sissili et esquisse pedologique.* Rapport technique No. 69. Bunasol, Ouagadougou, Burkina Faso.
Byerlee, D. Harrington, L. and Winkelmann, T. (1982), 'Farming systems research: issues in research strategy and technology design', *American Journal of Agricultural Economics,* 64, 5:897–904.
Chambers, R. (1983), *Rural development: putting the last first.* Longman. London.
—. (1994), *Challenging the professions; frontiers for rural development.* IT publications. London.
—. (1997), *Whose reality counts? putting the first last.* IT publications. London.
Chambers, R. Pacey, A. and Thrupp, L. A. (eds). (1989), *Farmer first: farmer innovation and agricultural research.* IT publications. London.
Chayanov, A. (1925), 'Organizalsiya krest yanskogo khozyaistva', translated as 'The theory of peasant economy' by Thorner, D. Smith, R. E. F. and Kerblay, B. (eds) in Shanin, T. (1975), *Peasants and peasant societies.* Penguin, Middlesex, pg. 35.
Christoplos, I. (1995), *Representation, poverty and PRA in the Mekong Delta.* Research Report No.6 from EPOS, Linkoping University, Sweden.
Cleaver, K. M. and Schreiber, G. A. (1992), *The population, agriculture and environment nexus in sub-Saharan Africa.* World Bank, Washington D.C.

Cliffe, L. (1987), 'The debate on African peasantries', *Development and change*. Vol. 18, Part 4, pg. 625–636.
Clifton, R. and Wharton, Jr. (1971), 'Risk, uncertainty, and the subsistence farmer', In, Dalton, G. (1971), *Economic development and social change; the modernisation of village communities*. Natural history press. London.
Cline-Cole, R. (1996), 'Colonial science and its relics in West Africa', In, Leach, L. and Mearns, R. (1996), *The lie of the land: challenging received wisdom on the African environment*. International African Institute. London.
Collingwood, R. G. (1940), *An essay on metaphysics*. Clarendon Press, Oxford.
Cordell, D. Gregory, J. and Piché, V. (1996), *Hoe and wage: a social history of a circular migration system in west Africa*. Westview press. London.
Cornwall, A. and Fleming, S. (1995), 'Context and complexity: anthropological reflections on PRA, Critical reflections from practice', *PLA Notes*, No.24, IIED.
Dahl, G. and Hjort, A. (1976), *Having herds*. Dept of Social Anthropology, University of Stockholm.
de Boer, W.F. and Kessler, J. (1994), *Le sytème d'élevage Peulh dans le sud du Burkina Faso: une étude agro-écologique du département de Tô (Province de la Sissili)*. Documents sur la Gestion des Ressources Tropicales 4. Holland.
de Boer, W.F. (1992), *Veaux, vaches et vegetation*. PDCS, SNV, Burkina Faso.
De Bolster, H. (1992), *Quel avenir pour Sapouy?*. unpublished project document, Oxfam-Belgique, Projet UPV/AGIS, Burkina Faso.
De Selincourt, K. (1996), 'Demon farmers and other myths', *The New Scientist*. No.2027. pg. 36–40.
de Vries, P. W. T. and Djitèye, M. A. (1982), *La productivité des pâturages Sahélians*. Cabo, Wageningen.
Delgado, C. L. (1979), 'The southern Fulani farming system in the Upper Volta: a model for the integration of crop and livestock production in the West African Savanna', *African Rural Economy*. Part 20. Michigan State University, USA.
Diarra, S. Defoer, T. and Hilhorst, T. (1995), *Note méthodologique: pour la cartographie paysanne du terroir villageois*. IER, Bamako, Mali.
Dickens, E. (1988 to 1995), Technical assistant for DED in Djibo, Burkina Faso.
Dobrowolski, K. (1958), 'Peasant traditional culture', In Shanin, T. (1975), *Peasants and peasant societies*. Penguin. Middlesex.
Dreze, J. and Sen, A. K. (1989), *Hunger and public action*. Oxford University Press. Oxford.
Dubois, M. (1991), 'The governance of the Third World; a Foucauldian perspective', *Alternatives*. Vol. 16, pg. 1–30.
Duperray, A. (1984), *Les Gourounsi de Haute-Volta: conquête et colonisation 1896–1933*. Franz Steiner Verlag Wiesbaden GMBH.
Duval, M. (1985), *Un totalitarisme sans etat, essai d'anthropologie politique à partir d'un village burkinabé*. Editions L'Harmattan, Paris
Economist Intelligence Unit (EIU). (1991), *Niger-Burkina country profile*. EIU.
Egging, P. (1990), *La capacité de charge du Département de Tô*. PDCS, Léo, Burkina Faso.
Eklan, W. (1960), *Migrants and proletarians: urban labour in the economic development of Uganda*. Oxford University Press. Oxford.
Engberg-Pedersen, L. (1995), 'Creating local democratic politics from above: the 'Gestion de Terroirs' approach in Burkina Faso', *Drylands programmes issue paper No. 54*. IIED. London.

References

Eriksen, T. H. (1995), *Small places, large issues; an introduction to social and cultural anthropology*. Pluto press. London.
Ernst, K. (1976), *Tradition and progress in the African village: the non-capitalist transformation of rural communities in Mali*. Hurst & Company London.
ETC International. forthcoming. *Participatory technology development training guide*. ETC Publications, Leusden, The Netherlands.
Evans-Pritchard, E. E. (1951), *Kinship and marriage among the Nuer*. Oxford University Press. Oxford.
Fafchamps, M. (1992), 'Solidarity networks in preindustrial societies: rational peasants with a moral economy', *Economic development and cultural change*. University of Chicago, USA.
Fairhead, J. and Leach, L. (1996), *Misreading the African landscape; Society and ecology in a forest-savanna mosaic*. Cambridge University Press. Cambridge.
FAO. (1983), *L'inventaire forestier national*. Ouagadougou. Burkina Faso.
—. (1990), Project document. BKF/87/020. Ouagadougou, Burkina Faso.
—. (1990), Project document. BKF/885/011. Ouagadougou, Burkina Faso.
—. (1996), *World Food Summit Final Report – Part 1*. FAO, Rome.
Faure, G. (1994), 'Mecanisation, productivité du travail et risques: le cas de Burkina Faso', *Economie Rurale*. Vol 219, pg. 3–11.
Fei quoted in Bendix, R. and Lipset, S. M. (1953), 'Class, status and power: a reader in social stratification', Free press quoted In Shanin, T. (1975), *Peasants and peasant societies*. Penguin. pg. 245. Middlesex.
Fleuret, A., (1986), 'Indigenous responses to drought in Sub-Saharan Africa', *Disasters*. Vol 10, Part 3, pg. 224–229.
Fortin, D. Lô, M. and Maynart, G. (1990), *Plantes médicinales du Sahel*. CECI-ENDA.
Galeski, B. (1963), 'Chlopi I zawod rolnika. Warsaw', quoted In Shanin, T. (1975), *Peasants and peasant societies*. Penguin, pg. 242. Middlesex.
Gardner, K. and Lewis, D. (1996), *Anthropology, development and the post-modern challenge*. Pluto Press. London.
Geerling, C. (1987), *Guide de terrain des ligneux Sahéliens et soudano-guinéens*. Agricultural University, Wageningen.
Giblin, J. Maddox, G. and Kimambo, I. N. (eds). (1996), *Custodians of the land: ecology and culture in the history of Tanzania*. Villiers Publications, London.
Gijsbers, H. J. M. Kessler, J. J. and Knevel, M. K. (1994), 'Dynamics of natural regeneration of woody species in farmed parklands in the Sahel region', *Forest, ecology and management*, Vol 64, Part 1.
Glantz, M. H. (1987), *Drought and hunger in Africa: denying famine a future*. Cambridge University Press. Cambridge.
Goodenough, W. H. (1955), 'A problem in Malayo-Polynesian social organisation', *American anthropologist*. Vol 57, pg. 71–83.
Governement du Burkina Faso. (1986), *Premier plan de développement de la Sissili*. Ouagadougou.
Gugler, J. and Flanagan, W. (1978), *Urbanisation and social change in West Africa*. Cambridge University Press. Cambridge.
Guijt, I. and Cornwall, A. (1995), 'Editorial: critical reflections on the practice of PRA', *Critical reflections from practice*. PLA Notes, No.24, IIED.

Guinko, S. and Pasgo, L. J. (1992), 'Harvesting and marketing of edible products from local woody species in Zitenga, Burkina Faso', *Unasylva*, Vol.43, Part 169, pg. 16–19.

Guyer, J. I. (1986), 'Intra-household processes and farming systems research: perspectives from anthropology', In, Moock, J. L. (ed). (1986), *Understanding Africa's rural households and farming systems*. Westview Press. London.

Hailey, (1938), *An African survey: a study of problems arising in Africa south of the Sahara*. Oxford University Press. Oxford.

Harrison, P. (1987), *The greening of Africa: breaking through in the battle for land and food*. Paladin. London.

Hart, K. (1982), *The political economy of West African agriculture*. Cambridge University Press. Cambridge.

Heidenreich, A. and Cherret, I. (1992), *An assessment of environmental NGOs in eastern and southern Africa*. HIVOS, The Netherlands.

Hill, P. (1977), *Population, prosperity and poverty: rural Kano, 1900 and 1970*. Cambridge University Press. Cambridge.

Hoben, A. (1995), 'Paradigms and politics: the cultural construction of environmental policy in Ethiopia', *World Development*. 23 (6), pg.1007–1022.

Hopkins, H. (1974), *Forest and savanna*. 2nd edition, Heineman. Portsmouth.

Howorth, C. (1992), 'Energy transitions in Africa', *Boiling point*, No. 27, ITDG.

Howorth, C. and Cliffe, L. (1991), *Manual for participatory approaches to rural development*. FAO, Rome.

Howorth, C. and Konaté, O. (1995), 'Agroforestry Farming Systems Research and an examination of traditional medicine in the province of Sissili, Burkina Faso', unpublished project document, Lutheran World Relief, Niger and UNAIS, Burkina Faso, York.

—. (1995), 'Traditional medicine and tree planting in Burkina Faso', *Baobab Journal*. Oxfam, ALIN, November.

Howorth, C. O'Keefe, P. and Kirkby, J. (1993), 'Whatever happened to Brazil, 1992: an earth charter for whom?', In, Dahl, J. Drakakis-Smith, D. and Närman, N. (eds). (1993), *Land, food and basic needs in developing countries*, University of Göteborg, Sweden.

Hyden, G. (1980), *Beyond Ujamaa in Tanzania; underdevelopment and an uncaptured peasantry*. University of California Press. USA.

—. (1983), *No shortcuts to progress: African development management in perspective*, Heinemann. Portsmouth.

—. (1986), 'The invisible economy of smallholder agriculture in Africa', In, Moock, J. L. (ed). (1986), *Understanding Africa's rural households and farming systems*. Westview press. London.

—. (1996), Pers.comm. via letter.

Illiasu, A. A. (1971), 'The origins of the Mossi-Dagomba states', *Research review*. pg. 95–113.

INSD. (1993), *Annuaire Statistique du Burkina Faso*. Government of Burkina Faso. Ouagadougou. Burkina Faso.

INYPSA/BDPA-SCETAGRI/SOPEX (IBS). (1994), *Cartographie complementaire de la province de la Sissili: notice cartographique*. Programme de développement rural dans la province de la Sissili, FED, Burkina Faso.

Ionescu, G. and Gellner, E. (Eds). (1969), *Populism: its meanings and national characteristics*. Weidenfeld and Nicolson, London.

Jeune Afrique Economique. (1993), No. 173, pg. 174–179.

Jones, G. H. (1936), *The earth goddess: a study of the farming on the West African coast.* Longman, Green. London.
Junzo, K. (1993), 'Oral history and the imagination of the past', *Annales – economies societes civilisations,* Vol 48, Part 4, pg. 1087–1105.
Kinsey, B. H. and Binswanger, H. P. (1993), 'Characteristics and performance of resettlement programmes: a review', In, Kinsey, B. H. Binswanger, H. P. and Christiansen, R. E. (eds), Rooyen, J van (ed), and Cooper, D. *Experience with agricultural policy: some lessons for South Africa.* World Development, Vol 21, Part 9, pg. 1477–1494.
Kirkby, J. O'Keefe, P. and Timberlake, L. (eds). (1995), *The earthscan reader in sustainable development.* Earthscan. London.
Kitching, G. N. (1982), *Development and underdevelopment in an historical perspective: populism, nationalism and industrialisation.* Methuen, London.
Klintz, (1982), 'Pastoralisme: agro-pastoralisme et organisation foncière: le cas des Peulhs', In, le Bris, E. le Roy, E. Leimdorfer, F. (eds). *Enjeux fonciers en Afrique noire.* Orstom, Bondy. Paris.
Konaté, O. (1993 to 1995), 'Technical Assistant in agroforestry and agriculture with ADESSI', Léo, Burkina Faso.
Kowal, J. M. and Kassam, A. H. (1978), *Agricultural ecology of savanna: a study of West Africa,* Clarendon press. Oxford.
Last, M. (1980), 'Conservative change proceedings. Conference on change in rural Hausaland, Baguda. March 1980', In, Richards, P. (1985), *Indigenous African Revolution.* Hutchinson. London.
Laurent, P. J. and Mathieu, P. (1994), 'Migrations, environnement et projet de développement. Récit d'un conflit foncier entre Nuni et Mossi, au Burkina Faso', In, *Cahiers du cidep 20: Migrations et access à la terre au Burkina Faso.* Academia and Harmattan. Paris.
Le Houérou, C. and Hoste, T. (1977), In, Breman, L. de Ridder, J. (1991), *Manuel sur les pâturages des pays Sahélians.* Kathala, Paris.
Le Roy, E. (1990), 'Le justiciable africain et la redécouverte d'une voie négociée de règlement des conflits', *Afrique contemporaire,* Vol.156, Part 4, pg. 111–120.
Leach, M. and Mearns, R. (eds). (1996), *The lie of the land: challenging received wisdom on the African environment.* International African Institute. London.
—. (1996), 'Environmental change and policy; challenging received wisdom in Africa', In, Leach, M. and Mearns, R. (eds). (1996), *The lie of the land: challenging received wisdom on the African environment.* International African Institute. London.
Les Atlas Jeune Afrique. (1993), *Atlas du Burkina Faso.* Les Editions, Paris.
Lévi-Strauss, C. (1963), *Structural anthropology.* Penguin. Middlesex.
Low, A. (1984), *Household economics in Southern Africa.* Mbabane, Swaziland, Typescript.
Maiga, A. (1987), *L'arbre dans les systèmes agroforestiers traditionnels dans la Province du Bazega.* Université de Ouagadougou – IDR.
Malinowski, B. (1950), (3rd Ed) *Argonauts of the western Pacific.* Routledge and Kegan Paul. London.
Marchal, J. Y. (1982), 'L'option pour l'extensif l'evolution de l'agriculture Mossi', *Economie rurale.*
Marx, K. (1850), 'Peasantry as a class', In Shanin, T. (1975), *Peasants and peasant societies.* Penguin. Middlesex.

Mathieu, P. (1994), 'Mouvements de population et transformations agricoles: le cas du sud-ouest du Burkina Faso', In, *Cahiers du cidep 20: Migrations et access à la terre au Burkina Faso.* Academia and Harmattan. Paris.

Mauss, M. (1966), (translated by Ian Cunnison). *The gift: forms and functions of exchange in archaic societies.* Cohen & West.

Meillassoux, C. (1981), *Maidens, meal and money: capitalism and the domestic community.* Cambridge University Press. Cambridge.

Messer, E. (1989), 'Seasonality in food systems: an anthropological perspective on household food security', In Shan, D. E. *Seasonal variability in Third World agriculture.* pg. 151–175.

Middleton, N. O'Keefe, P. and Moyo, S. (1993), *The tears of the crocodile; whatever happened to UNCED (1992?.* Earthscan. London.

Millington, A. C. Critchley, R.W. Douglas, T. D, Ryan, P. Bevan, R. Kirkby, J. O'Keefe, P. and Ryle, I. (1994), *Estimating Woody Biomass in Sub-Saharan Africa.* World Bank.

Ministère du Plan et de la Cooperation. (1988), *Recensement de la population, 1985: structure par age et sexe des villages du Burkina Faso.* INSD, Ouagadougou. Burkina Faso.

Mintzberg, H. (1994), *The rise and fall of strategic planning.* Prentice Hall, Hertfordshire.

Moyo, S. (1995), *The land question in Zimbabwe.* SAPES books, Harare.

Mukhin, V. (1888), 'Obychnyi poryadok nasledovaniya krest'yan, St Petersburg', quoted In, Shanin, T. (1975), *Peasants and peasant societies.* Penguin, pg. 242. Middlesex.

New Internationalist. (1995), Issue 268.

O'Keefe, P. and Smith, N. (1989), 'Geography, Marx and the concept of nature', *Antipode.* Vol 12, No.2.

O'Keefe, P. and Van Gelder, B. (1995), *The new forester.* IT Publications. London.

O'Keefe, P. and Wisner, B. (eds). (1977), *Land use and development.* International African institute for environment training, African environment special report.

O'Keefe, P. Raskin, P. and Bernow, S. (1982), *Energy in Kenya; opportunities and constraints.* Beijer Institute, Stokholm.

OCDE. Club du Sahel. CILSS. (1995), *Approche 'Gestion de Terroirs' analyse et évolution.* Mission de dialogue avec les projets GESTION DE TERROIRS/GR du Club du Sahel au Burkina Faso, au Niger et au Mali, 1994–95, Rapport de mission, OCDE, Paris.

ODA. (1997), *Natural resource systems programme.* ODA, London.

Olivier de Sardan, J. P. (1990), 'Populisme, developpementiste et populisme en sciences sociales: idéologie, action, connaissance', *Cartiers d'etudes Africaines.* Vol. 120, pg. 475–492.

Opeloye, M. O. (1996), 'Evolution of religious culture among the Yoruba of Nigeria', *Islamic Culture.* Vol. LXX, No.2.

Ouena, N. A. (1994), *Problematique de financement des activités des organisations paysannes par le credit culture attelée.* Memoire de fin de cycle des eleves – conseillers FJA, Ministère de l'Agriculture et des Ressources Animales. Burkina Faso.

Pearce, D. Markandya, A. and Barbier, B. (1992), *Blueprint for a green economy.* Earthscan. London.

—. (1994), *Sustainable development: economics and environment in the Third World.* Earthscan. London.

Peet, R. and Watts, M. (1993), 'Development theory and environment in an age of market triumphalism', *Economic geography.* Vol. 69, Part 3.

Platteau, J. (1991), 'Traditional systems of social security and hunger insurance: past acheivements and modern challenges', In, Drèze, J. Ahmad, E. Hills, J. and Sen, A. (eds). (1991), *Social security in developing countries*. Oxford.
Pottier, J. (1993), 'Migration as hunger-coping strategy: paying attention to gender and historical change', *Institutional issues in natural resource management*. Occasional Paper No.9, International Development Studies, Roskilde University, Denmark.
Pradervand, P. (1989), *Listening to Africa: developing Africa from the grassroots*. Praegar, New York.
Pretty, J. N. (1994), 'Alternative systems of inquiry for sustainable development', *IDS bulletin*. Vol. 25, Part 2, University of Sussex. Brighton.
Pretty, J. N. Guijt, I. Thompson, J. and Scoones, I. (1995), *Participatory learning and action: a trainer's guide*. IIED Participatory Methodologies Series, IIED, London.
Prudencio, C. Y. (1993), 'Ring management of soils and crops in the West African semi-arid tropics: the case of the Mossi farming system in Burkina Faso', *Agriculture, ecosystems and environment*. Vol. 47, pg. 237–264.
Rahnema, M. (1988), 'Power and regenerative power in micro-spaces', *International social science journal*. XL (118).
Redclift, M. (1987), *Sustainable development: exploring the contradictions*. Routledge. London.
Richards, P. (1985), *Indigenous african revolution*. Hutchinson. London.
—. (1995), 'Participatory Rural Appraisal: a quick and dirty critique', *Critical reflections from practice*. PLA Notes, No.24, IIED.
Roche, C. (1994), 'Operationality in turbulence: the needs for change', *Development in practice*. Vol. 4, Part 2.
Rostow, W. W. (1978), *The world economy: history and prospect*. MacMillan, London.
Sahlins, M. (1972), *Stone age economics*. Aldine Atherton Inc.
Samatar, S. S. (1991), *Somalia: a nation in turmoil*. A minority rights group report.
Sampson, H. C. Crowther, E. M. (1943), *Crop production and soil fertility problems*. The West Africa Commission (1938–39: technical reports (part 1), Leverhulme Trust, London.
Sauerborn, R. Adams, A. and Hien, M. (1996), 'Household strategies to cope with the economic costs of illness', *Social science and medicine*, Vol 43, Part 3, pg. 291–301.
Savonnet, G. (1970), *Pina: étude d'un terroir de front pionner en pays dagari (Haute Volta)*. Mouton & Co. Paris.
Savonnet-Guyot, C. (1986), *Etat et Sociétés au Burkina*. Karthala, Paris.
Sawadogo, K. Reardon, T. and Pietola, K. (1994), 'Farm productivity in Burkina Faso, effects of animal traction and non-farm income', *American Journal of Agricultural Economics*. Vol 76, Part 3, pg. 608–612.
Schreckenberg, K. (1995), 'The respective merits of RRA and conventional methods for longer-term research', *Critical reflections from practice*. PLA Notes, No.24, IIED. London.
—. (1996), *Forests, fields and markets: a study of indigenous tree products in the woody savannas of the Bassila region, Benin*. Ph.D. Thesis, SOAS, University of London.
Schumacher, E. F. (1973), *Small is beautiful: economics as if people mattered*. Harper and Row. London.
Scoones, I. (1995), 'PRA and anthropology: challenges and dilemmas', *Critical reflections*

from practice, PLA Notes, No.24, IIED. London.
Scoones, I. Thompson, J. (eds). (1994), *Beyond farmer first*. IT Publications. London.
Scott, J. C. (1976), *The moral economy of the peasant; rebellion and subsistence in Southeast Asia*. Yale university press. USA.
Sen, A. K. (1982), *Poverty and famines: an essay on entitlement and deprivation*. Clarendon Press, Oxford.
Sen, A. K. (1983), 'Poor relatively speaking', *Oxford economic papers*. Vol. 35, pg. 153–169.
Shanin, T. (1966), 'The peasantry as a political factor', In, Shanin, T. (1975), *Peasants and peasant societies*. Penguin. Middlesex.
Skinner, E. P. (1964), *The Mossi of Upper Volta: the political development of a Sudanese people*. Stanford University Press.
Slocum, R. Wichhart, L. Rocheleau, D. and Thomas Slayter, B. (eds). (1995), *Power, process and participation – tools for change*, IT publications. London.
Somé, S. and McSweeney, K. (1996), 'Assessing sustainability in Burkina Faso', *ILEIA Newsletter*. ETC Leusden, The Netherlands.
Songre, A. Sawadogo, J. M. and Sanogoh, G. (1974), 'Réalités et effets de l'émigration massives des Voltaïques dans la contexte de l'Afrique Occidentale', In Amin, S. (ed). *Modern migrations in West Africa*.
Sow, N. E. and Zombré, P. (1989), *Etude de l'occupation des sols*. PPDAK, Centre Régional de Télédéction, Ouagadougou, Burkina Faso.
Spencer-Trimingham, J. (1959), *Islam in West Africa*. Oxford
Stamm, V. (1994), 'Non commercial systems of land allocation and their economic implications; evidence from Burkina Faso', *Journal of modern African studies*. Vol 32, Part 4, pg. 713–717.
Strathern, M. (1988), *The gender of the gift: problems with women and problems with society in Melanesia*. University of California Press. USA.
Sutton, J. E. G. (1990), *A thousand years of East Africa*. British Institute in Eastern Africa, Nairobi, Kenya.
Thébaud, B. (1995), 'Land tenure, environmental degradation and desertification in Africa', *Drylands networks programme issues paper*. No.57, IIED. London.
Thomas, A. and Potter, D. (1992), 'Development, capitalism and the nation state', In, Allen, T. Thomas, A. (1992), *Poverty and development in the 1990s*. Open University Press.Milton Keynes.
Thomas, W. I. and Znaniecki, F. (1918), 'The Polish peasant in Europe and America', Dover publications. 1958. quoted In Shanin, T. (1975), *Peasants and peasant societies*. Penguin. pg. 242. Middlesex.
Tiffen, M. Mortimore, M. and Gichuki, F. (1994), *More people, less erosion; environmental recovery in Kenya*. John Wiley & Sons, New York.
Totté, M. (1994), 'Migrations internes, populations et environnement: migrants et autochtones dans leur rapport à l'espace du Sud-Ouest burkinabè', In, *Cahiers du cidep 20: Migrations et access à la terre au Burkina Faso*. Academia and Harmattan.
Toulmin, C. (1983), *The economic behaviour among livestock keeping peoples: a review of literature on the economics of pastoral production in the semi-arid zones of Africa*. Development paper No. 25, University of East Anglia.
Toutain, B. (1974), *Implantation d'un ranch d'embouche en Haute-Volta*. IEMVT, Maisons Alfort.
Twose, (1985), *Behind the weather: why the poor suffer most – drought and the Sahel*.